CW01455358

A TEXTBOOK
OF INTERNATIONAL LAW

GENERAL PART

By

ALF ROSS, L.L.D., Ph.D.

PROFESSOR OF INTERNATIONAL LAW IN
THE UNIVERSITY OF COPENHAGEN

THE LAWBOOK EXCHANGE, LTD.
Clark, New Jersey

ISBN 978-1-58477-707-6

Lawbook Exchange edition 2006, 2013

The quality of this reprint is equivalent to the quality of the original work.

THE LAWBOOK EXCHANGE, LTD.

33 Terminal Avenue
Clark, New Jersey 07066-1321

*Please see our website for a selection of our other publications
and fine facsimile reprints of classic works of legal history:*
www.lawbookexchange.com

Library of Congress Cataloging-in-Publication Data

Ross, Alf, 1899-
  A textbook of international law : general part / Alf Ross.
    p. cm.
  Originally published: London ; New York : Longmans,
    Green, 1947.
  Includes bibliographical references and index.
   ISBN-13: 978-1-58477-707-6 (alk. paper)
   ISBN-10: 1-58477-707-9 (alk. paper)
   1. International law. I. Title.
  KZ4002.R67 2005
  341--dc22   2006004688

Printed in the United States of America on acid-free paper

A TEXTBOOK
OF INTERNATIONAL LAW

GENERAL PART

By

ALF ROSS, L.L.D., Ph.D.

PROFESSOR OF INTERNATIONAL LAW IN
THE UNIVERSITY OF COPENHAGEN

LONGMANS, GREEN AND CO.
LONDON · NEW YORK · TORONTO

LONGMANS, GREEN AND CO. LTD.
6 & 7 CLIFFORD STREET LONDON, W. I

NICOL ROAD, BOMBAY, I
17 CHITTARANJAN AVENUE, CALCUTTA, 13
36A MOUNT ROAD, MADRAS, 2

LONGMANS, GREEN AND CO. INC.
55 FIFTH AVENUE, NEW YORK, 3

LONGMANS, GREEN AND CO.
215 VICTORIA STREET, TORONTO, I

FIRST PUBLISHED 1947

CODE NUMBER 80851 S
—
PRINTED IN DENMARK BY
A. RASMUSSENS BOGTRYKKERI
RINGKJØBING

CONTENTS

Chapter I.

THE CONCEPT AND PRESUPPOSITIONS OF INTERNATIONAL LAW

Chapter II.

THE SOURCES OF INTERNATIONAL LAW

Chapter III.

THE SUBJECTS OF INTERNATIONAL LAW

Chapter IV.

DELIMITATION OF THE SPHERES OF DOMINION OF STATES: THE TERRITORY

Chapter X.

CO-OPERATION OF STATES FOR THE PURPOSE OF SAFE-GUARDING COMMON INTERESTS

Chapter XI.

VIOLATION OF THE LAW. RESPONSIBILITY

Chapter XII.

THE SETTLEMENT OF STATE DIFFERENCES

FOREWORD

It is a pleasure to me to be allowed to introduce Professor Alf Ross' little book on International Law to English readers. He brings to the writing of this book a combination of qualifications which are not often found together in our English legal writers, a familiarity with philosophical concepts as well as a training in law. Such a combination is in the true Continental tradition, and if International Law is to be a genuinely international object of study, as it should be, it is very desirable that the students of one country should understand a method of approach which, though they may at first find it a little strange, comes naturally to those of another. An English reader will find, despite the novelty to him of the approach, that Professor Ross' conclusions more often than not are the same as those which he reaches himself by his different route. In any case for the lawyers of different countries to understand one another is to make their own small special contribution to that feeling of international community upon which the very possibility of an effective International Law depends.

Oxford, October, 1946.

J. L. BRIERLY.

PREFACE

This modest exposition of the fundamental features of International Law has been translated from the Danish original. It is not of course in any way intended to compete with the great standard works in which the English literature has always abounded, and which in recent times are so handsomely represented in *Oppenheim-Lauterpacht's "International Law"*. It is obvious that as a source of the data of International Law my book cannot offer anything that would justify a translation into a universal language. The reason why I have nevertheless wished to present this account to the English-speaking world is that I have here attempted an analysis of the fundamental concepts and problems of International Law on the basis of a specifically Scandinavian view of the nature of law and the aims of jurisprudence to which there is probably nothing exactly similar in the Anglo-American literature. I hope I shall shortly be able to publish these legal theoretical viewpoints in a book entitled "Towards a Realistic Jurisprudence", and until then I merely refer the reader to my earlier work "Kritik der sogenannten praktischen Erkenntnis" (Copenhagen 1933), the contents of which, however, are in the main philosophical.

It will perhaps be thought that this is not an auspicious time for publishing a textbook of International Law, now that the statesmen of the victorious Allied Nations are building up a new international system which is to create a possibility of liberty and peace in a world that was threatened with destruction by tyranny and barbarity. I do not think, however, that the new instruments, however powerful and important they will be, will essentially invalidate the theoretical analysis and criticism of the fundamental concepts and problems of International Law which form the nucleus of this book. I even venture to think that I have here expressed basic ideas which point towards the future course of development. I am here thinking especially of the concept of sovereignty and the dogma of the equality of states.

The not very easy translation has been done by Miss Annie I. Fausbøll, Copenhagen, to whom I owe thanks for her patience and interest in the task. My grateful acknowledgements are due to the Trustees of the Rask-Ørsted Foundation for a grant of funds to defray the expenses of translation and publication.

Copenhagen 1946

ALF ROSS.

Chapter I

THE CONCEPT AND PRESUPPOSITIONS
OF INTERNATIONAL LAW

§ 1.

THE CONCEPT OF INTERNATIONAL LAW

I. *The current definition.*

According to the current view *International Law* is the body of legal rules binding upon states in their relations with one another. Thus International Law forms a contrast to the law valid for individual states (e. g. British Law, German Law, Danish Law) which is called by a common name *internal* law, national law, state law, or municipal law.

This view is evidently based on the following presuppositions.

Legal rules are not ideas floating in the air but are associated as connected wholes, termed legal systems, with concrete human societies. International Law is such a legal system connected with a certain society, the society of states. Thus International Law is not contrasted with penal law, the law of persons, procedural law, or other similar groups of legal rules defined by their object, but forms a contrast to British, German or Danish law as individual legal systems.

Hence International Law is a separate legal system associated with a certain human society. But this society is not a new society co-ordinate with the British, German, or Danish society; it is a larger, more comprehensive community embracing all these as parts of a whole.

On the current view it is further supposed that the sum of the national systems plus International Law is exhaustive; or conversely, that the whole legal universe may be divided into the legal stystems valid in the individual states (national law) and the legal system valid for all states (International Law).

II. *The current definition is circular.*

This view is, as we shall presently see, not far from correct. But it is extremely incomplete as long as no clear definition is given of what is meant by a "state". For this is by no means self-evident. Experience shows a great variety of interdependent superior and subordinate legal communities each of which may in a certain sense be said to constitute an individual whole; thus for instance municipalities, districts, provinces, member-states, "ordinary" states, federal states etc. But at what stage of this mounting scale do we find a "state" in the sense borne by this word in the definition of International Law? Common linguistic usage as such cannot be decisive. In the U. S. A. the parts united are usually termed "states", but this does not necessarily mean that they are also states in the sense determining the concept of International Law.

Unfortunately the current expositions of International Law give no clear reply to this important question. For as a rule the term "state" is defined by its sovereignty — in a later chapter — and this term again by the relation of the state to International Law. Sovereignty, for instance, is defined as sole subjection to International Law, that is to say, as the quality of being subject to International Law alone, not to state law. But in that case the *definition given of the term "International Law" would be unmeaning.* We have here a vicious circle: in order to determine whether or not a certain rule is international we must know whether or not the legal community bound by it is a state. But in order to decide this question we must know precisely whether or not the rule in question is international. The term "International Law" is defined with reference to the term "state" and the definition of the term "state" again refers back to the term "International Law". A definition thus biting on its own tail is circular. The consequence is that on the point in question the definition is in reality a blank.[1]

---

[1] Often the constitutive factor in the concept of the state is not expressly defined as subjection to International Law, but indirectly the same result emerges from the fact that (externally) sovereignty is defined as independence. Since now it cannot be intended to deny that the sovereign state can be legally bound, e. g. by treaties, in its relation to other states, independence must mean independence within the limits of International Law, or sole subjection to International Law. Thus e. g. *Oppenheim*, International L..w, § 64; *Fauchille*, Droit international public, no. 164.

If the current definition of International Law is to be made consistent the object must be, therefore, to find a criterion for the term "state" which shall not be circular and at the same time shall *justify*[2] a fundamental division of all law into the species "Internal Law" and "International Law", so that these concepts, at any rate in the main, shall cover the phenomena which usually go by these designations. That any such criterion is to be found at all cannot be taken for granted. It is possible that the traditional attempt at a definition is wrong from the very start and that the investigation, therefore, must be resumed from an entirely different point of departure. But in the first instance it seems reasonable to try whether it would be possible to arrive at a tenable result by following up the traditional reasoning. For this purpose it will repay the trouble to explain in more detail, by way of introduction, the different manners in which a legal community may be built up into larger units.

These two examples may serve as typical instances of the prevailing doctrine. The circle recurs whenever the conclusions are based on these three elements:

1. A definition of International Law as the law valid between states,
2. A definition of the state by the concept of sovereignty, and
3. A definition — explicit or implicit — of sovereignty as sole subjection to International Law (§ 3. IV).

[2] A definition is a statement as to what the speaker intends to understand by a certain word. Hence a definition is not true or false but more or less convenient, it is not proved but is justified from various points of view. There are two formal requirements which a definition must satisfy unconditionally:

1. It must not be self-contradictory.
2. It must not be circular.

If these conditions are satisfied its convenience is estimated from two points of view:

1. Its relevancy, i. e. its value as an instrument for scientific exposition. It is a prerequisite that it emphasises such conditions of affairs as are decisive in the formulation of certain scientific propositions. Its value is measured by the capacity of the definition to formulate the scientific exposition in the simplest way.
2. Its convenience, i. e. its agreement with the traditional conception, in the sense that the definition in the main covers precisely those phenomena which usually, in the science concerned, are denoted by the concept defined.

These two evaluations may lead in different directions. Consideration for the relevancy of the definition may necessitate a departure from the traditional acceptation. Progress in science consists in great part in a delicate adjustment of concepts according to their relevance.

III. *The self-governing community.*

It is a fact that all law occurs as a development in a human community, a legal community. As a rule it has a territorial basis. Further, it is a fact that a legal community together with other co-ordinate legal communities may enter as an element into a common, larger, superior legal community. In Denmark, for instance, the municipal districts have the right to govern their own affairs under the supervision of the state. Thus each municipal district constitutes an independent legal community with its own special municipal law. But at the same time all Danish municipal districts enter as elements into a larger legal community, the Danish state. The latter again enters as an element into the international society of states. Often one or more intermediate links (district municipalities, member states, and the like), are introduced between the municipal district (or a similar legal community) and the state, just as a link may come in between the state and the international community, for instance a federal state. This affords a possibility for a smaller or greater number of stages in a pyramidal construction of the legal communities into more and more comprehensive units.

Now, it is important to note that when a subordinate community becomes part of a superior community this may happen in two essentially different ways.

Either it may be conceived that the superior community enters into *direct* communication with the individuals in the subordinate communities so that the more comprehensive, legal system is directly binding upon the individuals in the narrower spheres and is enforced by the central community's own organs. The law of the subordinate community is then only in force in so far as it is not supplanted by the law of the superior community. The latter therefore is said to possess a "higher legal power" over the individuals.

Or the connection between the higher order and the individuals may be *effected through* the incorporated community's own legal system and its enforcement of this. That is to say, the duty created by the higher legal order is never a duty imposed directly on the citizen but always on the subordinate community as a collective unit, viz. a duty for the latter to impose by its own law-creating and law-enforcing organs a certain state of law on the individuals. Hence, in this case, from the citizen's point of view, the subordinate community is the highest legal power which decides what is the law in force for him. Only the community as such, not the individual citizen, is subject to a higher legal order.

This contrast, however, is not absolute. Intermediate stages may be conceived in which the superior community in certain spheres of life may come into direct contact with the individual, while in others it must leave it to the subordinate community and its organs to carry out its purposes.

To express this condition of affairs more briefly the following definition may be put forward: a legal community is called *self-governing when and in so far as it is the highest legal power in relation to its individual members.*

We may then distinguish between

a. *fully self-governing* legal communities, that is to say, such as are self-governing in all spheres, and

b. *partly self-governing* legal communities, that is to say, such as are self-governing in certain spheres of life only, and

c. *non-self-governing* legal communities, that is to say, those whose law can in all spheres of life be supplanted by the law of the superior community.

It follows that a self-governing community may very well itself be subject to the law of a higher order of community. Only the latter law cannot then, as far as self-government goes, be directly binding upon the citizens.

To make it clearer what is meant by the contrast between self-governing and non-selfgoverning communities we may consider the Danish state and a Danish municipality respectively.

The municipality is non-self-governing[3] because it is not on any point the highest legal power with respect to its inhabitants. There is no sphere of life which is reserved for the municipal community in such a way that Danish legislation cannot interfere and directly bind each individual. It may also be said that Danish law is valid not only *for* the municipality but also *in* the municipality.

The Danish state, on the other hand, is fully self-governing, because on every point it is the highest legal power with respect to the citizens. There is no sphere of life where the law of a higher community is directly binding upon the individual Dane.

---

[3] According to the definition given this does not of course conflict with what is usually called municipal self-government, which I, to distinguish the concepts, will call municipal self-administration.

It is true that above Danish law there are legal rules of a higher order. But these are valid *for* the Danish state only, not *in* it.

As an example of a partly self-governing community may be mentioned the state of New York. Under the American constitution certain matters are referred to the independent and unchallengeable sphere of power of the individual states;[4] that is to say, in such a way that the federal authorities are debarred from interfering in these spheres, while in other domains the federation may legislate directly with a binding effect upon the inhabitants of the individual states. Therefore the United States themselves may be adduced as an example of a partly self-governing state. This shows that the absence of selfgovernment in a certain sphere may be due to the fact that in certain affairs the direct legal power is placed in the hands either of a superior or of a subordinate community. It is the same case viewed from two angles.

IV. *A new definition of the term International Law.*

I now propound the hypothesis that the current definition of the term "International Law" (as the law valid for states in their relations with each other) may be rendered more complete by replacing the term "state" implied in it by "a self-governing legal community".

Of course no definition of the concept of International Law is true or correct in itself. Here as in other cases of the delimitation of a definition we are alone concerned with the question of its suitability for scientific classification and its connection with the scientific tradition which the individual enquirer cannot abruptly disregard. It is this tradition which is determining for the presentation of the problem: in the present case a division of the total material of law into the two main species "International Law" and "Internal Law". The solution of the problem which is aimed at by the definition is that of finding the most natural or the most "essential" criterion for the distinction, that is to say, the criterion which brings to light the differences that are most important in a scientific-systematic respect. Our eyes will then be opened to the differences and the connection between the

---

[4] See § 36 Note 9.

phenomena, and the scholarly treatment of the material will gain in penetration and simplicity of formulation.[5]

On this view I am of opinion that International Law may conveniently be defined as *the law valid for (binding upon) self-governing communities*, the chief distinguishing mark being, then, that it is never directly binding upon individuals but must always be rendered effective through the medium of the internal law of the self-governing communities.

This implies that an obligation is present which may be ascribed to the self-governing community *as a whole*. In state law terminology the state may incur obligations towards the citizens with reference to its own legal system, e. g. to pay compensation for expropriation, to respect certain liberties and the like. Since, however, the self-governing community in the last instance controls these legal relations itself, such duties cannot be ascribed to the "state" as a term for the selfgoverning community as a whole. "The state" here stands for a certain branch of the administration, not for the self-governing community as a whole. Not until an obligation is present which the state cannot control in any of its ramifications, does the idea of International Law, a legal system above the state, arise; and it is to such relations alone that the above-mentioned definition refers. For similar reasons legal relations between a state and other states or private individuals, which are tried by the rules of civil law, fall outside International Law, even if it is, according to the circumstances, the civil law rules of an alien legal system which are applied. Such legal relations are present, for instance, if the state enters upon the purchase of a consignment of corn from a foreign state. The prerequisite for international legal relations is said to be that the self-governing community has acted *jure imperii*, not *jure gestionis*.

For the justification of the above-mentioned definition it may in the first place be pointed out that in the main it covers precisely those phenomena which according to the tradition have been conceived as international. As will be explained more fully in § 6, there can be no doubt that the rules which tradition conceives as coming under International Law are not as such valid in the national legal communities, but are only valid *for* these as collective units. A treaty between Great Britain and France, for

---

[5] Cf. Note 2.

instance, does not impose obligations on individual Britons which can be appealed to and enforced by British courts of law, but always merely creates an obligation directly binding upon the British state.

Only in certain border-line cases can the definition here propounded conflict with the current views. For if several partly self-governing states, as for instance the states of the U. S. A., are united by rules which are directly valid for the states and not for the individual citizen, then these rules must, according to the definition, be regarded as international no matter whether they are incorporated in a constitution or based on a treaty. But if the definition points to essentials and if it is defensible at all, a correction of the usual view on this point is well founded.

The crucial question will then be whether the definition stresses such a difference in essentials that it will justify a systematic division of all law into the species "International Law" and "Internal Law". This must decidedly be supposed. Already the century-old tradition in this sphere favours the assumption that good practical and theoretical reasons must be at the bottom of the distinction. And on second thoughts the supposition is confirmed that the justification of the division depends precisely on the criterion set up by the definition.

Thus from a practical point of view it is clear that it will be of interest to gather into one system all the legal rules which are directly binding upon the citizens of a certain legal community and are enforced by the courts of this community. Systematic considerations, too, will lead to the same result. The contents of International Law must on many points be supposed to have a distinctive stamp because its rules apply exclusively to states (self-governing communities). The intercourse here dealt with must in the nature of the case differ essentially from that of internal law, and this circumstance must be supposed to characterise International Law in all its stages, both the primary rules of intercourse, and the secondary rules of responsibility, as well as the tertiary rules of procedure (§ 8). As will appear from the exposition to follow, especially § 5, this is, in fact, the case.

However, not all the actual peculiarities of International Law are invariably and necessarily associated with its character as inter-state law. The imperfection resulting from the absence of a firm organisation through legislative, judiciary and executive authorities which now above all sets its sad mark on Inter-

national Law has not necessarily, as is often supposed, anything
to do with the nature of International Law. There is nothing to
hinder us from conceiving an effective development of power
and order in international affairs: as long as we are concerned
with an *international* order, that is to say, an order directly concerned with states, not individuals, it will, however, be necessary
to draw a radical distinction between International Law and
Internal Law. The present lamentable conditions in this domain
are not implicit in the nature of International Law. International Law is not "conceptually" but only "accidentally" imperfect
law.

It would be a different matter, on the other hand, if we conceived a development of international courts as courts of appeal
supreme over the national courts, (and international instruments
of power to enforce the judgments pronounced on individuals)
— that is to say, a system of law which, dispensing with the
intermediation of the states, *directly* regulated legal relations
between individuals and was able to supplant national lav. In
that case the fundamental difference between International and
Internal Law would disappear. The states would no longer be
self-governing, that is to say, they would not be the highest
legal power in relation to the citizens but subordinate parts of
a great world state. In other words, International Law must
necessarily be indirect law; its existence is bound up with that
of the self-governing communities.

I think I have here adduced good reasons to justify the
definition set forth above. These reasons can, however, only be
of a temporary character. It is in the succeeding treatment of
the individual problems of International Law that the definition
will be put to the proof. Here it will appear whether consistent
adherence to it will be possible. Incidentally it should be noted
that the justification of a definition can never be final. There is
always the possibility that by penetrating more deeply into the
correlation of the phenomena we may succeed in finding another
and more fruitful criterion of division.

V. *The relation of this definition to the current doctrine.*

The tentative definition here put forward of the term "International Law" may be regarded as completing and deepening the
traditional view, according to which International Law is the

body of rules valid for the states in their relations with each other. The term "self-governing legal community" should merely be substituted for the vague or circularly defined term "state". In this way the technical element determining the peculiar character of International Law in contradistinction to Internal Law is emphasised, at the same time as it is understood without difficulty that International Law is valid for other subjects besides states. For there are other self-governing communities in addition to states. Thereby the absurdity characteristic of several of the traditional expositions will be avoided: at the same time as these *define* International Law as the law valid for states they teach that others besides states may *exceptionally* be subjects of International Law. It would seem that juridical authors accustomed to operate with rules and exceptions transfer this scheme of thought to the definition of concepts, too, without understanding that its application here is a logical monstrosity. If a triangle has been defined as a figure formed by three sides it is a contradiction to add that occasionally there may occur a few triangles with four sides.

However, the agreement with the prevailing view is perhaps more apparent than real. For it turns out that the current doctrine, though it defines International Law as the body of rules *valid* for states, actually, when it comes to the point, attaches weight to another criterion, viz. that International Law is the body of rules *created* by the common consent or mutual agreement of states. According to this, then, no weight is attached to the particular character of the subject bound, but to the special nature of the *legal source* or the *basis of validity*. That this is really what is meant appears especially in the section dealing with the basis of the "binding power" of International Law. In all cases where this basis is sought in a "common consent" *(consensus omnium)*, *"reconnaissance" "Vereinbarung"*, a fundamental norm as to the binding power of agreements *(pacta sunt servanda)* or the like, it follows that the essential factor in International Law is its coming into existence: it is a *conventional law*, i. e. a law which has come into existence by an explicit or implicit agreement between equal members of a fellowship.

The prevailing doctrine does not see any essential difference between the two definitions. For it is taken for granted that states can only become subjects of duties by mutual agreement and conversely that an agreement between states normally only creates rights and duties for the contracting parties, the states. (Agreements favouring or encumbering third states are rare). The two points of view therefore may be combined in the formula: International Law is the body of rules which are created by agreements between states, and which normally therefore are binding upon states. This also affords a possibility of recognising and explaining that others besides states may exceptionally be subjects of International Law.

This view of International Law is the counterpart of the theory that the law within a state is law derived from a commanding authority. According to this, state law implies a relation of absolute superiority and subordination between the state power and the individual. The law, it is thought, consists of commands issued by a supreme ruling power which is present in every state. And it acquires its "binding force", its validity as law, from this power, because it is not only the highest physical power but also possesses *authority*, i. e. the capability of validly binding others. It is this authority which makes the law a spiritually valid order raised above brutal tyranny. As there is not in the society of states a corresponding, common superior ruling power, no source of International Law can be conceived other than the united wills of the states. These wills then are the highest source of all law, internally by virtue of authority, externally by virtue of *autonomy*, that is to say, the power of the will to bind itself validly. International Law, therefore, is also characterised as law of co-ordination in contradistinction to law of subordination.

This is the real core of the traditional definition of International Law: a legal rule is international when its sole[6] source is an agreement, while it is state law when it originates from an authoritative power.[7]

This doctrine which has deeply marked the scientific treat-

---

[6] This distinguishes International Law from the civil law of contracts which in the last instance springs from the authoritative command that agreements must be kept, cf. *Anzilotti*, Droit international, 44—45, 122.

[7] See e. g. *Anzilotti*, Droit international, 45—46: »Le rapport de prééminence et de subordination qui caracterise les organisations étatiques a eu pour consequence que la production des normes juridiques est devenue exclusivement, ou presque, l'oeuvre des organes placés audessus des associés, de telle sorte que la norme parait imposée par une volonté superieure *(commandement)*. Au contraire, entre les États cette norme n'est et ne peut être qu'un accord entre égaux *(promesse)*.«

ment of a number of seperate problems must be definitely rejected.

It is open to suspicion if only for the reason that it is not a realistic description of the legal phenomena but a speculative "explanation" of the "binding force" of the law conceived as a supersensual quality, cf. below § 4.

Hence it is not to be wondered at that the theory is quite unsuitable for a characterisation of international phenomena. It is a dogma which does not correspond to the facts that states can only be bound by explicit or implicit agreements. Common custom and general legal principles are also binding upon states that have not accepted them, especially newly formed states. Forcible fictions are then resorted to, custom is construed as a tacit agreement, and tacit consent feigned on the part of the newly formed states.

In addition, the distinction between law derived from agreements and law derived from commands is fluid. Consent may, as often exemplified in International Law, be *indirect,* that is to say, be consent to a certain authoritative order, instruments being created with a certain authority of command, hence a certain imperial power (e. g. the European Danube Commission). Further, as already stated, it is necessary, in order to avoid the worst absurdities, to assume that consent may also be *tacit* and *presumed,* or even *compelled* by the circumstances. But if we have gone thus far, there is nothing to prevent our construing state law as based on the autonomy of individuals. And as a matter of fact such theories have frequently been propounded. (The social contract theories and the more recent recognition theories).[8]

We may then establish the following propositions:

1. It is no certain criterion of the international character of a rule that it has come into existence by agreement.

2. It is no certain criterion of the national character of a rule that it has not come into existence by agreement.

Or more generally: The international or internal character of a rule of law is dependent on its *content* alone (whether or not it is binding upon a self-governing community) not on the *basis of its validity* (its coming into existence, possibility of amendment).

---

[8] See *Ross,* Theoriè der Rechtsquellen, Chap. VIII, Note 30.

Thus the origin of the rules in the autonomy of the parties is not suitable for defining International Law. On the other hand, it is true that the autonomy of the parties plays a much greater part in the International Law now in force than in internal law. For within current International Law there is no legislation or hardly any, that is to say no authoritative formulation of law, which is binding upon others than the parties concerned, cf. § 10. 1.

The view of the nature of International Law here expressed is presumably new in the literature on International Law. The author who comes nearest to it is, as far as I know, *Verdross* in his latest exposition (»Völkerrecht« 1936). Previously Verdross has defined International Law as a conventional law (founded on the norm *»pacta sunt servanda«*), and sovereignty (as determining the conception of the state and of Internal Law) as subjection to International Law only. In a paper published in 1930[9] I criticised this view from the same fundamental principles as I have asserted here. It may be supposed, perhaps, that this paper has not been without influence on Verdross's altered view. But even though Verdross now in principle defines International Law as law valid for sovereign legal communities, and further defines the sovereign legal community as the highest legal power in its relation to its individual members (i. e. as that which I have called a self-governing community) from which it would follow that the content of the rule alone, not the basis of its validity, is determining for its character as International Law, the agreement theory still haunts Verdross's exposition in places. Thus he constantly declares the sovereign state to be directly subject to International law« (völkerrechtsunmittelbar). If this is not to be a purely circular declaration, it must imply another definition of International Law, namely as a law of agreements (treaties). That this is what is meant in fact appears plainly from his doctrine of the unions of states. This is still in principle based on whether the union is founded on treaty or constitution (Cf. § 3, IV and § 17).

In the paragraphs to follow some separate aspects of the tentative definition of the term "International Law" will be dealt with in more detail.

---

[9] *Ross*, La souveraineté des États et la Societé des Nations, Revue de Droit intern et de Légeslation comparée, 1931, 652; 1932, 112; Völkerbund und Staatssouveränität, Z. für offentliches Recht, Bd. XI (1931), 441.

§ 2.
THE SUBJECTS OF INTERNATIONAL LAW

I. *Here we deal merely with the question as to who c a n b e subjects of International Law, cf. Chapter III.*

By the subjects of a certain legal order are meant the persons to whom the legal rules "apply", for instance by imposing duties on them, conferring rights on them, or investing their actions (e. g. their promises) with a special law-creating effect (a fuller explanation of the term will follow).

It must appear from the very content of a certain legal order who are its subjects in this sense. A legal rule which imposed certain duties but did not state on whom these duties were incumbent would in reality only be a meaningless fragment. Usually, however, the individual legal rule, as found for instance in a statute, does not itself give exhaustive information as to the persons to whom it applies. The statute of contracts, for instance, is not applicable to young children. But this does not appear from the statute itself but from the law of infants. The latter, therefore, is in reality a fragment which only forms actual legal rules in conjunction with other (incomplete) norms.

These fragmentary rules relating to the general conditions essential to being a subject of law in various relations are presented in the *law of persons.*

International Law, too, has its law of persons dealing with the general conditions and the various kinds of international subjectivity. The exposition of these rules is of course an exposition of the content of International Law and will therefore be postponed till a later chapter (III). The present chapter does not deal with the contents of International Law but only with the concept, that is to say, here the material to be dealt with in the sequel is delimited. But it follows from this alone that the International Law of persons must move within certain bounds. Here we shall deal solely with the question as to who *can be* subjects of International Law. In Chapter III it will be shown who *are* its subjects according to the International Law now in force.

II. *Only a self-governing community can be capable of international duties.*

International Law has been defined as the law valid for (binding upon) self-governing communities. It follows that *self-*

governing communities and these alone are capable of inter-national duties.

This, as already stated, is a consequence of the definition of International Law. But it may be asked whether this delimitation is convenient. Doubts must arise if legal rules can be shown to exist which bind individuals or non-selfgoverning communities and which still, according to the general view, cannot be said to belong to an internal legal system. For it is usually taken for granted that internal law and International Law should together exhaust all law. Below under V the legal position of the individual is mentioned. Here the question is discussed with a view to non-selfgoverning communities.

If for instance we consider municipalities, it will be clear that many of the legal rules applying to municipalities are, according to the general view, of an internal legal nature, since they are elements of the state organisation into which the municipalities enter as subordinate elements. Conditions would be otherwise if it could be shown that there existed legal rules binding munici-palities in their relations with foreign states or other munici-palities in foreign states. We might imagine, for instance, that a public legal agreement was entered upon by two municipalities belonging each to its own state. If now legal rules could be shown to exist, which made such an agreement binding on the munici-palities, these rules could not, according to the general view, be regarded as belonging to internal law. It would then have to be decided whether it would not be necessary to extend the defini-tion of International Law to comprise these rules too. I shall, however, try to prove that such rules can hardly be conceived to exist. And thus the problem too, ceases to exist.

That a legal duty is incumbent on a person means that a certain conduct is "demanded" of him in the sense that, if he does not comply with it (under certain more precisely defined con-ditions), he can be made *responsible*. Normally this takes place by the aid of courts by which the person is made liable for damages, punishment, or some similar *sanction*. The object of this procedure is of course that this possibility (in connection with other factors) shall induce the person on whom the duty is incumbent to fulfil his duty. Normally, therefore, there is no sense in imposing duties on acting persons if such an inducement must be considered excluded at the outset. This may be conceived to be the case especially for two reasons: Either because the subject lacks the mental qualifications for it; or because the action demanded is not within his *control*.

For the latter reason *self-governing communities alone are by nature suited* to be subject to international duties. For they and they alone can control the conduct, that is to say, the internal legal act, required of them as subjects of a superior legal system. For the self-governing communities were defined precisely as communities which, in internal matters, are the highest legal authority. The non-selfgoverning communities, on the other hand, are not themselves masters of their internal law and therefore lack the natural qualification for fulfilling duties in that respect.

It is for this reason that *legal relations between other than self-governing communities are practically inconceivable*. Even though an agreement between a municipality in a State A and a foreign state or community is regarded as binding, it would be unreasonable to regard the municipality as the subject under obligation. For the municipality cannot itself control the fulfilment of the obligation. The relation must therefore be understood to mean that the subject under obligation is the state A which controls the fulfilment of the agreement. As a natural consequence of this, according to International Law the agreement is only binding if it has been entered upon with the consent (sanction) of the state. Cf. § 37. I.

Hence we need not reckon with the possibility that there might be legal rules binding non-self-governing communities which yet, according to the general view, should not be regarded as belonging to internal law.

III. *A possible objection to the definition of International Law.*

It may possibly be objected against the definition of International Law as the law binding upon self-governing communities that the definition, having only regard to *duty*, does not in all cases contain an applicable criterion, namely not with respect to those legal rules whose purpose is to create either *rights* or *competences*, i. e. a power of creating law by certain actions. As a particularly important form of competence it is usual to mention the capacity of action, that is to say, the capacity of creating duties for oneself by one's own actions.

This objection is based on the widespread conception that "duties" and "rights" are co-ordinate fundamental legal concepts, and if this view were correct, the objection would be well founded.

But it is not correct. It arises from the fundamental conception that the law is a spiritually valid order, and that duties and rights are spiritual qualities or forces, which in a mysterious way are created by the law and are present in human beings. To a realistic view, in which the law is a socio-psychological relationship and individual duties or rights are typical situations in this relationship, the matter is quite different. If the terms "duty" and "right" are regarded solely as technical legal means of describing a certain relationship in the socio-psychological empirical reality it can be demonstrated that in the *last analysis every legal rule creates a duty*, or that all description of law can be reduced to a description of situations of duty. The situation "right" turns out, not to be a new situation co-ordinate with the situation "duty", but the *situation "duty" regarded in its relation to a certain individual other than that bound by the duty*. Several relations may here come into question, as well as several corresponding conceptions of rights. Of special interest is the direct relation of the content of the duty to the interest of another (the *interested party*) and the relation of the sanction to the person who by instituting proceedings is able to set the machinery of law in motion (the *prosecuting party*). Hence rights are in reality merely elements in a complete description of the duty situations.

If, for instance, A owes B £100 A is subject to a duty in the sense that if he does not pay in due time, he may be made responsible in court. That B has a corresponding right means two things: first that he is the party directly interested in B's fulfilment of his duty, secondly that he is the party who can make him accountable by instituting proceedings against him. Both things say nothing more than is already implied in a complete description of A's duty.

A fuller description and defence of these points of view will be found in my book "Towards a Realistic Jurisprudence", Chapter IX, to which the reader is referred.

The same applies to the legal rules which create a competence. Their content is to establish certain conditions — the law-creating actions — the incidence of which gives rise to duties. They are accordingly general indirect statements concerning concrete situations of duty.

Thus no legitimate objection can be raised because the definition only takes account of the duty situation.

IV. *An individual also may be the subject of rights.*

It follows from the above statement that an *individual* can never be capable of an international duty and consequently he cannot, either, be capable of international action. On the other hand, there is no conceptual objection to the individual being the subject of international rights, both as an interested party and as a party instituting proceedings. To what extent this is actually the case of course depends on the contents of International Law.

On the position of the individual in relation to International Law there exists a comprehensive literature whose controversies, however, are largely due to terminological obscurity. Three groups of views may be distinguished:

a. The current view takes it for granted that International Law only regulates relations between states and that only states, therefore, can have international duties and rights.

b. A school gaining more and more adherents recognises that states are the typical subjects of International Law but adds that individuals may, exceptionally, occupy the same position.

c. Finally some more recent authors contend that "the state" — just like other "persons in law" — is only a fiction of the brain and individuals are therefore, in all cases the true subjects of rights and duties.

Apart from the last, extreme, school based on special presuppositions, the obscurity is in great part due to the assumption, resulting from little clarified fundamental concepts, that the questions relating to the position of the individual as the subject of rights and duties must be dealt with and solved *en bloc*. As already shown, this is not the case.

Here we will discuss two questions:

1. Is it compatible with experience to assert that an individual can never be the subject of international duties?

2. Is it true that in the last analysis it is always the individual who is the real subject?

V. Is the individual actually never the subject of international duties?

In the literature reference has been made to a number of different cases in which recognised rules of International Law presumably create duties directly for individuals. Attention has been directed to the customary rule of the Law of Nations according to which *pirates* may be apprehended and punished by any state. The same applies to certain *war criminals* under the Treaty of Washington of Febr. 6 1922 concerning the use of submarines and poison gases in war. Under the Treaty of Versailles, Art. 228, Germany undertook to surrender to the Allied and Associated Powers any persons charged with committing acts in conflict with the laws and customs of war. Finally, the rules of the Law of Neutrality have been mentioned, which warrant certain sanctions (confiscation of ship and cargo) if *neutral persons* are guilty of breaking a blockade, carriage of contraband, or unneutral services. — In all these cases International Law seems to attach sanctions directly to certain actions performed by individuals, which means the same as creating a duty to avoid these actions.

This, however, is not correct. International Law does not enjoin that pirates, war criminals, and neutral persons are to be punished under the above-mentioned circumstances. International Law simply has not the organs to exercise such jurisdiction. The meaning of the aforementioned rules of International Law is merely that the states in these cases are authorised to exercise an extraordinary jurisdiction which would otherwise conflict with the law of aliens (§ 28. IV).[1] The punitive state therefore is not guilty of any act conflicting with International Law by omitting to exercise the sanction. The persons concerned are sentenced by national organs for transgressing national rules, and thus there is no international duty for the individual.

Nor can the *statutes of the International Court of Justice* be quoted as an example of international legal rules which directly bind individuals. The duties which these apparently impose on the judges e. g. to motivate the decisions, are not real duties but

---

[1] This appears plainly from the Treaty of Versailles, Art. 228, which begins: "The German Government recognises the right of the Allied and Associated Powers to bring before military tribunals persons accused of having committed acts in violation of the laws and customs of war."

a condition of the competence attributed to them as judges, the transgression of which may at most entail invalidity, § 59. V. We are then concerned with limits to the duty states undertake by submitting to the jurisdiction of the Court.

On the other hand, there are indisputable instances where international organs of administration, (e. g. the *European Danube Commission*), exercise direct administrative and judicial authority over individuals who are to a corresponding extent withdrawn from the supremacy of the state of sojourn.[2]

From my point of view I can only reply to this that under the definition posited here such phenomena fall outside International Law and that this segregation of them is presumably just. We have here actually a formation which merely differs in the extent of its authority from the federal power in a federal state. In that special domain — which in the cases concerned is very limited — the participating states are no longer the highest legal power in relation to their citizens, hence not fully self-governing, but have transferred part of their government to a common supreme authority. It is right therefore with several authors to regard the Danube Commission as the organ of a special "River State".[3] What may apparently make this view unacceptable is merely the idea that a federal state cannot be based on a treaty but always implies a "constitution". As I shall show later on (§ 17 cf. § 3 IV), this is only a prejudice arising out of the false theory of International Law as a conventional law.

VI. *Is it, nevertheless, in the last instance the individual who is the subject of international duties?*

The question as to the nature of "persons in law" is a very old moot point in juridical literature. It has been held that corporate units such as joint stock companies, municipalities, and

---

[2] The "European Commission" was established by the Paris Convention of 30. March 1856 and its authority extended by the Congress of Berlin Act of 1878 and the London Agreement of 10. March 1883. The peace treaties after the first World War and the Danube Acts of 23. July 1921 maintained the arrangement. This withdrew the river from the mouth up to Braila with appertaining plants, as well as the functionaries of the Commission, from the territorial supremacy of the adjoining states. Cf. *Strupp*, Wörterbuch, II. 476 and III. 871—72.

[3] See *Knubben*, Die Subjecte des Völkerrechtes, 416.

states which are mentioned and treated in positive law as if they were persons co-ordinate with physical persons are in reality only constructions of the brain which may perhaps be useful aids in the technique of scientific exposition, but do not denote any actually existing new subject. The legal rules express themselves as if such persons existed, but actually they do not. They are phantoms or fictions. In a truthful description there only occur individual human beings, and in a truthful analysis of law only rights and duties for these.

With respect to International Law such viewpoints lead to a denial of "the state" as an independent subject of law. *Scelle*, for instance, says that in principle the law consists of competences which are ascribed to certain wills. But only individuals have wills. It has never been possible to prove the existence of a collective brain or other collective organs. If several people join in a group no new supreme individual comes into existence. The special group phenomena can only be explained by the interaction of the individuals acting in concert. In a marriage the husband and wife may influence each other, but it has never been shown that the result of their interaction was a new individual furnished with an independent will, e. g. "the household". Even so with the state. In a state with 20 million inhabitants there are not 20 million and one persons. The simple fact is that in the group there are some who are representatives and some who are represented in a certain partnership of interests. The collective interests are taken care of by the representatives, and to ascribe rights and duties to the group itself, i. e. the state, really means that these belong to the representatives.[4]

If this view were correct, the definition of International Law here advanced would be inapplicable, at any rate without an essential correction.

It is easily seen that the above-mentioned theory implies that rights and duties are qualities which are created by the law and are associated with a certain will. This brings the problem into connection with the epistemological question whether collectivity possesses an independent will which can be the "upholder" of a legal capacity or quality. If collectivity is not a new "entity", it is difficult to see *where* or *with whom* the rights

---

[4] *Scelle*, Droit des gens, I. 9 f.

and duties should be found. As to this both defenders and deniers of the existence of the person in law are agreed.

There is no reason, however, to enter into the epistemological speculations on the existence of an independent group entity. In a realistic consideration of the function of the law the question as to collective subjects of law has nothing to do with these. Collective subjectivity to law simply expresses situations of rights and duties which differ from the usual types by the fact that the different elements in the situations which usually bear some relationship to one and the same individual here bear a relationship to several different individuals.

An obligation for A generally means that, if A does not act in a certain way, proceedings may be instituted against him; A is the subject both of conduct and of responsibility.

A right for A generally means that A is able to institute proceedings with the effect that for his benefit a certain mode of action can be enforced on the part of the person bound; A is the subject both of proceedings and interest.

An obligation for a collective body on the other hand, means that if X does not act in a certain way the responsibility will rest with Y. And similarly with a right. Here then the subjective relationships are divided between several persons. It is then impossible to find again the typical (combined) situation of rights, either with X or with Y as the subject. Since, however, the brain cannot rid itself of the customary scheme, according to which duties and rights are a substance "found in" certain subjects as beings furnished with a will, we are forced either to seek such a being in the collective unit (the organic theories) or to seek the subjectivity to law in the separate individuals (the mechanicists). Both theories are equally beside the mark. The real facts are that the *typical (combined) situation of rights is not present at all, but a non-typical divided one.* This does not exclude the possibility, however, that it may be convenient to use as a *term for this non-typical situation* the expression that the *collectivity is the subject of law* if only we realise that the phenomenon here concerned is not identical with the typical situation of rights.

Normally it would be absurd to apply a sanction to Y because X does not act in a certain way, or to let proceedings instituted by X lead to an advantage for Y. If there is to be any sense in such a procedure, it is evident that X and Y must have interests in common. It is this solidarity which is the socio-psychological reality of the group and gives a meaning to collective situations of duties and rights.

For instance, the duty for a joint stock company to pay taxes means that if the director of the company does not pay the taxes due a fine will be imposed on the assets of the company, that is to say, on the shareholders.

Similarly with the rights of a joint stock company and the rights and obligations of a state.

Notably it will be seen that it is misleading — as contended by the above-mentioned theory — to interpret rights and duties for a corporate body as identical with the rights and duties of the organs of the corporate body. If it was the director of the joint stock company who was liable to pay taxes, it must mean that he was liable to pay the fine out of his private means. Similarly the international sanction would be directed against the state organ. But this is not the case.

The real situation when we speak of duties and responsibilities for a state is, then, that actions performed by certain persons (the competent organs) have the consequence that certain others (the citizens in general) are held responsible. This schism is obscured by the application of the current scheme of thought to a situation of duty with the "state" as a new independent subject. It is then said that it is the state itself which is bound by its own actions. Thus, even though this is only a manner of speaking, it is nevertheless felt to be a natural expression of that solidarity of interest which unites "organs" and "citizens". That action and responsibility are attributed to the same subject, "the state", expresses the circumstance that owing to group solidarity their association is practically not felt to be absurd.

§ 3
THE CONCEPT OF SOVEREIGNTY

I. *The function of the concept of sovereignty in International Law: It is considered to determine the status as subject of International Law and to be the source of a series of sovereign rights.*

The term "sovereignty" has played a very great part both in the scientific treatment of International Law and in practical political terminology. But there is hardly any domain in which the obscurity and confusion are as great as here.[1] It is not only that there are almost as many definitions of the term "sovereignty" as there are authors, but also that there is no agreement as to *what purpose is served* by this concept in International Lav. Often there is no clarity at all on this point. Lengthy discussions about the correct definition of the concept abound, but not one word in them makes it clear what scientific interest attaches to the positing of such a concept.[2] It is overlooked that the subject of science is problems and their solution. The formation of concepts is merely a means towards that end, hence every concept must be associated with a definite problem. That the above concept can still play such a dominant role in spite of much criticism is no doubt connected with the fact that emotional ideas of the sublimity and sacredness of the power of the state are more or less consciously associated with it.

Under these circumstances an exact criticism would have to be directed against each single definition of the concept of sovereignty. Such a task could not of course be carried out within the scope of this exposition. It is necessary, therefore, at the

---

[1] As a forbidding example of the complicated profundity to which the doctrine of sovereignty has given rise we quote the following definition from Knubben:

"Souveränität ist der Sachervalt, dass Staaten von den in ihrem Substrat zur sozialen Gesamtheit zusammengeschlossenen Einzelmenschen als deren bzw. deren Gesamtheit Organ (im untechnischen Sinne) nämlich als Normenquelle und evtl. auch (so vor allem im Völkerrecht) als Normenadressat eines Rechtes geschaffen bzw. anerkannt werden, und dass dann die Staaten hinsichtlich der Schaffung dieses Rechtes auf Grund jener allgemeinen Kompetenz, jenes Zurechnungsprozesses für sich nun ihrerseits nicht auch wieder eine andere juristische Person, sondern nur sich selbst bzw. zumindestens auch sich selbst (ihre Mitbeteiligung) für die Schaffung des Rechtes gelten lassen, und dass die Staaten hinsichtlich der Geltung jenes Rechtes (insonderheit des Völkerrechts) auf Grund jener generellen Kompetenz, jenes Zurechnungsprozesses, weder die Einzelmenschen, noch für sich ein andere juristische Person, sondern nur sich selbst bzw. auch sich selbst als Normenadressaten, Zurechnungspunkte für die subjectiven Rechte und Pflichten jenes objektiven Rechtes gelten lassen. Kurz: Souveränität hat der Staat, insofern und insoweit er Zurechnungs-Endpunkt ist." (*Knubben*, Die Subjekte des Völkerrechts, 173).

The rest of us, who feel somewhat harassed by German syntax as displayed in this piece of scientific prose, permit ourselves to doubt disrespectfully, like the child in "The Emperor's New Clothes", whether there is anything but quite ordinary nonsense behind all this solemnity.

[2] This applies, for instance, to *Sukiennicki*'s monograph "La souveraineté des États."

expense of exactitude, to try to point out some main lines which recur again and again in the current conceptions.

In broad features, then, it may be said that in the first place the concept of sovereignty serves to characterise the subjects of International Law, or at any rate the subjects of International Law *par excellence*. It is taken for granted that International Law is the law binding upon states (or at any rate primarily upon states). The question will then again be what are the main characteristics of a state in contradistinction to subordinate territorial law communities, as e. g. a municipality. Three factors are usually mentioned as constitutive of a state viz. a human population, a territory as the basis of it, and a legal order which organises the group into a unit. But these marks alone are not able to separate the state as a subject of International Law from other communities organised on a territorial basis. The decisive mark of distinction is found precisely in sovereignty. The latter, then, is formally a *certain quality of the state* (or the legal order of the state) by which it differs in principle from other communities in such a way as to *qualify the state to be a subject of International Law*.

In what does this quality materially consist? The reply to this question typically tends to show that the state is the "highest order" or the "highest power". This is manifested *internally* by the fact that the state is absolutely the *highest ruling power* which does not know of any other power by its side or above itself; and *externally* by the fact that the state is *legally independent* of other states even though it must recognise these as its equals.

Sovereignty, thus defined, is, then, primarily determining for the position of the state as a subject of International Law altogether. But, in addition, it is held that from sovereignty there arise a number of rights for the state. As *internal sovereign rights* are generally mentioned the right to possess its own political organisation, the right to possess its own legislation and administration. It is often assumed that internal sovereignty is divided into a "territorial supremacy" and a "personal supremacy", a right to state-legislation and administration with respect to all persons and things found on the territory following from the former; and a corresponding right with respect to a certain circle of persons (the citizens of the state), no matter where they are, following from the latter. As *external sovereign rights* are mentioned full capacity of action under International Law — more especially the right to diplomatic intercourse (the right to send envoys) and the right to conclude treaties — further the right to wage war, the right to equality and respect, the right to inviolability of territory and citizens etc.

In recent times the practice of enumerating specific sovereign rights has mostly been discontinued, but *internal self-government, full capacity of action* and an *extensive freedom of conduct* are still taken to be effects of sovereignty.

II. *Regarded as a description of "self-government" sovereignty is indeed determining for the status of a community as a subject of International Law, but no sovereign rights can be deduced from this circumstance.*

The idea of something that is in a certain sense "supreme" is then, as is also inplied in the word itself, the central factor of the concept of sovereignty. There is in fact undoubtedly something correct in this idea when soberly and more accurately formulated. Above (§ 1. IV) I have attempted to vindicate the view that an appropriate definition of International Law is based on the term "self-governing community", that is to say, precisely the community which is the supreme legal power in relation to the citizens. *If* therefore the supreme (internal) power is not to mean anything but a *descriptive term* for the condition of affairs that there is not within the state any power which the legal order of the state cannot supplant; and similarly, *if* "legal independence" means that there is not outside the state any power which can supplant the law of the state in its direct relation to the citizens, then sovereignty in its two branches is *merely another term for self-government.*

Interpreted in this way it is correct to say that "sovereignty" (self-government) is the element which is determining for the position of a state as a subject of International Law (a subject of international obligation). This is a simple consequence of an appropriate definition of International Law. A plurality of "sovereign" (self-governing) states is a prerequisite of International Law without which no "Society of Nations" would exist but a total world state.

On the other hand — and this is a very important point — it is *quite baseless to deduce any rights whatever* for the "sovereign" state from "sovereignty" in this sense. "Sovereignty" involves no other consequences than that of the "sovereign" community being invested with the duties (and rights) called international. What these duties and rights are cannot be deduced from this definition but depends solely on the content of the norms of International Law actually in force. The fact that it has nevertheless been supposed that anything whatever could be "deduced" from "sovereignty" must be a *sign that the concept has been interpreted in another than the aforementioned purely descriptive sense,* in which it is identical with "self-government". In order to understand this it is necessary to glance at the historical development.

III. *Historically the concept of sovereignty is rooted in mystic ideas. The absolute concept of sovereignty is incompatible with the assumption of an International Law.*

When in the Middle Ages "sovereign" princes or city states were referred to, those were meant whose decisions with respect to their subordinates could not be appealed to a higher authority. Owing to the peculiar feudal system with its widely extended allotment of state power to independent feudal lords (barons) the concept could be applied to units we should not nowadays regard as states *("Cascuns barons est souverains en se baronnie")*. On the other hand both the emperor and the pope attempted to assert supremacy in relation to the regal power by putting themselves at the top of the feudal pyramid and characterising the kings as their vassals. Thus at any rate the imperial and papal jurists preferred to describe the state of affairs. But the facts were not in agreement with the theory. In the course of the 14th and 15th centuries the French kings stabilised their power more and more, both internally and externally. They put down the independence of the barons by fighting, and emancipated themselves from all dependence on the emperor and the pope (in secular matters). They defeated feudalism both in its inner and outer ramifications and created the modern centralised absolute state. It was this political development which found its theoretical expression in *Bodin's* doctrine of sovereignty.

Bodin emphasises the necessity of a central power in the state. In every community worthy of the name of a state there must necessarily be a supreme power whose will is law, and which is therefore itself raised above all laws. For no community can keep together without such a supreme power which forces its members to constitute one body. In a sound state this supreme power should be vested in one man, the king. The supreme power is not, however, unlimited self-glorification. It is subject not only to divine laws and natural law (hereunder also, according to the view of that day, International Law), but also to certain fundamental laws which constitute the very foundation of kingship. Finally the sovereign must also respect the family and private property, which is supposed to follow from the very aim of state creation.[8]

From this it would seem that the concept of sovereignty merely served to describe a certain actually existing state of law which is regarded as constitutive for the idea of the state. But this is not really the case. The concept of sovereignty can be traced far back into the political thought of the Middle Ages and has always been connected not with the fact of state power, but with the question of its *right, validity* or *legitimacy*. All medieval political thought centres round the problem: whence is the legitimate authority of the political power and the consequent obligation of obedience derived? And the answer is given in the various theories of the origin and content of sovereignty. Some maintain that sovereignty was originally vested in the people which by a contract had more or less completely transferred it to the prince. Others, on the other hand, thought that the prince had derived sovereignty directly from God. It is clear that here the word cannot be meant to denote a positive state of law. Sovereignty here means *the invisible mystic power or ability to create valid law* which is the source of all positive law and which is referred to as a substance "found" somewhere, and capable of being transferred from one party to another just as a visible object is transferred.

Sovereignty in this mystic sense is of course a mere fiction. Logically it takes its rise from the fact that ideas of law which only have meaning within a system, or on the assumption of an extant state power, are transferred to this system or this state power itself. There is no sense in asking by what right an ex-

---

[8] See *H. W. Carlyle* and *A. J. Carlyle*, A History of Medieval Political Theory in the West VI (1936), 417 f.; *I. W. Allen*, A History of Political Thought in the Sixteenth Century (1928), 407 f.

isting right is a right. Psychologically the concept is explained
as a rationalisation of certain peculiar emotional experiences of
inner constraint (moral validity) which accompany positive law.

This mystic sense has since then clung to the concept of
sovereignty in all its shapes. 'The decisive feature in this connection is not, however, a critism of the concept but the circumstance that the conception of sovereignty as a supernatural
source of power *explains why it was thought possible to deduce
from sovereignty a number of sovereign rights* as the immediate
effects of its supersensual force.

In Bodin's time "sovereignty" was thought to be inherent in
a certain person, the prince, a view which is naturally adapted
to the construction of the absolute state. Later on in the constitutional states, it was not possible similarly to point to a
single person as invested with this mysterious sovereign power
and it was therefore attributed to the state as such. In the 19th
century this reasoning was especially supported by *Hegel's*
philosophy. To Hegel the state is the conscious manifestation of
spirit in the world. The state is God's course in the world. Its
foundation is absolute reason, manifesting itself as will. The will
of the state therefore is absolutely "sovereign", that is to say,
it knows no other law than the welfare of the state itself and is
therefore the only source of all legal validity.

The consequence of this philosophy, which became widely
diffused in the 19th century, must, in fact, be that the existence
of International Law is incompatible with the assumption of
such an absolutely supreme will of the state independent of
everything else. How should the state be subject to International
Law at the same time as its own unrestricted will is the supreme
law and the source of all law? Some authors, in fact, drew the
following conclusion: International Law is not valid for a state
any longer than it serves that state's own interests. But as a rule
it was attempted, by ingenious constructions of the same kind as
the attempts to square the circle, to combine the idea of absolute
sovereignty with the existence of an International Law. This
purpose was especially served by the theory of the "self-limitation" of the will of the state: The sovereign will of the state
voluntarily, in its own interest, submits to international duties.
Hence International Law, like all other law, derives its validity
from the will of the state, it is "external state law". It is readily
seen, however, that this construction is impossible. An obligation

which is dependent on the will of the person bound is no real obligation. Either we must in all seriousness accept the idea that the state is only bound by its own will, but if so there is no real obligation, no real International Law. Or else we must seriously accept the international obligation, but in that case the state is bound by other factors than its own will, and the latter then is not "sovereign".

IV. *The modern concept of sovereignty (sole subjection to Inter-ternational Law) is neither suited to be a criterion for the position of a state as a subject of International Law or to be a source of the effects of sovereignty.*

After the impossibility of the construction of self-obligation had been realised, most authors resorted to a *narrowing down* of the concept of sovereignty. Sovereignty, it was said, does not mean absolute unrestricted power but *power within the limits of International Law.* The absoluteness of sovereignty is not the extent but the basis of its power. A state is sovereign when its power is *primal,* i. e. merely limited by International Law. If, on the contrary, its power is derived from and thus limited by a higher constitution, that is to say by state law, not by International Law, the state is not sovereign. Sovereignty briefly expressed is *sole subjection to International Law.* On the other hand, it does not affect sovereignty that the power of the state is largely limited, if only these limitations are based on International Law (treaty). In this way the essential elements of the inherited concept of sovereignty are thought to have been preserved, while that incompatibility with the existence of International Law that wrecked the concept of absolute sovereignty has been avoided. The notion is retained that the will of the state is alone able to create law. But this manifests itself in two ways, internally as dominion (*imperium,* authority), externally by an autonomous creation of law in conjunction with other state wills by means of agreements. It is true that the sovereign state is bound, but only by such obligations as it has itself consented to by agreement or understanding. *The sovereign state is independent of all alien dominion.*

From this it will be seen that the definition of sovereignty as sole subjection to International Law is closely bound up with the definition of International Law as a *conventional law.* The element which is of fundamental importance in this definition of sovereignty — that sovereign power is alone bound by International Law — only acquires its real meaning if it is added: and thus alone by obligations which the state itself has undertaken by agreement, and which, therefore, in so far are rooted in the will of the state itself and not in alien dominion.

This is the core of all the more modern theories of sovereignty; decisive importance is attached to the *basis of validity* for the obligations incumbent on the state, and it is thought that this formal element is determining for the status of the state as a subject of International Law, and for the fundamental effects of sovereignty: internal self-government, full power of action, and extensive freedom of conduct.

This doctrine is not, at the outset, apt to inspire confidence. It is based on the distinction between law derived from agreements and law derived from commands which, as we have already shown (§ 1. V), is of speculative origin, and quite fluid in its practical application. In addition it must *a priori* seem quite improbable that it should be the formal foundation of the obligations, not their content, which determines the legal position of a state. This objection is confirmed on further reflection.

A. The attempt to *characterise the subject* of International Law, the sovereign state, by the criterion of "sole subjection to International Law" is evidently meaningless if with the prevailing doctrine we take it for granted — as most of the adherents of the theory do — that International Law is defined as the law binding upon states. It is said first that International Law is the law binding upon states; next that states are the communities which are bound solely by International Law. This is evidently a vicious circle. In order to decide whether or not a community is a (sovereign) state we must first know whether or not the rules by which it is bound are international. But to know whether or not a rule is international we must first know whether or not the subjects bound by it are (sovereign) states.

It is a disgrace to us that such an obvious absurdity marks the current theory of International Law.

The definition of sovereignty as sole subjection to International Law therefore only acquires sense provided International Law is at the same time defined as the law derived from agreements. As shown in § 1. V, this definition is not, however, tenable.

B. It is impossible to deduce *self-government* from sole subjection to International Law. Whether or not this state of law is present must depend on the contents of the rules applying to the community, not on the basis of their validity (treaty — constitution).

1. Even if a state A is subject to a superior constitution, there is nothing to prevent the content of this being, precisely, to give full or partial self-government to A. (The states of the U. S. A., for instance, have partial self-government).

2. Conversely, though A be only bound by treaty there is nothing to prevent the content of this treaty consisting, precisely, in A entirely or partially submitting its internal decisions to the control of another state, A's self-government being abolished to a corresponding extent (e. g. in a federal state founded by treaty).

C. It is impossible to deduce complete *capacity of action* from sole subjection to International Law. Whether or not this legal position is present must depend on the content of the legal rules valid for the community concerned, not on their formal basis.

1. Even if A is subject to a constitution there is nothing to prevent the content of this being, precisely, to give A full or partial power of action (thus the member-states of the imperial German Reich had partial capacity of action).

2. Conversely, though A be only subject to treaty there is nothing to prevent the content of this treaty being, precisely, that A entirely or partially transfers its power of action to another state (thus in a protectorate founded by treaty).

D. It is impossible to deduce *extensive liberty of conduct* from sole subjection to International Law. To what extent liberty of action falls to the state must depend on the content of the obligations incumbent on it, not on their formal basis.

1. Even if A is subject to a constitution there is nothing to prevent this leaving A extensive liberty to act as it likes.

2. Conversely, though A be only bound by treaties there is nothing to prevent these imposing such extensive obligations on the state with respect to home and foreign affairs that its liberty of action is in the main abolished. It may have bound

itself with respect to its constitution, its commercial policy, its administration, its tariff policy, cultural policy etc. Such states are referred to as pseudo-sovereign states.

This schematic view will have shown that there is no connection between sole subjection to International Law and the effects of sovereignty. A couple of examples to the contrary will clearly illusrate this.

A state A concludes a treaty with the state B by which B acquires the right to military occupation of A and supervision of the administration of the country, at the same time as B takes charge of the foreign affairs of A. According to the current theory the state A is a sovereign state, since it is only bound by treaty.

Another state, X, is included with other states in a common federal constitution according to which a federal power is established in a very few inessential domains, while the federal states in other respects retain self-government and capacity of action in external affairs. According to the current theory such a state is not a sovereign state, since it is subject to a constitution.

A theory leading to such absurd results has condemned itself. We are then led to admit that formal sovereignty *only typically*, not necessarily, is connected with the effects of sovereignty, whereby the whole question becomes involved in a superfluous complication.

Whether a certain legal position is established by treaty or conferred by constitution is often a rather unimportant matter of form. If, for instance, we consider the former Bohemian-Moravian "protectorate", the decisive factor in its position was the content of the rules applying to its relation to Germany. Whether these rules were formally established by treaty or imposed by a constitution or German state law would seem to be without any real importance whatever. Only a mystico-magical train of thought could lead to the result that in the first case the arrangement was still a manifestation of the original sovereignty of Czechoslovakia.

That the current conception must be false is confirmed when we consider what is the actual distinction between treaty and constitution. If we disregard all mystic notions and dwell alone on the positive legal facts, the distinction refers solely to a difference in the *conditions of amendment* of a certain order.

An order is based on treaty when it can only be altered by the consent of all those bound; it is based on constitution when it contains or implies a procedure of amendment different from this. It is now clear that nothing whatever can be inferred about the content of an order from the conditions of its amendment. But this is, precisely, what the current theory attempts to do.

V. *The concept of sovereignty must be replaced by the concepts "self-government", "capacity of action", and "liberty of conduct".*

It follows from the criticism here passed that the current concept of sovereignty consists of a goodly portion of mysticism and a consequent confusion of various real legal functions. Our task must be to overcome the idea of sovereignty as a substance or a unitary quality from which various effects follow, and instead present the separate *"effects of sovereignty" as positive legal situations created directly by rules of law.* The following three special functional concepts will then replace the substantial concept of sovereignty:

1. *Self-government* in the sense previously stated. This is the original core of the concept of sovereignty, which may be retained. This concept is (by definition) determining for the capacity of international obligations and thus for the status as subject of International Law.

2. *Capacity of action.* Whether or not a self-governing state also has power of action depends on the content of the rules binding the state — no matter whether these rules are formally based on a treaty or on a constitution.

3. *Liberty of conduct.* Absolute liberty of conduct is enjoyed by no state. Every international norm, especially every treaty, restricts the state's liberty of action. The extent of a state's liberty of action is the sphere of action not affected by general or special international norms.

Similarly a state's dependence on another state — and hence according to the current terminology, its lack of soveverignty — may mean three different things, which need by no means occur together:

1. Abrogation or limitation of self-government when a second state controls the first state's internal affairs.

2. Abrogation or limitation of the capacity of action when a second state acts in external affairs on behalf of the first.

3. An unusually far-reaching limitation of the state's liberty of conduct in favour of another state (right of occupation and the like).

VI. *The unfortunate consequences of the traditional doctrine of sovereignty.*

A. The current doctrine of sovereignty thus in the first place shows a *methodical unsoundness* which is apt to have a damaging effect on the scientific treatment of International Law. Wherever we meet with arguments in which a certain legal status is deduced from the sovereignty of the states we have a typical example of that *conceptual jurisprudence* which should be a thing of the past in the modern science of law. In reality nothing can be deduced from the concept which has not been arbitrarily introduced into it. We can, if we like, call a state sovereign when it has self-government, when it has capacity of action, or when it has the usual extensive liberty of conduct. But we can never "deduce" any of these things from a certain "quality", sovereignty, which is anything else than the various legal rules determining the position of the state in each of the three above-mentioned relations. Unfortunately such unreal conceptual constructions are still extensively met with in scientific literature as well as in the reasoning of legal decisions.[4]

B. But, in addition, the doctrine of sovereignty has a *practical political tendency*. Whether one feels sympathy with this is a matter apart, falling outside the scope of science. On the other hand, a protest must be entered against the creation through the doctrine of sovereignty of a quasi-scientific motivation of certain political tendencies.

It is primarily the concept of absolute sovereignty which involves a tendency hostile to a development of International Law. The notion of the state's absolute self-glorification and lack of restriction by anything but its own will and its own welfare is an idea which, strictly, must lead to a denial of all International Law. At any rate it is apt to render suspect any

---

[4] See e. g. *Loder's* and *Weiss'* dissentient votes in the Lotus judgment (1927) Publications of the Permanent Court, Series A, No. 10.

development of international solidarity owing to the emotional attitude which fears that such a development will threaten the mystic "sovereignty" of the state.

But even the more restricted concept of sovereignty, too, acts in the same direction. If we regard sovereignty formally as a certain quality determining the character of the state as state, and at the same time materially as a freedom of conduct of a definite extent, we are easily, by confusing the issues, led to the result that there must be a certain sphere of liberty which belongs unconditionally to the state as state. This is expressed in the theory of the *"reserved domain"* which is supposed in principle to lie outside the regulation of International Law and within the exclusive competence of the state. Under this head are subsumed for instance immigration questions, the economic policy of states, and national status. But actually there is no sphere of life which cannot give rise to international conflicts and be the subjects of international regulation. To what extent this will be the case at any time depends solely on the actual development of International Law. But the theory of the "reserved domain" tends to check this development.

The *unanimity principle* too, according to which no state can be bound by a resolution it has not adopted itself, and the principle of *the equality of states* are ideas which by virtue of the concept of sovereignty acquire an absolute dogmatic validity that forms an essential obstacle to the development of an international organisation (cf. § 34).

It applies to all cases that the mystical, vague, ambiguous concept of sovereignty marked by an emotional attitude is a means well suited to mobilise natural egoistic tendencies of the state opposed to the desire for an international organisation and solidarity, and to lend to these tendencies, hostile to International Law, a semblance of an objective motivation.

§ 4.
THE BINDING FORCE OF INTERNATIONAL LAW

The current expositions of International Law usually contain in the preamble a section on "the basis of the binding force of International Law". It is taken for granted that International Law, like other law possesses a "binding" capability or force to "impose obligations" and it is then asked whence this "force" is derived, or how this effect can be explained.

Now what is actually this "obligation" and "binding force" here implied? To a realistic consideration the law is a socio-psychological relationship of motives which release actions, and of actions which again create motives. The individual legal obligation is a term for a typical situation in this relationship. That situation is characterised by various motives typically arising in the person on whom the obligation devolves. These are partly founded on his fear of counteractions (sanctions: punishment, compensation, and the like), which may normally be expected to happen if he does not act in a certain way (fulfil his obligation). But, partly they appear to the individual, in a manner almost incomprehensible, as independent of his own interests with a purely commanding character as an urge to do "the right thing". It can be shown that we have a mechanism of motive which in a peculiar manner has been built up in the individual through influences from his first infancy and which now acts automatically and suggestively without any connection with the conscious endeavours and interests of the individual. In this way these impulses acquire to the individual an obscure commanding, categorical character interpreted as a "conscious-ness of duty", a "sense of duty" or "liability" in a legal moral sense. (Exactly the same mechanism of motive comes into play with respect to purely moral duties).

If the expression "legal obligation" is taken in this socio-psychological sense, an explanation of the binding force of the law cannot mean anything but a more detailed *socio-psychologi-cal account* of the conditions under which the above-mentioned peculiar feeling of legal obligation arises.

It is not, however, such an explanation that is sought when one enquires into the basis of the binding force of the law, more par-ticularly of International Law. This is connected with the fact that duty is not usually interpreted realistically, but — actuated by deep feelings of respect for something exalted and by the religious and metaphysical traditions of centuries — men inter-pret it as an experience of a *supernatural, spiritual order, a specific spiritual validity,* truths of a peculiar kind which do not "describe" but "demand", and which in the last instance are ascribed either to a divine source or an absolute spirit or reason inherent in man himself.

As already stated, this point of view is grounded in profound feelings and obtrudes itself with an almost invincible power. But it is at variance with the methodical principles which are the basis of all modern science, and which have proved their fruitfulness by the magnificent results to which they have led. If once we accept an objective spiritual interpretation of the consciousness of duty we become involved in a number of difficult problems as far as law is concerned. For it is conspicuous that the legal order is in many ways conditioned by human arbitrariness, external power and historical accident. The content of the law is clearly, at any rate to a great extent, determined by certain historical human law-creating acts and has no spontaneous validity by virtue of its inner moral-spiritual rightness. This raises the question how the law as a "positive" order is capable of creating "valid" obligations. How can it be explained that certain human law-creating actions are able to produce anything else or more than merely causal consequences in the world of physical and psychical reality, namely, an obligation in an ideally valid sense?

This has at all times given rise to much speculation. It is the fundamental problem of all traditional philosophy of law, and the theories vary with the different — more or less obscure and unconscious — views held concerning the nature of supersensual validity. I will not enter more closely into these theories, not even in their special relation to International Law. For according to my fundamental view they are all sham theories about sham problems. For the reader's enlightenment I will merely briefly state the chief theories of the "foundation" of the "binding force" of International Law.

A. *The will theories.* Very often the foundation for all legal obligations has been sought in the *will of the person* on whom the obligation is imposed. It is perhaps felt to justify the demands and possible compulsion of the law if it can be asserted that the person compelled has of his own accord given his consent to the compulsion. In this way the unpleasant fact of brute force seems to have been eliminated. From this point of view there has been an attempt to "explain" national law by a social contract between individuals, and similarly International Law by a mutual agreement or contract between the "sovereign" wills of the states. In International Law this point of view is — as we have seen — still common though in the general theory of law its untenability has long been realised.

B. *The idealistic theories.* The will theory has met with objections partly because it is an obvious fiction that all International Law implies agreement on the part of the parties bound, partly because it has been contended that no fact as such, not even a party's own will, can in itself explain the origin of an ideal validity. If a fact can create a valid obligation it must be because a higher valid norm confers this power on it. What is valid can only be deduced from a higher validity. From such points of view upholders of idealistic natural-law theories have contended that all law, International Law too, derives its validity from certain *objective ideas,* especially the idea of justice, which reveal themselves in the human mind and manifest themselves in a number of particular maxims, of which positive law again is a still more concrete application dependent on particular circumstances.

C. *The postulate theories.* The view leads to the difficulty that the validity of positive law becomes dependent on its agreement — even though loose and indirect — with certain objective ideas of justice. The existence of the law as a historical fact, its "positivity", seems to conflict with this. An attempt has then been made to combine positivistic (A) and idealistic (B) views by reducing the objective ideas to postulates, i. e. assertions incapable of proof which science is obliged to take for granted in order to "explain" the validity of law, and the contents of which are determined precisely in such a way that this validity covers positive law. Mostly under the influence of the will theories some authors have thought it possible to lay down the maxim *"pacta sunt servanda"* as the postulate or fundamental norm of International Law, while others, more attracted to the idealistic theories, have found it necessary to operate with a whole series of postulates.

Herewith this train of thought has in reality come to the end of its tether. If it is necessary, in order to explain the binding force of law, to resort to postulates incapable of proof, whose content conforms, precisely, to that which is to be explained, we may as well abandon all "explanation" and simply regard "the obligation" as a socio-psychological phenomenon.

§ 5
THE CHARACTER OF INTERNATIONAL LAW

I. *Is International Law actually law?*

It is an age-old controversial question whether International Law is actually law, or an order of a looser, more especially moral character. The great majority of authors on International Law hold that International Law is actually law; but particularly among the more philosophical authors there are a good many "International Law deniers".

On a superficial view the question must indeed appear doubtful. A sceptical attitude comes natural in an age which has seen the bankruptcy of the League of Nations and seen many other more or less sincere idealistic attempts to prevent war by international agreements wrecked. We have seen solemn agreements regarded as a mere scrap of paper. But it is not enough that the law is trampled under foot when it conflicts with strong interests. Just as offensive to the general sense of justice is the chaotic uncertainty that prevails in many domains with respect to the question of what is right. It is an ancient experience that both the contending parties maintain that right is on their side, and often they will both be able to do so with a certain amount of *bona fides*. For in extensive spheres of International Law there is a complete lack of clarity and certainty as to its contents. Nor is there any magisterial power which can stop the dispute and decide with authority what is to be valid as law. Far less is there any power which can enforce the commands of the law on those who will not obey. Therefore brutal violence, war, the great chaos, is unavoidable.

In this situation scepticism is quite understandable. That it may sometimes lead to scoffing and ridicule of International Law is perhaps at bottom a manifestation of the self-torturing protest of an offended sense of justice against recognising as justice this inverted picture of its ideals. But, on the other hand, it must not be forgotten that this is due to a onesided consideration of particular sections of International Law, viz. the law of war and the law for the prevention of war. Of course these are the sections that most closely affect us all. But it should not on that account be forgotten that there are other parts of International Law which have created civilised human intercourse of the very greatest importance. If we would picture to ourselves the contributions made by International Law we should think of the Universal Postal Union rather than of the Briand-Kellogg pact. Indeed, apart from the political part of International Law we may perhaps maintain with Brierly that International Law functions and is obeyed just as certainly as any part of national law.[1] Thus it would be quite misleading to characterise the world-embracing community of the Universal Postal Union as a merely moral order. It is just as good law as any corresponding national phenomenon.

Incidentally, an exaggerated importance has generally been attached to the question as to the legal character of International Law.[2] It is merely a question of terminology. International Law will neither be the better nor the worse for being called one thing or the other. It must be remembered that it is we who group and name things from certain points of view, and that these designations do not determine the nature of the things.

It is because of this that, traditionally, the problem as to the character of International Law is discussed in a curiously inadequate manner. The question is generally decided directly by a comparison with national law. It is then pointed out that it is true that International Law has neither a legislative, a judiciary, nor an executive power corresponding to these phenomena in national law. But, the reply is, on the one hand there are approaches to this in International Law, and on the other hand there are also within national law domains where these factors are more or less wanting (primitive law, parts of public law, especially constitutional and administrative law).

But the problem cannot be treated rationally in this way. It is not possible by a direct comparison of different phenomena to see whether or not they can be subsumed under the same concept. We cannot judge by a direct comparison whether or not the whale is a mammal. The "mammalian quality" is not a quality inherent in the thing itself, but something we ourselves establish by a definition. It must not be supposed that the things in themselves are grouped around a certain "nature" or a certain "idea" which we merely contemplate passively. Conceptual segregations cannot be compared to islands or continents

---

[1] *Brierly*, Law of Nations, 60.
[2] See e. g. *Lundstedt*, Superstition or Rationality in Action for Peace?

which are sharply marked off by nature from each other, but
to the meridians of longitude and latitude we imagine to be
drawn on the globe for our own guidance.

Such guidance can only be obtained by a conceptual charting
of the total group of phenomena with which we are here concerned (legal, moral, and similar phenomena). We can then
afterwards by these means determine the conceptual position of
International Law. Of course it is a lengthy task to justify the
criteria by which the conceptual distinctions can best be drawn.
I cannot here enter more closely into the subject but must be
content to state the result at which I have elsewhere arrived.[8]

When law and morality are contrasted it is generally said that
law is a "positive", morality a "natural" order. The inner
meaning of this is that law depends on human arbitrariness and
external power; its content varies with time and place according
to the interest and will of the potentates, and its validity as law
depends on the fact that it is backed by an effective executive
power. Morality, on the other hand, is a revelation of the eter-
nal; its laws derive their substance from the ideas of pure
reason and are directly valid by virtue of their inner truth.

Behind this metaphysical interpretation lie certain psychological realities, a difference in the way in which the moral
and legal feelings of validity arise and are experienced. Even
though the moral experiences of validity are of a social origin
there is, nevertheless, the possibility of a wide individual margin.
Morality knows no external legislator or judge, conscience is the
supreme arbiter. Therefore the moral experiences present
themselves as direct revelations, to conscience, of an actual rightness. Law, on the other hand, is experienced as a *social order*,
that is to say, as given with the community in which one lives
and independent of the conscience of the individual — in the
same way as, for instance, the rules of chess. The actual circumstances causing this difference in the experience of validity,
must be sought in the fact that the legal experiences arise and
develop under the pressure of an effective machinery of compulsion for the enforcement of certain pre-established rules. It
is this institutional factor which gives to the legal experiences

---

[8] Cf. *Ross*, Kritik, Chap. VII, and Towards a Realistic Jurisprudence,
Chap. IV, 3.

their peculiar character of "social order" or "positivity". Two elements are implied in this. The law is

    a. authoritatively established (conventional)[4].

    b. enforced by compulsion (enforceable).

Morality has neither of these qualities.

There is, however, an intermediate form, too, so that we get the following scheme:

A. *Personal morality*
    not conventional
    not enforceable.

B. *Conventional morality* (custom and usage, fashion, deportment, politeness, rules of the game):
    conventional
    not enforceable.

C. *Law:*
    conventional
    enforceable.

The three groups are not sharply marked off but pass gradually into each other. The rules laid down in group B are often — in contrast with those of law — unorganised, arising spontaneously out of the community.

In this system International Law must most naturally be placed in group B. For in International Law there is a considerable authoritative laying down of rules. It is no question of conscience what is International Law. In this point International Law differs decidedly from morality proper (personal morality), a fact which has generally been overlooked by the "international law deniers". On the other hand, International Law on the whole lacks an effective instrument of enforcement by compulsion. A reference to war as a self-administered enforcement of law replacing the organised enforcement is out of the question. For war lacks both the regularity of application and certainty of result (for the defeat of the lawbreaker) which characterise the enforcement of law by compulsion in a state.

Nevertheless, it would not be right to characterise International Law as "conventional morality". International Law is

---

[4] It should be noted that the term "conventional" is used here in another sense than that above in § 1. V in the connection "conventional law".

undoubtedly felt to be valid as law. This is due to the fact that the fundamental maxims of International Law, for instance the maxim *"pacta sunt servanda"*, agree in substance with the maxims of national law and therefore — since it is the same persons acting in different situations — acquire a character of legal validity derived from national law. If the maxim that agreements must be kept had not thousands of years' prescriptive standing as positive national law and thereby had become fixed in men's minds as a legal maxim, the maxim *"pacta sunt servanda"* would not, either, have been experienced as a legal rule.

International Law is of a conventional non-compulsory order with a derived character of law.

This is a characterisation of International Law such as it has developed, but is does not apply — a fact which is often overlooked — to the concept of International Law. A development of an international organisation and the use of force towards states might be imagined without International Law vanishing on that account. International Law will exist as long as its subjects are the self-governing states and not individuals.

*

If we compare International Law in its present stage of development with the national systems of law we cannot help realising that in many respects International Law is an order of a much weaker character with respect to its ability to direct human conduct towards social purposes. The following points may especially be emphasised:

II. *The anarchical character of International Law in the absence of an obligatory administration of justice and an organised force.*

According to general International Law states are under no obligation to submit their disputes to a legal settlement, and apart from the unsuccessful attempt in the Covenant of the League of Nations, International Law has hitherto lacked rules concerning organised means of compulsion against those who are found guilty of a violation of International Law. The effects of this shortcoming are, as already indicated, extremely varied with respect to the different parts of International Law. For the law of war and the law for the prevention of war it is catastrophic. In these domains even the semblance of a state of law may be worse than nothing at all. The solemn phrases and promises induce a belief in the man-in-the-street that law and order have replaced lawlessness. When later on unchecked force brutally rends this illusion, a reaction may easily set in, so that the value of all International Law and all international efforts to create a better world are regarded with cynical doubt.

In my opinion there can be no question that the way onward towards the overcoming of the former condition of anarchy can only be traversed step by step, along with a development of an organised power for the enforcement of law in international intercourse. All idealistic talk about a change of heart, a raising of the standard of morality and the reliance on good faith and promises — which are not the result of an effective organisation but are imagined to be produced by mere verbal appeals — is a naive misconception of the laws by which a community is built up. The necessary power may be conceived to be procured by a single state setting itself up as lord over the others (within a certain area) or by a co-ordinate co-operation being established for the maintenance of peace between the states as members of a league. The latter proceeding is of course attended with great difficulties. On the other hand it is the only possible one if the peace is not to be bought at the expense of liberty and humanity. The two ways correspond respectively to dictatorship and democracy in interstate affairs. The victory of the allied nations has saved Europe from slavery under a German supreme state. But it is an imperative necessity to understand that the freedom which has been won for the peoples by such enormous sacrifices can no longer mean the lawless, self-glorifying arbitrariness of "sovereignty", but freedom under law and order in the commonwealth of nations. It is the hope of mankind that the United Nations' organisation will be a step towards the realisation of this object.

III. *The static character of International Law in the absence of legislative power.*

One of the greatest dangers to peace comes from the markedly static character of International Law. It must be kept in mind that the most serious conflicts in a community are not conflicts about what is law but about what ought to be law (cf. § 59. III). Within the state the mechanism of legislation opens up the possibility of a peaceful smoothing out of the conflicting interests of the groups. Even the wages conflict has to a great extent been regulated by law. And although of course not every interest can press home its claim, the mere circumstance that the claim can be made and defended in a lawsuit means an essential remission of the conflict. Otherwise in International Law. Here, so far, there is a lack of every mechanism of legislation, that is to say, a laying down of what is the law which is binding on others than those who assent. The development of international courts is entirely unimportant in this connection. What is required is not a decision on the basis of law already in force, but a political revision of extant treaties and relations of power. The dogma of the sovereignty and equality of states constitutes an essential obstacle to the idea of international legislation. But as long as this is not removed there is no other way to the solution of a conflict of interest than a voluntary understanding between the parties or — war. In this respect too we must set our hopes on the new international organisation.

IV. *The uncertain and rough character of International Law as customary law.*

Though the rules of International Law have to a great extent been fixed through treaties, especially collective law-making treaties, still by far the greater part of general International Law is based on customary law. The result of this is that only an extremely uncertain and rough formulation of the contents of International Law is possible. Customary law is the law implied in the practice of states. But it will often be beset with great difficulty and uncertainty to find the legal rule which is the common denominator of a great number of actions. And in the nature of the case rules which have come into existence in this manner will show a tendency to be of a certain hard-handed rude character. The finer shades imply explicit formulation. Therefore International Law often bears the stamp of a primitive simplification compared with the minutely analytical quality of national law. Precision and refining of the rules of International Law can be conceived to be attained in two ways. Either by codification in collective treaties, or through the development of an ample fixed legal practice of a court whose decisions will have a determining influence on the international conception of law. The experience so far gained in the first respect is not encouraging. Here the *law of the lowest standard* applies, on the analogy of the economic law that base coins will oust good ones. If agreement is to be reached it will easily become the standard of the most backward state in law and culture which will decide the norm (the Codification Conference at The Hague 1930!). On the other hand, there is every hope that a continued development of the practice of the International Court which is now resurrected in a new shape will gradually lead onward to the goal.

V. *The non-social character of International Law.*

Compared with national law International Law has a very modest range. On perusing a textbook of International Law the reader will be surprised to see that by far the greater part of the rules presented have the character either of presuppositions for or of supplements to the actual material rules for social intercourse; examples of this can be seen in the rules regarding the subjects of International Law (states etc., their capacity for obligation and action, composite states, state succession); the rules regarding treaties (as the formal procedure for creating special International Law); rules dealing with violations of International Law (the consequences of having violated the central norms); and finally the rules for the settling of disputes (international process). The central rules themselves fill only a small volume. In addition, they are in the main restricted to a formal delimitation of the competence of the states, their living space. Of norms intended to render state intercourse harmonious with due regard to other interests, a social co-ordination for the promotion of common purposes, general International Law knows very few. It contains nothing about the burning questions as to the raw materials of the world; economic policy; density of population; immigration and emigration and the other incendiary subjects in international politics. All these questions come within the "reserved domain". Formally International Law gives each individual state "liberty" to adjust these problems as it likes. But in reality this liberty only means that every state must fight by itself for its own interests against all others. International Law is very largely non-social law, because it leaves fundamentally opposed interests to adjustment by fighting and force (see also § 31).

The development has brought about a schism here. When the economic system was more primitive international relations could more easily be left to lawlessness. Economic unity and with it economic dependence was much less. Nowadays the very advanced division of labour and industrialisation in connection with the development of the means of communication and the increase in the population have taken away all possibility of dividing up the whole world into more than a very few comparatively independent economic "spaces". There is now hardly any single state which can be enough unto itself. The interdependence of the states is greater than ever before. A change in the economic policy of one country may bring about ruin for the population of large portions of the population in another country. We are all parts in a great aggregate of production. Thereby political power becomes a decisive economic factor and strained relations between the nations due to economic causes are more intense than ever before. The more ramified, the more closely welded together and complicated the economic system becomes, the more easily can it be used as an instrument for economic political control and exploitation. Just as earlier advancing industrialisation created a greater interdependence between capital and labour, but for that very reason also a possibility of conflict and exploitation which rendered a social regulation necessary, so also the increasing international interdependence creates matter for strife and exploitation which necessitates international regulation. As long as no plan and order is introduced into international co-operation, economic factors will always be a source of wars.

VI. *The small number of the subjects of International Law.*

A peculiar trait of International Law is, as emphasised by *Brierly*, the small number and great difference of its subjects.[5] National law can formulate its rules with a view to typical situations which recur with tolerable uniformity in a great number of cases. National law can approximately regard its millions of subjects as interchangeable entities which function in abstractly determined situations ("creditors", "debtors", "successors" etc.). This is largely impossible in International Law. Many problems of International Law require a detailed individual decision with due consideration for the special conditions in each state, rather than abstract regulation. The reason why it has so far been impossible to find a solution of the

---

[5] The Rule of Law in International Society, N. T. 1936 appendix, 8.

question of the extent of the maritime belt is probably that a solution by means of abstract rules is not possible at all on account of the great individual differences between the actual conditions and interests. The ideal solution might be conceived to be a complete marking out of the limits of each maritime belt on a map of the world.

But even in the fields where International Law actually operates with abstract rules, these must for the same reason acquire a strained character, threatening every moment to make them illusory, in the face of the enormous actual heterogeneity of the subjects. Who can believe that it is really possible to lay down rules which can be applied without difference to a world power and a Lilliput state? If International Law is to be more than an illusion for the maintenance of abstract ideals of equality, it is inevitable that it should largely take into consideration (especially in the rules of organisation) the actual differences between the states, especially the extent of their political power. The small states must give up their jealousy, and legally, too, allow the great powers the dominant rôle which is actually their due. A schism between law and reality can never serve a sound development of the law but only an idle vanity. But unfortunately, here too, the ideology of sovereignty and the dogma of the absolute equality of states prevents a sound evolution (§ 34).

§ 6
INTERNATIONAL LAW AND INTERNAL LAW

I. *Survey of the theories.*

There exists a comprehensive literature on the relation between International Law and Internal Law. The fundamental disagreement concerns the question to whether International Law and the various national systems, taken together, can be said to form a unity, a universal system of law, or whether International Law must be said to constitute an independent system by the side of the others. The former theories are called *monistic,* the latter *dualistic.* Unfortunately it is anything but clear what is meant in this connection by the slogans "monism" and "dualism". It may be seen therefore that one author adduces the same facts in support of monism as another regards as a proof of dualism. In so far the dispute is merely a dispute about terms.[1]

Up to the time of the first world war the dualistic view, especially as formulated by the German *Triepel* and the Italian *Anzilotti,* prevailed absolutely. But since then monism has gained considerable ground, supported particularly by the so-called "Vienna school" (*Kelsen, Verdross* et al.). A concurrent cause was perhaps the fact that monism in a way harmonised well with the first post-war political tendencies by asserting the primacy of International as compared with National Law. Later, however, there has probably been a reaction. The more recent treatments of the subject, particularly the thoroughgoing investigations of *Walz,* in my opinion decidedly favour adherence to the traditional theory.

A. According to the *dualistic* theories International Law and Internal Law differ because they partly spring from different sources, partly refer to different subjects (states — individuals). From this it again follows

a. that the two systems differ in *content* or subject-matter, International Law regulating relations between states, Internal Law that between individuals or between the individual and the state;

b. that the two systems can have no influence on each other's *validity:* the validity of an internal norm as such depends solely on its conformity to the constitution and is not affected by its relation to International Law or the reverse.

c. that the two systems can never become actually *opposed* to each other: they are not concerned with the same subject-matter.

Nevertheless they are connected with each other:

a. International Law *demands* that national law should have a certain content. The international norm is directed towards the state and demands that it shall create by means of its organs a certain internal state of law. In relation to the demands of International Law, national law may be either *indifferent* or *relevant;* in the latter case either *in conflict with* International Law or *in harmony with* it: if in harmony with it either *permitted* or *commanded* by International Law.

As a rule the international norm is not content to demand a

---

[1] *Mirkine-Guetzévitch,* Droit constitutionnel international, defends monism but does not explain what he means by it and does not adduce any fact which, in my opinion, is incompatible with dualism.

certain act of legislation, but primarily aims at the actual enforcement of the law in the civil administration and the administration of justice. At any rate a certain state of legislation does not conflict with International Law merely because it opens up possibilities of actions at variance with International Law.

b. International Law and internal law may each of them be formulated as a *reference* to the other system in the same way as a national system (in its interlegal norms, cf. § 7) may make reference to another national system. Such a reference involves a *transformation* of the received norm with respect to its source as well as to its subject and content.

B. The *monistic* theories exist in variants differing widely from each other.

Monism with *state law primacy* is the term used when International Law is conceived to be an element of the individual national system (we have here a pluralism properly speaking). This view is a natural consequence of the absolute concept of sovereignty and the theory of the self-limitation of the power of the state. The rules of the constitution concerning the authority to conclude treaties are then understood to imply a voluntary subjection to the treaties as well. International Law is "external state law".

It is evident that the monism of state law is rendered abortive by the fact that not all International Law is treaty law. In addition, the construction of self-obligation is incompatible with the recognition of a true obligation. This conception may therefore be left out of consideration.

Monism with *International Law primacy* is the term used when International Law is viewed as a kind of general constitution delegating to each state its competence for internal legislation within the scope of International Law. In this way International Law will be, as it were, the apex of the pyramid in a universal legal system. Just as the municipality and its legislative power is grounded in the state, the state itself is grounded in International Law. This view exists in a radical and in a moderate form.

The *radical* variant seriously considers the idea of the derived character of national law and draws the conclusion that internal law loses its validity as such if it conflicts with International Law.

There cannot be any doubt, however, that this is in the most obvious way at variance with the facts. No matter what "logical" arguments may be brought forward in favour of state law as a law of a lower order bound to yield to International Law, it is an incontrovertible fact that it does not actually do so, (cf. below under II A). But when "logic" leads to a conflict with facts it is all the worse for "logic" (which of course has never been any tenable logic). This theory, too, may therefore be left out of consideration.

The *moderate* variant admits the existence of a national law conflicting with International Law. But, it says, this is not incompatible with the unity of the system. The same thing occurs within the internal system when a legislative act is maintained as valid in spite of its conflict with the constitution, viz. when the courts have no competence to judge in questions concerning the constitutional character of the legislation. In such cases an "error clause" must be presupposed in the constitution which at the outset renders legitimate possible errors brought about by actions ultra vires. The same construction may be seen when state law conflicts with International Law. (Common to both cases is the circumstance that the transgression need not involve invalidity but may manifest itself merely in a responsibility for the violation of the law).

C. The *choice* therefore can only be made between the dualistic theory and the moderate monistic theory with primacy for International Law. Apart from disputes about words the core of the dissension is this: is the legislative power of the state given by International Law or does it exist indepently? Is International Law a "general constitution" or does it confine itself to making demands on states which existed, temporarily and logically, before and independently of International Law?

Logically, both constructions are no doubt possible. That is to say, the legal relation between International Law and state law is reconcilable both with the one and the other theory. But the question to whether or not a certain rule of law exists has not been decided by the fact that its assumption is logically possible, i. e. without it coming into conflict with other rules. The question of the existence of a law is in the last instance always a question of certain *socio-psychological* realities. Such realities, however, are not found behind the logically possible assumption of a "general constitution". The national legal systems are not felt to be derived from International Law, they are felt to be original. The validity of state law is a fact, which has its socio-psychological foundation in internal functions of intercourse. To attempt to "legitimise" this fact through an international general constitution is an empty superfluous construction very far from reality. To a psychological consideration conditions are, as we have seen (§ 5, I), on the contrary just the reverse, namely that the validity of International Law is deduced from internal law.

The dualistic construction must therefore be regarded as the correct one. National Law is not derived from International Law. International Law and National Law are independent systems. Their interconnection lies partly in the demands International Law makes on National Law, partly in references to one another.

II. *The relation between International Law and internal law before a national forum.*

"Dualism" is merely an abstract outline. What is really of interest is to see what the connection between the two systems actually looks like on closer inspection. Let us first consider the matter from the angle of internal law.

A. *Internal law is valid even if it conflicts with International Law.* — In accordance with the dualistic fundamental view it must be maintained that in internal legal relations, that is to say, in cases that are settled *in national courts, the law of the land, and that only, applies,* and that even if it conflicts with International Law. Before the national forum, therefore, the maxim applies that "*the law of the land cancels International Law*".

Formally this holds good without exceptions. No matter to what extent experience shows that International Law is actually taken into account in national courts, it must in any case be interpreted to mean that here we have an explicit or implicit acceptance on the part of national law of the rules of International Law, that is to say, a transformation. Even according to a system like the Spanish under the constitution of 1931, which at the outset assimilates internal law to International Law and denies internal validity to any law conflicting with

International Law, this harmony is due precisely to the contents of the Spanish law itself. The Spanish law-courts, too,
have since then used Spanish law alone, namely the constitution
and its general acceptance of the norms of International Law.
As the harmony between the two factors is thus wholly dependent on the pleasure of one of them, there is, in principle, always
the possibility of a disagreement (in the present case, by a
Spanish constitutional act).

But in the great majority of cases the possibility of a national
law conflicting with International Law but still retaining its
national validity is quite clear. *Walz* has undertaken to show
this by a careful review of a series of leading systems of law.
He points out how a long series of judicial decisions according to
American, British, and German law are based on the point of
view that it is a matter for the courts of the country alone to
enforce the law of the land whether or not the latter is at
variance with International Law.[2] A single example must suffice
to illustrate this. The *Mortensen-Peters* case (1906) was concerned with a Danish shipmaster who had fished in Moray
Firth in a place which presumably, according to International
Law, was outside English territorial waters[3] but beyond any
doubt within a territory where fishery was prohibited by British
(Scotch) law.[4] A passage in the judgment ran thus:

> In this court we have nothing to do with the question of
> whether the Legislature has or has not done what foreign powers
> may consider an usurpation in question with them. Neither are
> we a tribunal sitting to decide whether an Act of the Legislature
> is ultra vires as in contravention of generally acknowledged prin-
> ciples of International Law. For us an Act of Parliament duly
> passed by Lords and Commons and assented to by the King is
> supreme, and we are bound to give effect to its terms.[5]

Consequently Mortensen was sentenced to pay a fine, but
after diplomatic representations on the part of the Danish

---

[2] *Walz*, Völkerrecht und staatliches Recht, § 10.

[3] Cf. on bays § 23, III with Note 1. The fishing took place more
than 3 nautical miles from the coast.

[4] Under Art. 6 of the Herring Fishery Act for Scotland 1889 beam and
otter trawling was prohibited within a certain distance from the Scotch
coast, namely, in Moray Firth within a line drawn from Duncansby
Head to Rattray Point.

[5] Quoted from *Walz*, l. c. 181.

Government the fine was remitted. There can be no clearer example of the conflict between the national and the international decision.[6]

B. *But internal law to a certain extent seeks to exclude conflict with International Law by reference.* — Even though internal law is thus absolutely valid in the national courts, it has to submit to the international demands for a certain formulation. These demands may be conceived to be fulfilled by the legislature in numerous relations expressly paying attention to the international commands and taking care that the law is formulated in accordance herewith. In practice such a detailed procedure will be very troublesome and unreliable. The national systems therefore generally contain explicit or implicit norms more or less comprehensively making reference to International Law and transforming the rules of the latter into national law. It may also be said that, corresponding to the interlegal norms of national law, there are certain norms which make reference to International Law. The extent of this embodiment cannot of course be settled as a matter of principle. It is entirely dependent on the discretion of the individual legal systems. I may mention examples of the different types. A distinction must be made between the way in which customary law and treaty law respectively are incorporated in national law.

1. *Customary law* (including treaties which have gained general recognition).

a. *Incorporation of customary law as a whole.* This type has its historical origin in England and is expressed in the formula "*international law is part of the law of the land*". This sentence is derived from natural law. In an age in which common law was conceived to be a manifestation of natural common sense, as it was revealed through the living oracles of the law, the English judges *(Blackstone)*, it would be natural to regard International Law, which was also considered to have taken its rise in *ratio naturalis* and *consensus omnium*, as simply one com-

---

[6] To do away with this discrepancy the Trawling in Prohibited Areas Prevention Act was passed in 1909, according to which no prosecution can take place if the prohibited fishing methods have been exercised more than 3 nautical miles from the coast, but the fish so caught may not be landed or sold in the United Kingdom.

ponent of common law. Later on the condition of affairs has correctly been understood to be that the maxim is itself merely a customary rule of the common law.

By a long series of judical decisions[7] it has been established that the maxim only applies to customary law (and other generally accepted law) which demonstrably, in practice, has been acknowledged by England, and only gives the transformed law validity as common law. It may therefore be displaced by a statutory rule to the contrary, cf. *Mortensen-Peters*.

A well-known case, the *Franconia case (Regina v. Keyn*, 1876) has given rise to doubts as to the scope of the rule. A German steamship, the Franconia, collided in English territorial waters with a British steamer, one person being killed. Before an English court proceedings were instituted against the master, Keyn, for manslaughter, but at the highest tribunal he was acquitted on various grounds, partly on the view that even if International Law places the territorial waters under the control of the littoral state and authorises the latter to exercise jurisdiction there, such an international rule would not afford a basis for punishment if the British penal code had not included the territorial waters under its domain. And from an historical interpretation of the penal laws in force this was not deemed to be the case. *Walz*[8] and others think that this restricts the said rule to apply only to rules of International Law which are binding and not merely permissive. In my opinion, however, no restriction is implied in the rule but the result simply follows from the fact that in a case such as this the rule has hardly any practical significance. What would the transformation of an authorisation mean? It could at most be conceived as a constitutional rule to the effect that according to British law the territorial waters are included in the domain in which English government authorities have the usual competence to legislate and exercise jurisdiction. That a man could be punished merely according to such a rule of competence must at any rate be excluded.

The rule in fact caused the passing of the Territorial Waters Jurisdiction Act 1878, which extended British criminal jurisdition to the territorial waters.

---

[7] See especially *West Rand Central Gold Mining Co. Lt. v. the King* L. R. [1905] 2 K. B. 391) cf. *Walz*, l. c. 275 f.

[8] L. c. 180.

The maxim "international law is part of the law of the land" at the emancipation of the American colonies passed as a part of common law into American law and has since been firmly established there.

A similar provision after the English pattern was incorporated in the German Weimar Constitution of 1919 Art. 4 *(Die allgemein anerkannten Regeln des Völkerrechts gelten als bindende Bestandteile des Reichsrechts)*, and from there passed into the former Austrian, Esthonian, and Spanish liberal constitutions.

b. Presumably everywhere the *rule of interpretation* is accepted that in doubtful cases, that is to say, where the wording is ambiguous, national law must be interpreted in the way which will give the best agreement with International Law. Where there are no clear indications of the reverse it must be assumed that the legislator has not intended to legislate in conflict with International Law.

c. In countries which, like Denmark and most others, do not know any rule, established by law or custom, for incorporation en-bloc of the generally acknowledged International Law, the above-mentioned interpretation will, however, hardly suffice. There is reason to believe that the tribunals will to a great extent come to the same results as in the case of an incorporation, by implying, or by their interpretation introducing, such corrections as are necessary to make national law accord with International Law. For the fact is that the British system is not based solely on ideas of natural law but is also sustained by the claims of practical life which must be felt with special force in a country like Great Britain with its highly developed intercourse with other nations. It would often lead to undesirable results if the courts were to base their decisions on a national law in conflict with International Law. As a rule, however, it may be taken for granted that the legislator has not really intended to legislate in conflict with the principles which are recognised by the country itself in its intercourse with other states. If nevertheless the wording of the law does not accord with these, it may be due to the fact that the legislator has simply forgotten to take into account these more exceptional conditions with which he will often not be closely acquainted, amongst other things because Customary International Law has not been fixed by clear rules, but must first be deduced from the practice of the states, and the recognition this has found in the particular state itself. Starting from such considerations we may probably *presume*, at any rate in countries such as Denmark where the courts have considerable libety in their interpretation of the law, that national law must be interpreted with such reservations as will make it agree with generally accepted International Law. Danish law, for instance, does not state that foreign state property cannot be seized or that customs officers cannot arrest a person on a ship in the open sea. Nevertheless the rules in question must no doubt be understood with the restriction which follows from generally accepted International Law so that actions at variance with this must be regarded as invalid and will perhaps involve responsibility for neglect of duty.

The difference between this presumption and the rule of interpretation given under b lies in the fact that it can be applied even where national law by its wording is unambiguous.

The difference from the British system is not then very great. In Great Britain too International Law must yield to later, opposed, legal provisions. Actually the difference lies merely in the fact that while the problem is clearly presented and definitely solved in English practice, none of these things is the case under Danish law. The maxim "international law is part of the law of the land" is undoubtedly an element of common law, but the corresponding conjectural rule in Danish law is merely based on more loose indications and estimates as to how the courts would presumably react if the problem were clearly presented. But it may also be imagined that the same principle will not be followed in all cases but that there will be an adjustment to circumstances and the practical interests concerned in the various situations. I should think that according to the nature of the case it will be much the same in other legal systems which, like the Danish system, do not contain any fixed, recognised rule concerning the incorporation of international customary law in the national law.

d. Finally, national law often contains *scattered references* to generally accepted International Law, see the Danish Penal Code § 12, German Penal Code (1927) § 6.

2. *Treaty Law.*

a. *Automatic transformation* at the ratification and proclamation of the treaty in the law gazette.

According to Art. 6 Part 2 of the American constitution the following rule applies:

This Constitution, and the laws of the United States which shall be made in Pursuance thereof; and all Treaties made, or which shall be made, under the Authority of the United States, shall be the supreme Law of the Land; and the judges of every State shall be bound thereby, any Thing in the Constitution or Laws of any State to the Contrary notwithstanding.

According to Art. 2 Part 2 the power of making treaties lies with the President with the consent of a majority of two-thirds of the Senate.[9]

It follows that as soon as the President has lawfully ratified the treaty (and published it) it is automatically, by virtue of Art. 6, transformed into American law with validity as union law. That is to say, it cancels earlier union law, but may be itself supplanted by later union law. It takes absolute precedence of the laws and constitutions of the individual states.

This rather unique rule, (which, however, recurs in the Mexican and Argentine constitutions as well as the Spanish constitution of 1931) is originally grounded in the endeavours of the American constitution to strengthen and guarantee the unity of the union.

Naturally, Art. 6 only applies to treaties, the contents of which are formulated in a sufficiently concrete way to refer directly to the legal status of individuals (self-executory treaties), hence not to treaties that only proclaim certain principles which require to be formulated in more detail by law.

b. Even in states that do not know any rule corresponding to Art. 6 of the American constitution and thus require an ordinary act of legislation for the transformation of the treaty, *a similar result can be attained indirectly.* We are here thinking of constitutions according to which the consent of the legislative assembly is always or as a rule required for the ratification of

---

[9] It has not been settled whether this power also extends to domains which according to the constitution are reserved to the legislative power of the single states. There exist a number of dicta from the Supreme Court of Justice which deny this. On the other hand treaties have in several cases been respected by the Court, even though they encroached on such domains. These dicta and decisions cannot be made to agree, cf. *W. W. Willoughby*, The Constitutional Law, 2. ed. (1929) §§ 310—13. If the power of the president to conclude treaties is recognised as unlimited it will mean that the self-government of the states is abolished to the same extent as the Union has actually concluded treaties which interfere in the domains otherwise reserved to the states.

the treaty by the head of the state. If this consent is given in the shape of a statute, and if this statute granting consent is also interpreted as an anticipatory transformation act, an automatic transformation to national law will then occur as soon as the treaty has been ratified (and proclaimed).

This practice was usually followed under the earlier German constitution of 1871 as well as under the Weimar constitution.

The usual practice is, however, that the treaty as such it not transformed but that it is carried through by an adjustment of the national law in the ordinary way of legislation.

This is the system in England where there has always been a sharp distinction between the power of the crown to conclude treaties (formally without consent) and the legislative power of Parliament. In Denmark too, the two elements in the process are normally kept distinct.

The procedure under this system also differs from the preceding ones in the fact that the law enacted for the execution of the treaty only contains those elements of the treaty which are intended to be law in the state concerned. As a mutual agreement the treaty of course also contains elements relating to conditions in the other contracting state. In automatic transformation, on the other hand, it is the undifferentiated text of the treaty which is turned into law (treaty law). It is then the task of the courts to segregate the ideal element which is to be valid as law of the land.[10]

d. As far as treaties are concerned the following *rule of interpretation* may perhaps be laid down. In doubtful cases, that is to say, where the wording of the national law is ambiguous, it must be interpreted in such a way that it most nearly agrees with treaties already in force. But otherwise there can be *no presumption* — as is the case with generally recognised Law — that national law is to be interpreted in accordance with treaties made. The above-described consideration does not apply in this case, seeing that the legislator must be assumed to have had knowledge of the rules formulated by the treaty.

---

[10] The same thing may occur by transformation by the ordinary means of legislation, when, exceptionally, the whole treaty is turned by legislation into law, instead of segregating the suitable elements.

C. *In relation to a concrete case the reference of National Law to International Law may have a double form.*

It may either refer directly to a norm which determines the *main question* in issue; for instance, when the penal code makes reference to the international rule of the immunity of envoys — in relation to a case which concerns the question of the liability to punishment of an ambassador.

Or it may refer to a norm which will only serve to decide a preliminary question. How this is to be understood may be explained thus. A legal rule associates the legal effect with certain conditioning facts. Now it may happen that a legal rule R_1 contains among its conditioning facts some facts the occurrence of which cannot be settled without examining the available facts in relation to another legal rule R_2. It is this estimation in relation to R_2 which is called a preliminary decision in a case that requires to be judged directly in relation to R_1.

If, e. g., it has any bearing on the calculation of taxes whether a man is married or unmarried, the establishment of his marital status is a prejudicial decision in a case concerning his duty to pay taxes.

The rules of International Law can be of importance in manifold ways in deciding such prejudicial questions, as will be shown by a couple of random examples quoted below.

In a vindication with respect to personal property it is of importance to know beforehand whether the present owner or a predecessor gained possession of the property by robbery or the like. (In that case a claim for restitution will be recognised). If, however, the owner derives his right from a compulsory relinquishment made in a foreign state, rules of International Law must settle the question whether it has been a case of mere robbery or a confiscation by the state which, as a legal action of the state, must be respected in other countries. (See the case *Luther v. Sagor*, 1921,[11] § 18. IV.).

In a case where a person during the first world war had insured himself against the possibility that peace should not have been concluded between England and Germany within a certain date, it was — when the "conclusion of peace" is interpreted as a legally qualified term — a prejudicial question of International Law whether or not peace had been concluded at the time stipulated. See *Lloyd v. Bowring.* 1920[11].

---

[11] The case is mentioned in *Scott*, Cases on International Law.

III. *The relation between International Law and Internal Law before an international tribunal.*

Conversely, from the standpoint of International Law it holds good, formally without exception, that in international legal relations, that is to say, in cases which are decided *in international courts, International Law applies and International Law only,*[12] and that even if national law is an obstacle to the fulfilment by the state of international obligations. Before an international tribunal, then, the rule applies that *"International Law nullifies the law of the land"*.

It is another question, however, whether "specific performance" can always be demanded of the state bound, so that it must change its laws, more especially its constitution, so as to be able to carry out the actions demanded of it. If this would cause excessive disturbance, the state must be able to satisfy its obligation by paying compensation. An example will illustrate this *(City of New Orleans v. Abbagnato,* 1894[11]). In 1894 Abbagnato and 10 other Italians who had been taken into custody in New Orleans charged with the murder of the head of the police in that city (though several of them had already been acquitted) were lynched by a mob that made its way into the prison. During a lawsuit connected with this affair it was admitted that the authorities of the town, including the mayor and the police, had been cognisant of the intended action against the prisoners, but had nevertheless failed to do anything for their protection. The President expressed his regret for what had happened to the Italian government and declared that he would apply for a grant for compensation (which was not warranted under the law in force) to the families of the murdered men. The Italian government was not satisfied with this offer, but made the further demand that the leaders of the mob should be tried and punished in accordance with the laws of the land. "With this demand the government of the United States could not comply, however willing it was to do so. It is well known that the federal courts have no common law jurisdiction in

---

[12] In contrast with internal law. On the other hand, it may be that the international court, in accordance with the autonomy of the parties recognised by International Law, either must decide the matter on the basis of certain rules laid down by the parties, or pass judgment ex *æquo et bono,* cf. § 59, IV.

criminal matters, it was impossible, therefore, to institute a criminal suit against these persons in those courts; and as the states are wholly independent of the federal government in respect of such jurisdiction, it was equally impossible to compel the government of Louisiana to institute such proceedings. The government of the United States was therefore quite helpless in this aspect of the case, and could only listen to the complaints of Italy and try to explain to her statesmen the intricacies of the United States Constitution" (cited from *Scott*, Cases, 123). It is true that we might reply to this that it was in the power of America to change her constitution on this point. That, however, would seem to be too much to ask, and ultimately the Italian government did agree to receiving a pecuniary compensation.

Otherwise similar rules apply here as described under II. International Law may by *reference* convert national law into International Law. A general but very vague reference to this is found in the Statue of the International Court Art. 38, part 1 c, according to which the Court in its decisions must apply "the general principles of law recognised by civilized nations" (i. e. in their internal law) (§ 12).

§ 7.
INTERNATIONAL LAW AND INTERLEGAL LAW

By "interlegal law" we here mean what is usually called "private international law". Normally it is both hopeless and inadvisable to try to alter a generally accepted terminology, but in this case linguistic usage is so misleading that it seems to me right to make the attempt. For "private international law" is neither private nor international. The last point is, indeed, controversial, cf. below. But it is generally acknowledged that, besides a private international law in a narrower sense, there is also, similarly, a processual, penal, constitutional, and administrative international law.

The legal rules here concerned are incontestably those that are applied by a national tribunal. They are, therefore, by definition formally elements of national law. They decide the question whether a lawsuit shall be judged materially by the law of the land or, if not, by which particular foreign legal system. Formally, therefore, in so far as foreign law comes into play, they consist in *references* to foreign law which convert the contents of the latter into national law.[1]

Such a reference of course is always dependent on the presence in one respect or another of "foreign elements" in the lawsuit in question. These may consist in a certain connection either with the population of a foreign state or with its territory, see also below § 28. IV.

Of course it is true here as in all other spheres that International Law may make certain *demands* on national law, in this case on the interlegal rules of national law. And as a matter of fact, International Law really makes various demands in this respect, and more than is often supposed by "nationalist" theorists. Further, as we have seen, there is more or less a presumption that internal law may have incorporated, or may be interpreted in accord with, generally accepted International Law. In this way it may come about that International Law as transformed national law is applied to a certain extent in these cases, but that does not change the fact that the interlegal rules are, none the less, national law.

Though interlegal law is an element of national law, nevertheless special circumstances come into play which may explain the view, widespread especially in earlier times, according to which interlegal law was regarded as an international arrangement, above the states, the task of which it was to delimit the competence of the various legislations in relation to each other. The principal reason why we trouble to set up rules of interlegal law at all and why all cases are not simply tried according to the law of the land is the fundamental assumption that it is just and desirable that any matter whatever should be tried by the same material law apart from the accidental circumstance whether the case is brought before the courts of one country or another: *any tribunal, the same law (the principle of uniform judgment).* It is now clear that this ideal would not be realised if the courts in a state always applied the country's own law. Hence interlegal rules must be introduced. But this is not enough in itself. For the ideal will not be attained either, if the interlegal law in the various states has not the same contents. With a varying tribunal the same case will then be judged now according to one, now

---

[1] We also include in interlegal law the norms determining (1) whether the courts of the country are competent to try a certain case; (2) to what extent foreign judgments are given legal or executive force in the country.

according to the other material law. We can therefore say: inter-legal law, by its very nature, is only of value to the extent that it is international in its contents. Consequently the political discussion of interlegal problems assumes the appearance of an attempt to find a *common international* arrangement, and that fact has no doubt contributed to the origin of the interna-tionalist theories.

§ 8
THE SYSTEM OF INTERNATIONAL LAW

Before we can proceed to an exposition of the contents of Inter-national Law two requirements must be fulfilled. First, it must be settled what rules are international and thus the subject of the exposition. As the reader will already have perceived, that is the task to be solved in the first chapter of this book, which deals with the *concept* of International Law. In this connection the presuppositions of International Law are likewise discussed, as well as its general characteristics and its relation to internal law.

Second, since the exposition is to be an exposition of the law in force — and not of merely imaginary or desirable norms of international content — it must be explained under what con-ditions a rule which, according to its formulation must be inter-national, may be regarded as expressing *current law*. This question is dealt with in the doctrine of legal sources which is presented in Chapter II.

In chapters III—XII follows the *dogmatic* exposition of the content of the international rules. The systematics of this ex-position are presented in the schematic representation on page 76.

The importance of this schematic representation will best be gathered from the exposition itself, particularly the in-troductory remarks to chapters III, IV, VI, VII, X, XI, and XII. Provisionally the following comments may be made.

At the centre of every legal system we find the *central rules of intercourse* which make the conduct that it is desired to realise in the intercourse of the members a duty.

But these rules are in several respects fragmentary, that is to say, they do not acquire their full meaning until they are viewed

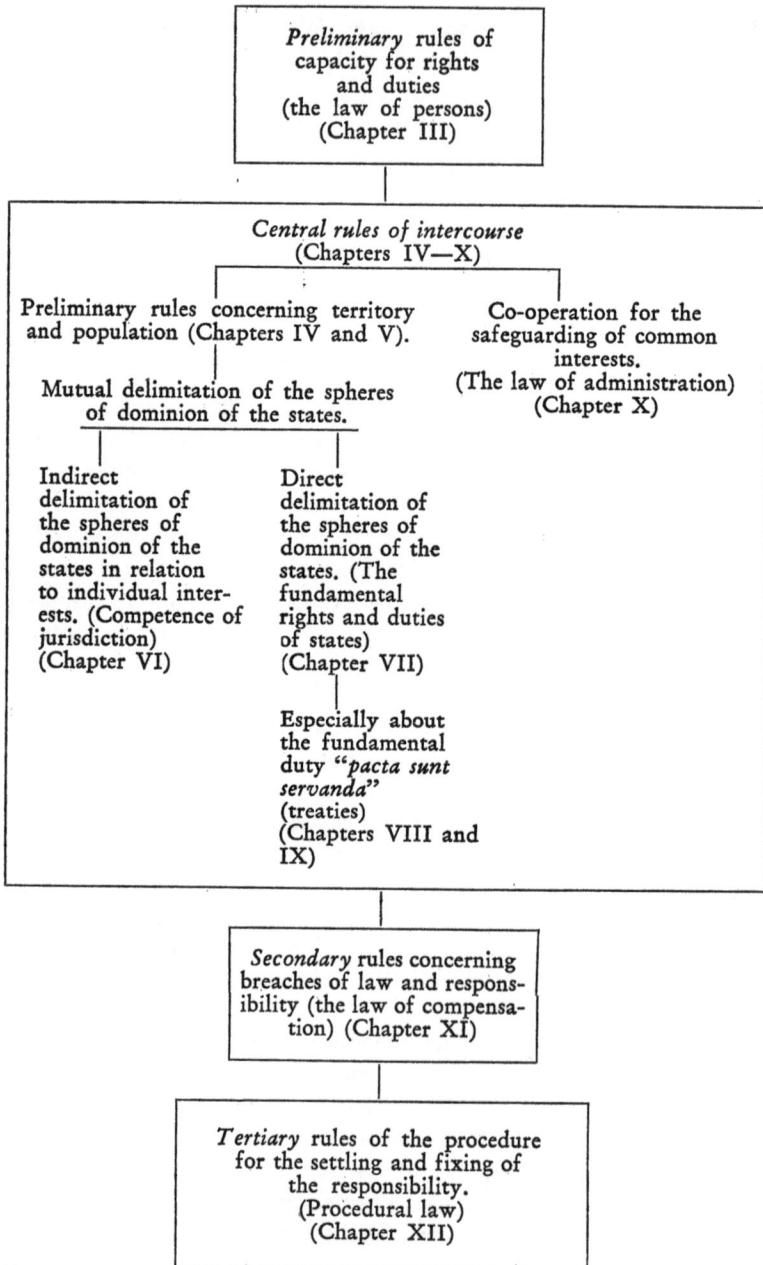

Preliminary rules of
capacity for rights
and duties
(the law of persons)
(Chapter III)

Central rules of intercourse
(Chapters IV—X)

Preliminary rules concerning territory
and population (Chapters IV and V).

Co-operation for the
safeguarding of common
interests.
(The law of administration)
(Chapter X)

Mutual delimitation of the spheres
of dominion of the states.

Indirect
delimitation of
the spheres of
dominion of the
states in relation
to individual inter-
ests. (Competence of
jurisdiction)
(Chapter VI)

Direct
delimitation of
the spheres of
dominion of the
states. (The
fundamental
rights and duties
of states)
(Chapter VII)

Especially about
the fundamental
duty "*pacta sunt
servanda*"
(treaties)
(Chapters VIII and
IX)

Secondary rules concerning
breaches of law and responsibility (the law of compensation) (Chapter XI)

Tertiary rules of the procedure
for the settling and fixing of
the responsibility.
(Procedural law)
(Chapter XII)

in connection with other complexes of rules, which are themselves of course also fragmentary if considered in isolation.

In the first place, the individual rule of intercourse which imposes a duty does not indicate in more detail on whom it imposes the duty. Information on this point is found in the *preliminary rules concerning the capacity for legal rights and duties,* the Law of Persons. These are therefore first presented in Chapter III.

In the second place, a legal system — in contrast with moral rules — cannot stop at the mere act of prescribing a certain conduct as duty. In case the central primary norms of intercourse are contravened, it is not enough to note this and perhaps disapprove of it, but, according to certain rules, there arises a definite responsibility for the contravener of the duty. The primary rules must therefore be supplemented by *secondary rules relating to breaches of law and responsibility.*

In the third place, a well-developed legal system does not stop at imposing duties (primary and secondary), but in cases of dissension and reluctance to comply prescribes, *in tertiary rules, a procedure* for the binding settlement and, if necessary, compulsory fixing of the responsibility (process). In this point, however, International Law is greatly lacking. The rules under this head are presented in Chapter XII.

The central rules of intercourse themselves are dealt with in Chapters IV—IX. They fall into two main groups, viz. partly rules in the main merely intended to delimit the spheres of dominion of the various states for the purpose of separating them and avoiding infiltrations and conflicts; partly rules aiming at a social co-ordination for the safeguarding of common interests. The first group has chiefly only negative or preventive, the latter positive or constructive objects.

The mutual *delimitation* of the spheres of dominion of states is based on two fundamental concepts: the *territory* of a state and its *population.* The more precise meaning of these is defined in preliminary international rules, which are presented in Chapters IV and V.

The delimitation itself comprises two sections. One deals with the *limits to the power of a state directly with respect to individuals* and so indirectly with respect to the foreign state that safeguards the interests of the individual. It refers to the rules of jurisdictional competence which are presented in

Chapter VI. The other deals with the *limits to the power of a state directly with respect to other states.* This section deals with what was formerly termed the doctrine of the "fundamenal rights and duties" of states — Chapter VII.

One of these fundamental duties is the duty of keeping agreements once entered upon. The particular rules as to when a binding agreement exists are presented in two chapters on treaties — Chapters VIII and IX.

The international *law of social co-ordination,* the rules of co-operation for the safeguarding of common interests, is based almost exclusively on treaty and is to that extent presented in Chapter X.

*

I believe that the succeeding exposition will prove the convenience and fruitfulness of this system, which is based on the fundamental structure characterising all legal systems (according to the scheme: preliminary, central, secondary, tertiary rules), and yet at the same time adapted to the peculiarities of the international system (the subdivisions within the central rules). The expert reader will see that the result is a construction which without entirely breaking with the tradition has necessitated essential rearrangements of the material both broadly and in detail.

Notably, I believe that the new place given to the rules concerning the territory and population of states, which are traditionally referred to the international law of persons, will prove well founded.

Chapter II

THE SOURCES OF INTERNATIONAL LAW

§ 9

THE TERM "SOURCE OF LAW" AND THE GENERAL THEORY OF LEGAL SOURCES

Treaty and custom are usually mentioned as the sources of International Law. Recently "general legal principles" are often said to be a third source. Very little clarity prevails, however, as to what facts and problems are actually dealt with in the maxims of the doctrine. As a rule it is not explained what is meant by the term "source of law". But without such an explanation it is not possible to know, either, what, strictly speaking, is meant by saying that something, for instance a treaty, is a source of law. It is necessary, therefore, by way of introduction, to say a few words about the term "source of law" in general.

The traditional doctrine of the sources of law is based on the view that all law derives its specific validity from coming into existence in certain forms. Sources of law, then, denote precisely those forms from which it can be deduced what is valid as law. That for instance "statutes" are sources of law would mean that everything that had come into existence in the shape of a statute (by means of legislation) is valid as law. Therefore the sources of law are the basis of the scientific exposition of the law as well as of concrete judicial decisions. In accordance with this view judicial decisions are conceived as a mere *application* of the rules given in the sources for the situation to hand. The task of the judge is to *ascertain* what is the law according to the sources of the system, and then *logically to subsume* the concrete facts under the given rules.

This view of the nature of a judicial decision is erroneous. In the first place because the application of a given rule is something more than a merely logical subsumption. Secondly, and especially, because to a great extent judicial decisions are not an application of rules already given. Even though it is true that the law as a social order has a tendency to objective establishment or formulation (§ 5. I), nevertheless the concrete decisions arise largely out of impulses not previously established by rules.

Altogether, the notion that the "validity" of the law can be "deduced" from certain sources is metaphysical. It is based on the implication that the "validity" is of a supersensual nature. It then becomes the task of the doctrine of legal sources to solve the curious enigma how certain specially qualified events in the empirical world are capable of producing anything but merely causal effects. The sources are the channels through which validity pours into the world of reality and lends to the law its "binding force" (§ 4). To a realistic view the validity of the law is in the last resort a manifestation of certain socio-psychological facts. For the genesis and development of these, however, the regular "enforcement" by the courts of law is of decisive importance. When a client asks his solicitor what is "the law" in a certain situation, the practical import of this question is how legal proceedings, if instituted, will be judged by the courts. The same interest is at the bottom of jurisprudence as a practical branch of learning. From this point of view another task will devolve on the doctrine of the sources, viz. an analysis of the general factors determining the content of the concrete legal ideas. This analysis is best carried out where the legal ideas are put to the most thorough and serious test, viz. in the concrete judicial decisions immediately before their enforcement. Here, after mature deliberation, thought is converted into action, which itself reacts on the thoughtful conception of the law. The judicial decision is the pulse of legal life, and it is here that the analysis of the legal sources comes into play. A source of law, then, means *the general factors (motive components)* which *guide the judge when fixing and making concrete the legal content in judicial decisions.*

As already mentioned, these factors cannot be restricted to notions of certain rules already formulated. As we know, the formulae are not an end in themselves, but serve to realise certain social interests, purposes, ideas, and considerations which exist, and conflict, in a certain community. Nor is the judge an automaton, but a living member of the community who feels that it is his task to materialise the living tendencies lying behind the formulated rules, and who first gives them their true meaning and scope. Considering these socio-psychological facts, it may be said in general that every judicial decision is determined by three co-operating groups of factors, viz.

a. The legal maxims authoritatively *formulated* in accordance with certain rules. Using an abstract common term, this legal source may be called *"statute law"*.

b. The not formulated, yet *partly objectified,* rules of conduct emerging from the precedents of the courts themselves, and from the legal customs of those subject to them. By virtue of the tendency to objective regularity, the courts of any legal system will be inclined to decide a case according to the same points of view as have been determining in other similar cases Therefore the *precedents* of the courts will always be an important factor, whether precedents are formally recognised as binding (as in British doctrine) or not. Since each judgment only settles the case at hand, it will always be more or less uncertain what general rule can be deduced from precedents. The rule is not authoritatively formulated (like statute law), but must first be "deduced" with more or less certainty from previous decisions.

The legal notions which have become objectified in the *legal customs* of those subject to the law have a similar effect.

Using an abstract common term, this group of factors is designated *"customary law"*. In these cases the feeling of validity is due, not to an authoritative formulation, but to the capacity every regularly observed social order has of investing itself with a character of validity (" the normative force of facts").

c. The *free,* not formulated, not objectified factors spontaneously arising in the judge as the mouthpiece of the community to which he belongs and which he serves. We are here concerned with a multiplicity of considerations and motives which it is not easy to class or describe. They are partly notions of social interests and ideas that underlie the formulated or objectified rules, partly ideas of behaviour with a merely moral stamp of validity, i. e. such as have not yet the character of an objective social order. There are, further, reflections in which consideration for the concrete situation and its interests comes into the forefront at the expense of the general rules. In short, there are all those motivating factors which arise quite naturally in a responsible individual who understands that it is his mission to exercise a social function and not only mechanically to apply certain rules. Using a somewhat misleading common term, this group of factors might, with adherence to the traditional terminology, be called *"the legal principles"*.

As will be seen, our tripartite division of the factors that constitute the judicial decision is based on the degree of their objectivity. This is greatest for the formulated rules, least for the spontaneous factors. It is never entirely nil, however, in so far as the judge always feels his task to be a social function, not a subjective matter of taste. It is expressed in the current demand that at any rate he is to look at the case "through the eyes of the community". On the other hand, it is clear that the judicial decision is not given merely on the basis of rules previously established. It is never merely "application of the law", but always to a certain extent *"creation of law"* also. Therefore the judicial decision can never be calculated with accuracy beforehand, and "the law" is something else than a set of given rules. This must be taken into consideration in all exposition of law. The farther one moves away from the objective formulations the more subjective in character will the exposition of law necessarily become. Notably it must be borne in mind that "law" and "morality" cannot be sharply separated. Moral factors enter into the process of motivation in the judicial decision. But in this way they are so elaborated that as integral elements of "practice" they acquire legal validity.

For many reasons the doctrine shows an evident aversion to admitting the presence in judicial decisions of relatively subjective factors and thus of the law-creating function of the courts. An attempt is made, therefore, to present the case as if the free judgment can be "deduced" from certain principles (as an objective form) in the same way as a rule of law can be deduced from the statutes. As such principles "the idea of justice", "natural law", "science as a source of law", "social utility", "the nature of the case" have at different times been adduced (as an objective standard for the "best" solution) — all of them fictions meant to conceal the absence of objectivity and serving to give to one's own subjective evaluation of the relevant considerations a false colouring of objective learning. Incidentally, it is symptomatic that though these principles differ widely from each other in their theoretical formulation, there is no difference to be felt in the results they lead to in practice. The reason is that they are merely labels stuck on to the content, which in each concrete case has been produced by many co-operating factors.

§ 10
THE SOURCES OF INTERNATIONAL LAW

The preceding abstract exposition of the sources of law rests on general socio-psychological experiences and is therefore universally valid. Each positive doctrine of the sources for a special legal system must fill in the details in this abstract scheme.

The sources of International Law are, then, the general factors (motive components) that determine the concrete content of law in international judicial decisions. But now the difficulty arises that there does not in interstate relations exist a regular obligatory administration of justice similar to the activity of the courts within the state. In principle all international judicial decisions are based on the voluntary agreement of the parties which also in principle decides on what grounds the matter shall be settled. Thus there is nothing to prevent the decision being based on more or less arbitrary instructions, and an analysis of such decisions cannot, therefore, form the starting point for an enquiry into the sources of International Law. The point of departure must be those cases which are referred to "judicial decision" without more detailed instructions or merely with a very vague indication of the grounds for the decision to which no qualifying importance is attached in practice ("according to law and equity" etc.).

If only for this reason the instructions in the Statute of the Permanent Court of International Justice, Art. 38, cannot formally constitute the foundation for the doctrine of the sources of International Law. To this must be added that the doctrine of the sources can never in principle rest on precepts contained in one among the legal sources the existence of which the doctrine itself was meant to prove. The basis of the doctrine of legal sources is in all cases actual practice and that alone. The attempt to set up authoritative precepts for the sources of law must be regarded as later doctrinal reflections of the facts, which often are incomplete or misleading in the face of reality.

On this basis the following sources of International Law may be shown to exist:

I *Treaties.*

In International Law — in contradistinction to the internal systems — formulated law is only known as based on the *autonomy of the parties* concerned, that is to say, law created by an agreement between the parties bound. Doctrine gives to such international agreements the common designation of treaties. On the other hand, International Law does not, in principle, know legislation, that is to say a formulation binding on all. This contrast is not absolute, however. The parties can by treaty give their binding consent to the founding of an organ, which is granted authority to bind the contracting parties by its resolutions, without their renewed consent. Approaches to such a legislation in special domains are indeed found in International Law.[1]

But even without indirect consent there are in interstate relations a few feeble approaches to legislation. A treaty which has won general consent, especially on the part of the leading powers, will often have such weight attached to it that it will become binding on outside states, too, as a manifestation of a universal conception of what is right. To refer this effect to tacit consent or to a later formation of customary law will often be illusory. It may also happen that a treaty arrangement consciously lays claim to a more far-reaching effect. Thus the Great Powers, after the upheavals of the Napoleonic wars, attempted to establish a kind of European Directorate — first by the Holy Alliance, later by "the European Concert" — for the maintenance of the existing conditions. This effort manifested itself in the proclamation on several occasions, especially in connection with the conclusion of peace, that the treaty arrangements made under this direction were sustained by common European interests and were valid as *droit public européen.*[2] This implied the postulate

---

[1] See e. g. the Polish-Allied minority treaty 28. June 1919 Art 12, and the Versailles treaty of the same date, Art. 422.

[2] Already the declaration of 20. Nov. 1815 (Paris) as to the neutrality of Switzerland pronounces this to be "dans les vrais intérêts de la politique de l'Europe entière." At the conferences in London in 1830 and 1831 the powers maintained that the newly created Belgium was bound by the "European" treaty obligations encumbent on Holland. The treaty of the

that as an objective political status the arrangement was to be binding on all European powers. In several cases this point was in fact carried. We may mention in particular the demilitarisation of the Åland Islands. An agreement directly binding on Russia, the then owner of the islands, was concluded on this question in the Convention of Paris (1856). After Finland had broken away from Russia in 1917 a dispute arose between Sweden and Finland about the sovereignty over the islands. Prompted by this the Council of the League of Nations appointed a committee of jurists to give an opinion on the legal status of the islands. The committee declared (1920) that since the powers had in 1856 intended to create a special international status for the islands in the common European interest, the agreements must still be valid as long as they were not replaced by others, so that any interested state could demand their observance. The council accepted this standpoint.

The existence of a valid treaty implies that the agreement has come into existence in accordance with the rules for the valid conclusion of treaties. It would therefore really be in place to present these rules here. But in accordance with the usual practice this is reserved for separate discussion in a later chapter (IX).

While all treaties, no matter what their content, are equally important in the case of a judicial decision, they are not of equal interest for a scientific exposition of International Law. Just as an exposition of a country's national law cannot, of course, have the object of describing the countless concrete situations of contract law which exist at a certain moment, but must keep to the general legal rules which are valid in the abstract for a great many situations (the so-called "objective law"), so also an exposition of International Law must confine itself to the discussion of the treaties which are generally valid, or are valid for a great many states, and which according to their content aim at establishing (or codifying) general rules and not only at regulating a concrete situation. On this view a distinction may be drawn between *general* and *special treaties*, between *law-*

Peace of Paris of 1856 expressly on several points purported to create *"droit public européen"*, thus e. g. in Art. 15, where it is declared that the rules of the Congress of Vienna concerning the traffic on international rivers should in future constitute part of "le droit public de l'Europe", cf. *Gihl*, International Legislation, 58.

making treaties and *contract treaties*. It is the general law-making treaties that are of interest in a scientific exposition.

As will be understood, the distinction between law-making treaties and contract treaties (and between general and special treaties) is relative and dictated solely by the practical necessity of confining the scientific task within certain limits. A rather widespread theory, according to which there exists a funda-mental difference between *Vereinbarungen* (law-making treaties) and *Verträge* (contract treaties) must therefore be rejected. On this theory the basis of the former is a union of parallel wills directed towards the same aim, an actual common will, whereas that of the latter is wills with different but mutually corre-sponding aims, supplementing each other as contribution and counter-contribution. Only a real common will can create "objective law", that is to say, not merely subjective rights and duties. This distinction has no foundation in fact and has been fostered solely by a speculative desire to find a specific source of International Law which should differ from the ordinary agree-ment. That it is a purely speculative product also appears from the fact that it is without any functional importance at all in questions concerning the conclusion of treaties, their validity, legal effects, etc.

As examples of general law-making treaties may be mentioned the Declaration of Paris on maritime law (1856), the Hague Conventions of 1889 and 1907 for the Pacific Settlement of International Disputes. Brierly states that in the period 1864—1914, 257 treaties of this kind can be enumerated, in the period 1917—1929, 229.

II. *Precedent and custom.*

As non-formulated but partly objectified sources of Inter-national Law may be mentioned precedent and custom.

Precedent may be defined as earlier judicial decisions in which a body of rules is more or less plainly objectified. This source is as a rule not mentioned in the usual expositions and Art. 59 of the statutes of the Permanent Court expressly dissociates itself from the British doctrine of the binding force of precedents. In Art. 38, No. 4, too, the judicial decision is not mentioned as an actual source but only as "subsidiary means" to deciding what is law. Nevertheless it necessarily follows from the tendency of the law to regularity that precedents must exercise a decisive influence on later decisions. The reluctance to admit this is connected with the reluctance to concede that courts are law-creating. Hence the illusion that practice is merely "subsidiary means", and not an actual source. And as a matter of fact courts as well as the authors constantly quote precedents in support of their results. In the face of this everything else is merely futile speculation.

That this fact has not so far been recognised is connected with the circumstance that until quite recently there did not exist any permanent, organised court. It is understandable that arbitration tribunals instituted ad hoc have not the same authoritative binding force on each other as the decisions of a permanent court. There is reason to believe that gradually, as the number of precedents of the Permanent Court increases, an international judge-made law will be established by practice, a law which will be of the greatest importance by giving to International Law that stability in which it is now so wanting. Whether or not the court formally believes in the binding force of precedents is actually of no great consequence.

By *custom* as a source of International Law I mean the legal rules which are more or less plainly objectified in the practice of the states.

Customary International Law may be either *special* (comprising only a small number of states) and then binding on these only; or it may be *general* (comprising the great majority of states, particularly the leading states) and is then binding on all states, on such, too, as have not taken part in the process of objevtivation, either because there was no occasion to do so or because they have only recently come into existence.

The central factor of customary law, which affords the actual motive for the courts to take custom into consideration, is the legal attitude manifested in it. In a legal order which like International Law is based in the main on autonomy, not on authority, the legal attitude of those subject to it must naturally be of decisive importance. The external actions in which custom finds expression are then, in the main, only of importance as affording proof of the existence and earnestness of this attitude (the states having ordered their conduct in accordance with it).

A state's international attitude may reveal itself in *all acts of state* that are connected in some way or other with International Law. This applies in the first place to such actions as appeal directly to other states. Thus for instance the claims addressed to or recognitions given to foreign states; the procedure adhered to in the conclusion of treaties; the reception and sending out of envoys, and all diplomatic negotiations. But it also largely applies to such actions as merely directly or indirectly, actually or contingently, affect the interests of other states. Thus for instance the way in which foreign ambassadors and citizens are treated, the conduct of states towards foreign vessels in territorial waters, their legislation and administration in matters relevant to other states and their interests, their judicial decisions in so far as these are based on International Law. A study of interstate custom cannot therefore be confined to a consideration of the actions of international legal organs, it must also be directed towards internal acts of state both factual and legal. Factual events, diplomatic documents, instructions for diplomatic organs, legislation, administrative acts and legal decisions are the material from which the implied legal views must be deduced.

An act of state is only of interest in so far as it gives evidence in some way of an international legal attitude. It may be imagined to do so in several ways. An action (or the failure to act) may be based on the implication that the state was *bound* to act; or it may express a *legal claim;* or merely imply that the action was *permitted*[3] (not prohibited) by International Law, (normally every single act of state must be based on that implication); or finally (though rarely) it may imply that the action by the acting party himself was regarded as *conflicting with International Law.*[4]

Hence the existence of a custom requires to be proved not only

---

[3] Especially in connection with the fact that other states have not protested though there were reasonable grounds for doing so, cf. the judgment in the *Lotus* case (Perm. Court Publ. series A No. 10), p. 29, cf 20 and 23. It will often be difficult to say whether the absence of a protest may be considered equivalent to acquiescence in a certain course of conduct. The decisive point must be whether or not, according to the usual view in state practice, there have been reasonable grounds for protest.

[4] That a state of law may be experienced psychologically in the ways here indicated, is not at variance with the fact that all description of law can logically be reduced to a description of situations of obligation, cf. § 2. III.

by the occurrence of certain objective actions but likewise by the subjective psychological presuppositions owing to which they have been carried out. The latter part of the proof will, by the nature of the case, often be difficult to furnish but in practice this seems to be of small consequence. As a rule the subjective background will be sufficiently clearly reflected in the objective situation. This is especially true in so far as a legal claim is concerned or merely an implication that a certain course of conduct is not prohibited. It is commonly only in the case of obligations that a doubt may arise as to where the line should be drawn with respect to concessions made merely out of friendliness or courtesy. The line of demarcation will indeed tend to be obliterated because every actual custom will in the long run be apt to create a corresponding feeling of being bound or of obligation.

The difficulty connected with proving the subjective aspect of custom has led to the theory that the psychological element does not really play any independent part. The judge freely decides when he will regard some external regular conduct as sufficient to constitute a legal custom, and the doctrine of a necessary "*opinio juris sive necessitatis*" merely has the ideological function of obscuring the judge's free law-creating activity in establishing what is customary law.[5] This view, however, goes too far. The fundamental factor in legal custom is the implied legal attitude and this will reveal itself in most cases. The Permanent Court too recognises the necessity of taking the subjective side into consideration, see for instance the judgment in the *Lotus* case (No. 10) p. 28. But it is true that tribunals and courts rarely enter upon an effective enquiry into the evidence for it, and that to a certain extent it is discretion that determines whether or not a custom is recognised. In so far there is judge-made law.

As will appear from the preceding part, time-honoured practice is not a necessary element in customary International Law. Its only importance will be to strengthen the evidence for the existence and earnestness of the attitude. But in itself there is nothing to prevent the attitude manifesting itself with sufficient distinctness by isolated actions, for instance by parallel acts of legislation in internationally relevant questions (e. g. on

---

[5] *Hans Kelsen*, Théorie du droit international coutumier, Rev. intern. de la théorie du droit, 1939, 253 f.

foreigners' liability to punishment for actions committed outside
the territory of the punishing state). The decisive point can only
be that this conduct has been followed in so far as there was
occasion to do so. Conduct which is only observed now and
then does not testify to a real legal conviction. Then, at any rate,
it must further appear that the deviations were regarded by the
acting party himself as conflicting with the law.

It will likewise appear from what has been said that the subjective element in custom cannot be confined solely to the implication of an obligation for the acting party but may have
other forms.

In these two respects this exposition differs from the prevailing doctrine, according to which custom requires, objectively,
uniform conduct over a long time, and subjectively, *opinio
necessitatis sive juris*.

III. *The free factors.*

When finally we come to the free, determining factors in
the motivation process of judicial decisions the enumeration of
definite "sources" is excluded by the nature of the case, the
special feature being, precisely, that the considerations, the
cultural factors, which are the living soil of all formulated law,
come spontaneously into the forefront in connection with the
contemplation of concrete cases. It is this which is called
by the current terms "legal principles", "the nature of the
case", "the idea of law", "scientific law", and the like. Any
attempt to name specific "sources" beyond this must necessarily
imply a certain, even though slight, objectivation.

In recent times, thus also in the Statutes of the International
Court of Justice, Art 38 part 1 c, *"the general principles
of law recognised by civilised nations"* are mentioned as an
independent source of International Law. The principles here
alluded to are the fundamental legal principles common to
human civilisation, recognised in the various internal legal
orders, such as certain processual maxims, certain fundamental
rules concerning the invalidity of contracts, certain human
fundamental rights, and the like. It is beyond doubt too that
such considerations actually form an element in international

judicial decisions.[6] But it would be a mistake to think that we have here a "source" in the same objective sense that treaties and partly precedent and custom are sources of International Law. The difference is best seen by the fact that while an abstract development — that is without regard to particular legal questions — of the rules given in treaties and partly also (though less certainly) the rules following from precedent and custom would be possible, such an abstract development of what follows from "general legal principles" would be quite unfeasible. It would only be possible in relation to a concrete situation or at any rate in relation to particular legal questions and would in any case have an extremely vague, very subjective character.

The same applies when — in accordance with Art. 38 part 1 d of the Statutes — the *teachings of the most highly qualified publicists* are mentioned as a "source" or a "subsidiary means" of determining what is law. In both cases we have pseudo-objectivations meant to conceal the fact that the courts are law-creating, not only law-applying, in so far as the active factors are not previously objectivated. A law-creating element also asserts itself in the "deduction" of the rules of customary law from the practice of the states, and incidentally also, since objectivation is never complete, in the interpretation and application of treaties. In addition it must be borne in mind that the different categories of sources denote *co-operating* factors in the judicial decision, so that there is always — actually or potentially, patently or covertly — a creative element inherent in it.

---

[6] See *Verdross*, Völkerrecht, § 15 and the literature cited there. Note also the following passage in the *Lotus* judgment (Perm. Court Publ. Series A. No. 10) pp. 30—31: "Neither the exclusive jurisdiction of either state, nor the limitation of the jurisdiction of each to the occurrences which took place on the respective ships would appear calculated to *satisfy the requirements of justice* and *effectively to protect the interests* of the two States. It is only *natural* that each should be able to exercise jurisdiction and to do so in respect of the incident as a whole. It is therefore a case of concurrent jurisdiction" (author's italics).

§ 11.
THE INTERRELATIONSHIP OF THE SOURCES
(INTERPRETATION)

As just stated, the various sources denote *co-operating* factors in the judicial decisions. Hence there can be no question of some being primary, others subsidiary.

This co-operation is most clearly seen in the relation between the objectivated sources and the free factors. The effects of the free factors especially manifest themselves in the *"interpretation"* of the objective sources. That is to say, the result actually emerging from a co-operation between the objectivated sources and the free factors is — in order to conceal the creative activity — fictitiously ascribed to the objectivated sources alone and is said to be "deduced" from these by "interpretation". The interpretation is then supposed to be a logical elaboration of the given material, whereby its true content is objectively revealed. A distinction is usually made between the *interpretation* proper of the directly given content (a linguistic and teleological interpretation) and the *development* of the indirect content through certain conclusions, especially antithetical and analogical. But all this is fictitious. All interpretation is *pragmatic,* not logical, that is to say, it is determined not objectively but according to its value in relation to certain implied intentions, ideas, interests. In short, interpretation is a co-operation between the objectivated and the free factors.

A special form of interpretation is the deduction of *"principles of International Law"* from the material immediately given in treaties and especially in customs. These principles must then be distinguished from the "general principles of law" previously mentioned, which are derived from national legal material.

As far as the relation between several objectivated sources is concerned, the general rule applies that a later source takes precedence of an earlier one, whatever the form of objectivation may be (a later treaty takes precedence of an earlier treaty, custom etc.). Further, a special rule to a certain extent takes precedence of a general rule no matter what its age or form.

§ 12.
THE OFFICIAL DOCTRINE OF THE SOURCES OF LAW

The Statute of the International Court of Justice, Art. 38 provide that

The Court, whose function is to decide in accordance with International Law such ‚disputes as are submitted to it, shall apply:
a. international conventions, whether general or particular, establishing rules expressly recognised by the contesting states;
b. international custom, as evidence of a general practice accepted as law;
c. the general principles of law recognised by civilized nations;
d. subject to the provisions of Article 59, judicial decisions and the teachings of the highly qualified publicists of the various nations, as subsidiary means for the determination of rules of law.
This provision shall not prejudice the power of the Court to decide a case *ex æquo et bono,* if the parties agree thereto.[1]

As stated in § 9, the article cannot form the basis of the doctrine of international sources of law, but must in the main be taken to be analogous to a scientific theory. A less happy formulation might, however, easily have landed the Court in difficulties even though the internal psychological laws for the application of the legal rules have always in practice proved stronger than authoritative precepts conflicting with them.[2] It is a fortunate thing, however, that the precepts of the sources are so spacious that they will hardly prevent a natural development of practice. That the Statute, for dogmatic reasons, maintain a distinction between the sources proper and mere "subsidiary means" is of no consequence in this respect. On the other hand, it is important that the article, in addition to treaty, custom and practice, also mentions "general principles of law" and "the teachings of the most highly qualified publicists" as a basis for the decisions of the court. This opens a place for the free non-objectivated factors. It is of less interest to establish what precisely should be understood by "general principles of

---

[1] Cp. § 59. IV.
[2] See *Ross,* Theorie der Rechtsquellen, III, 1 and 2 on the prohibition introduced by a French decree of 16/24 Aug. 1790 for the judge to interpret the law.

law recognised by civilised nations". In practice the free factors will after all become more or less masked as an "interpretation" of the objectivated sources. The history of the genesis of the article favours the interpretation that they are the general principles of law which are the common pillars of the various national systems of law. The warrant for applying "principles of International Law" must then be sought in No. 2, these being said to be implied in international custom.[3]

As minor strictures on the formulation it may be said that No. 2 only mentions general custom, and that custom is mentioned as evidence of practice. Custom is a practice evidencing a certain conception of law.

§ 13
POSITIVISM AND NATURAL LAW

The traditional doctrine of the sources of law is not (cf. § 9) based on a realistic analysis of judicial decisions, but rests on speculative reflections on the origin of the metaphysical validity of the legal rules. A distinction may here be made between positivist and naturalist theories.

The *positivist* theories take it for granted that all International Law is conventional law (§ 1, V) and that all validity of International Law is in the last instance derived from a union of the wills of the sovereign states. Only what emanates from the wills of the states, and thus has a positive character (based on experience, established by human beings, in contrast with what flows from pure reason), is accepted as valid law. In principle, therefore, only treaties are recognised as a source of International Law. In addition, however, custom is recognised, but is then regarded as a tacit agreement or an indirect expression of the will of the states, whereas all other sources of law are rejected.

---

[3] From the preparatory work to the Statute of 1920 it must be taken for granted that in No. 3 at any rate the common national legal principles must have been kept in view. These have in part been regarded as a kind of universal human common law or a universal human objectivation of the *droit naturel*. It cannot, however, have been intended to exclude the application also of international principles deduced from international custom, but it has not been clear whether the warrant for this should be sought in No. 2 or No. 3.

The *naturalist* theories, on the other hand, in numerous ramifications, start with the assumption that according to its nature the law is a supersensually valid order, and must, therefore, also in the last instance derive its validity from a supersensual source. In manifold ways, on the basis of different philosophies, this source has been sought in the will of God, pure reason inherent in man, the idea of justice, social solidarity etc. A common feature in all cases is that the positive law is regarded as historically conditioned, more or less imperfect, *attempts* to realise the claims of the true idea of justice, its validity being ultimately derived precisely from this idea. To be consistent one must with *Hegel* picture reality itself as a progressive revelation of the absolute idea.[1] On this assumption it is natural to recognise besides the positive sources in which the idea of justice only reveals itself imperfectly and indirectly also the idea of justice itself (natural law, justice etc.) as a subsidiary, supplementary, and directing source.

While the positivist theories prevailed in the 19th century, an ever stronger reaction against them has set in in the 20th century. The renaissance of natural law is often mentioned. Besides the two traditionally recognised sources, the existence of "a third source" has been asserted as an expression of the natural principles of law ("general principles of law", "the idea of justice" and the like).

As will appear from the above, there is undoubtedly something right in this reaction. There are sources of law other than those positively formulated. In so far one must agree with the naturalist theories. But this does not mean that there are also "natural" (supersensual, *a priori*) sources of law, but merely expresses the socio-psychological reality that judicial decisions, as described above, are also determined by spontaneous free factors of many kinds. There is an *ambiguity* in the term "positivism". It can both be defined as "what is based on experience" and as "what is formally established". The reaction against positivism is justified with respect to the latter, but not with respect to the former meaning. A realistic doctrine of the sources of law is based on experience but recognises that not all sources are positive in the sense that they are "formally established".

---

[1] Cf. *Ross*, Towards a Realistic Jurisprudence, Chap. II, 6.

Chapter III

THE SUBJECTS OF INTERNATIONAL LAW
(The Law of Persons)

§ 14
CAPACITY FOR INTERNATIONAL DUTIES[1]

In § 2 it was explained that International Law too has its law of persons, i. e. legal rules establishing the ordinary conditions for being subject to law in various relations, viz. being respectively capable of duty, capable of action, and capable of rights (capable of interests and capable of prosecution).

As regards the capacity of duty it has been shown that according to the concept of International Law it can only belong to self-governing communities.

But this does not mean that every self-governing community is in fact also capable of international duties. Since it is the

---

[1] Usually the law of persons, municipal as well as international, is concerned with the term "legal capacity" in the sense of the capacity of possessing rights and duties. This concept is based on the false presupposition that rights and duties are correlated counterparts, mystical qualities produced by the legal system in its subjects, and that legal capacity is therefore one and undivided in the two relations. As shown above, (§ 2, III) this is not the case, and it is therefore necessary to divide the concept into two: the capacity of duties and the capacity of rights. In municipal law the obscurity of the concept has not caused very much damage, because the two capacities, according to the law in force, nearly always coincide. It is difficult to mention subjects of rights who cannot at the same time also be subjects of duties (perhaps young children, fetuses, animals) or conversely, subjects of duty who may not also possess rights (slaves). Otherwise in International Law. Here the distinction is essential because the individual may be and actually to a wide extent is the subject of rights, but never the subject of duties. It is precisely because this distinction has been overlooked that a hitch seems to have occurred in the question as to the position of the individual in International Law.

concern of every legal system to indicate what persons are bound
by its rules — or these would have no definite subject — it
depends on the contents of International Law whether its rules
are binding on every self-governing community or only on some
of them. With this question we will now deal.

At present the following kinds of self-governing communities
exist: on a *territorial* basis: *states* and *local insurgent parties;* on
a *non-territorial* basis: the *Roman Catholic Church.*

Of these the states are practically by far the most important
and this explains why International Law is often, *pars pro toto,*
designated as the law that is valid for states.

I. *The State.*

By a state we here mean a *stabilised, self-governing legal
community on a territorial basis.* What a "self-governing legal
community" means has already been explained (§ 1. III). That
it has a territorial basis signifies that the community is individu-
alised and thus is distinct from others owing to the fact that its
organs for the enforcement of the law function regularly
within a particular territory. That it has been stabilised means
that it has gained lasting firmness, internally as well as externally.

Of course the current political, diplomatic, national, or international linguistic usage may not always adhere to this definition of the term "state". But that is of no consequence. The
important fact is merely that this definition emphasises self-
government as the factor which is, technically, a condition
of subjection to International Law[2] and thus in a convenient
way characterises the concept "state" as a term for the typical
subjects of International Law. This does not exclude that in
other relations, especially in other branches of science, it may
possibly be practical to formulate another concept of state.

Is every state a subject of International Law? This cannot be
maintained without reserve. According to its historical origin
International Law only comprises the "Christian European
States" (the fact that in other parts of the world, too similar
particular systems may have arisen is thus disregarded). But

---

[2] It should be noted that the term "subject of International Law", here
and in the sequel where the context cannot give rise to doubt, is sometimes
used for "subject to international duties".

both the limitations indicated by this definition have disappeared
in the course of the 19th century. As early as 1783 the circle
of subjects was extended to the American Confederation, and
in the first decades of the 19th century to the new independent
states in Central and South America. By the treaty of Paris
in 1856 Turkey was admitted to the "European Concert", and
gradually Japan and the remaining considerable Asiatic powers
followed. In our day the Universal Postal Union comprises all
civilised states throughout the world, and thus it may probably
be said that any state that comes up to certain very low
standards of civilisation and is actually in regular communication with other states is now a subject of International Law.
Excluded are solely certain primitive principalities and tribes
if their organisation can be regarded as that of a state at
all.

Since self-government may be complete or partial, there exist
states with full and states with partial self-government.

States with *full self-government* are the highest legal authority
in all spheres in relation to their citizens. They are therefore
without restriction subjects of International Law in relation to
every international norm which can be applied according to its
content. As previously stated, self-government is not excluded
by the fact that a state is subject to a higher legal order (a special
international legal order), whether this be based on a constitution or a treaty, as long as the import of this order is to give to
the state full and intact self-government.

States with *partial self-government* are only subjects of International Law within the range of their self-government, that is
to say, only in relation to those norms of International Law, the
fulfilment of which comes within the power of the State itself.
But it does not matter whether the higher order that determines
the extent of their self-government is based on a constitution
or on a treaty. A limitation in their self-government implies
that the direct legal power in relation to their citizens is divided
between a subordinate and a superior authority. From the point
of view of the participating parties the relation to the superior
instance may be based either on equality or on inequality.

A. Restriction in the capacity for duties on the basis of
equality: Member state — federal state. — The first case is present when two or more states are restricted in their self-government by a common superior federal power, formed of repre-

sentatives of the participating states in such a way that certain matters are reserved for the individual states, while others come directly under the federal power. The *member* states as well as the *federal state* are then only in part self-governing. They have each of them their spheres in which they are the highest legal power in relation to the citizens. Hence the federal state is an independent state side by side with the member states. Thus the term U. S. A. denotes 49 different states, viz. the 48 member states and the federal state. Each state has its own organs, legislative, executive and judicial, each its own citizens and territory, though so constituted of course that the citizens and territory of the individual states constitute parts of those of the federal state.

And now what is the position in regard to the capacity for duty for the member state and the federal state respectively? Since both have self-government, each in its own domain, the point of departure must in principle be that they are both subjects of duty within the range of self-government. Here however special circumstances in some degree complicate the situation and render necessary a deeper-going analysis and a creation of new concepts. It should be remembered (§ 2. VI) that the typical situation of duty for A implies that A is he of whom a certain conduct is "required", with the effect that if he does not act in accordance herewith, he will be responsible. Thus A is both he whose conduct determines whether or not there is a breach of law and he who must take the responsibility for it. He is the subject of conduct as well as the subject of responsibility. Now, however, the fact is that towards a third state the federation must take the responsibility for the actions of the member state (§ 55). Hence this means that in *reference to the third state* the typical situation of duty does not occur at all. It would be equally misleading quite summarily to designate either the member state or the federal state as the state subject to duty. The actual state of affairs can only be described by calling *the member state the subject of conduct* and *the federal state the subject of responsibility.*

That the member state is the subject of conduct must be maintained because that state, and that only, which has the power of action (self-government) and is thus able to fulfil or violate a duty, can be designated as the one bound to carry out a certain conduct-content. In this connection we may refer to the judgment mentioned above on p. 72 in the *City of New Orleans v. Abbagnato* which plainly illustrates that it was the State of Louisiana and not the Federal State which committed the breach of law, even though the Federal State had to assume the responsibility.

On the other hand, as regards the *mutual relations between the member states* or between these and the federal state the normal conditions obtain that each of these is an international *subject of duty within the range of its self-government*. This view is confirmed by numerous judgments concerning relations between the member states of the U. S. A. in which the decision was, subsidiarily, based on the general rules of International Law.[8] This establishes that the states are subjects of Interna-

---

[8] *Virginia v. Tennesee* (Supreme Court of the United States, 1892. 148 U. S. 503, 13 Sup. Ct. 728, 37 L. Ed. 537, Scott, 252): In 1802 the states of Virginia and Tennessee entered into an agreement which settled a prolonged boundary dispute between them. The boundary was marked off and the agreement solemnly ratified by the legislative power of both states in 1803. During the lawsuit in 1892 Virginia asserted that the agreement of 1802 should be declared invalid as entered upon without the consent of Congress, and the boundary verified in accordance with the older rights of the state. The case was settled by the Supreme Court against this assertion partly on the basis of the *general international principles* of the acquisition of territory by prescription. In support of this decision were adduced pronouncements by the two authorities on *International Law*, *Vattel* and *Wheaton*. Further the agreement of 1802 was clearly regarded as an *international treaty*. The judgment quotes a statement by Justice Story in which it is said: "It is part of the *general right of sovereignty belonging to independent nations* to establish and fix the disputed boundaries between their respective territories ... This is a doctrine universally recognised in the *law and practice of nations*. It is a right equally belonging to the states of this Union, unless it has been surrendered under the Constitution of the United States. So far from there being any pretence of such general surrender of the right, it is expressly recognised by the Constitution, and guarded in its exercise by a single limitation and restriction, requiring the consent of Congress" (author's italics). From this it would seem that the states are regarded as subjects of International Law that have preserved their international legal status and rights with the sole limitation that follows from the constitution of the United States. The consequence of this must be that the American Supreme Court in so far functions as an international court. But the judgment also seems to accept this consequence. It says about the case: "It embraces a controversy of which this court has original jurisdiction, and in this respect the judicial department of our government is *distinguished from the judicial department of any other country*, drawing to itself by the ordinary modes of peaceful procedure the settlement of

tional Law. At the same time the consequence must be accepted that the federal constitution, in so far as it contains rules concerning the mutual relations between the member states or between these and the federal state, is a special part of International Law — in spite of the fact that it is a "constitution", not a "treaty" (§ 1. V).

This exposition of the position of the member state in reference to International Law differs from the prevailing view which would only regard the member state as an international person in so far as it has preserved competence to act in external affairs by sending and receiving envoys, concluding treaties etc. that is to say, in so far as it is capable of action in external affairs. This view is due to an unwarranted confusion of the terms capacity for duty and capacity of action. It is a well known fact that a person can be liable to duties though he has

---

questions as to boundaries and consequent right of soil and jurisdiction between states, possessed, for purposes of internal government, of the powers of independent communities, which otherwise might be the fruitful cause of prolonged and harassing conflicts". It seems to be plainly expressed here that the court, as something out of the ordinary, regards itself as competent in disputes of an international nature.

Virginia v. West Virginia (Supreme Court of the United States, 1911. 220 U. S. 1., 31 Sup. Ct. 330, 55 L. Ed. 353, Scott, 81): During the Civil War the western provinces of Virginia remained loyal to the Union. After they had broken off from the mother state in 1861 and constituted themselves as West Virginia a law was passed in 1862 according to which the new state was to take over part of the debts of the mother state. The case was concerned with the question as to how this part was to be assessed. The judgment says: "The case is to be considered in the untechnical spirit proper for dealing with *quasi-international controversy*, remembering that there is *no municipal code* governing the matter, and that this court may be called on to adjust differences that cannot be dealt with by Congress or disposed on by the legislation of either State alone. Missouri v. Illinois 200 U. S. 496, 519, 520, 26 Sup. Ct. 268, 50 L. Ed. 572: Kansas v. Colerado, 206 U. S. 46, 82—84, 27 Sup. Ct. 655 51 L. Ed. 956". This must mean that the conflict must be judged according to international legal principles. This also accords well with the rest of the judgment. It is discussed whether there exists an agreement between the two states, and whether the aim of the debt as incurred either for the benefit of local interests or for the benefit of the welfare of the whole state may have any influence on the question of apportionment. The latter considerations have reference to a well-known rule of International Law, cp. § 19, II B.

See also the Constitution Art. I, sec. 10, cl. 3, which entirely coordinates inter-state agreements with agreements with foreign powers, and more detailed references to the precedents and the literature in *Oppenheim* I, 162, note 1.

no capacity of acting himself. What complicates the matter is not the capacity of action but the placing of the responsibility.

(The founding of a federal state need not affect the capacity of action of the member states beyond the self-evident fact that capacity of action now only means capacity of action in reference to affairs within the scope of self-government. But often the capacity of action of the member states is entirely or partly transferred to the federal power. In that case there exists also a confederation of states, cf. § 15).

B. Restriction in the capacity for duties on the basis of *inequality: Vassal state — suzerain state.* — When two or more states are united in such a way that the federal power (to which part of the government falls) is not exercised by representatives of the participating states, but by one of these only, there is a restriction in self-government and thus in the capacity for duties on the basis of inequality. The subordinate state is called a *vassal state,* the superior state the *suzerain state,* the relation between them one of suzerainty or vassalage. Whether this relation has been established by treaty or by constitution is of no consequence. The vassal state is partly self-governing, the suzerain state in reality consists of two states: a fully self-governing state and a partially self-governing state in relation to the citizens of the vassal state. (Often, too, the capacity for action has been transferred to the suzerain state. In that case there exists at the same time a relation of protectorate between them, cf. § 15).

According to a widespread view, however, the state is not a subject of International Law until it has been *recognised* by other states, cf. below § 18 III.

II. *The local insurgent party.*

This means a *non-stabilised, self-governing community on a territorial basis.*

The difference between a local insurgent party and a mere group of insurgents lies in the fact that in the first case it is implied that the insurgents have succeeded in establishing themselves in a particular part of the territory of the state and there have organised themselves with a government which is able *to assert itself effectively* as an organised power in the area and as a fighting power in respect of the mother state. Such a government is called a *local de facto* government (in contradistinction from a general *de facto* government which is a designation for a government that has acquired the power in the state by a revolution, § 36, II). This organisation is a pre-requisite if we are to speak of a self-governing community on a territorial basis. Incidentally it does not matter whether it is the aim of the insurgent party merely to separate the area from the mother state, or on the contrary to arrogate the entire power in the state.

The local insurgent party is distinguished from the state by its non-stabilised, provisional character. It is so to speak an embryonic state as long as the fight lasts. It depends on the issue of the fight whether or not a state is to be born.

Such a local rebellious party (if formed within the domain of the society of nations) is a subject of International Law, even though owing to its temporary character all the norms of International Law cannot come into play. It is of special importance that the rules concerning war and neutrality will probably be applied with a view to the fight against the mother country and in relation to a third state, cf. below § 18, V. But the law of peace also may come into use. The local insurgent party can for instance conclude treaties concerning the protection of alien citizens and enter into diplomatic relations with a third state. As an example it may be mentioned that during the last war several of the allied nations had diplomatic representatives with de Gaulle's insurrectionist government.

According to the prevailing doctrine, however, the rules of International Law do not come into use until the local insurgent party has been *recognised* as a belligerent by the mother country or a third state, cf. below § 18, III and V.

III. *The Roman Catholic Church.*

The Roman Catholic Church constitutes a self-governing community in ecclesiastical affairs, and its subjection to International Law is now generally recognised. According to the nature of the case it is, however, only a few of the norms of International Law, especially those concerning diplomatic relations and the concluding of agreements, which come into consideration as applicable to this subject.

The agreements entered upon by the Pope on behalf of the Roman Catholic Church are called *concordats*.

Different from the Roman Catholic Church is the *Vatican State*, re-established by the Lateran Treaty of 1929, by which Italy surrendered the small piece of its territory on which the Vatican stands to the Papal See and acknowledged the full independence of the latter. Here then we are concerned with a real state on a territorial basis, no doubt the smallest in the world. It stands in a relation of vassalage to the Roman Church.

§ 15
CAPACITY FOR ACTION UNDER INTERNATIONAL LAW

Capacity for action is usually defined as the ability to impose duties and confer rights upon oneself by one's own actions. The concept is then of importance in two relationships: the actions in question may either be declarations of will, especially agreements, or breaches of law. But these two relationships must in reality be sharply distinguished from each other. For by the definition any subject of duties possesses the ability to impose duties on himself (or exceptionally on others, § 55) in breaches of law. The person on whom a duty is imposed is the same who may contravene it, whereby a responsibility arises. The concept "capacity for action" must therefore be limited to denote the ability to acquire rights and impose duties on oneself by one's *own declarations of will*, especially by agreements (treaties) and the consequent power of taking action externally in relations with other states[1] by one's own representatives.

Which of the subjects of international legal duties likewise possess the capacity for action is of course a question for International Law to decide.

The main rule here is that *every* subject of a duty likewise possesses capacity for action (in the same proportion as it has self-government). General International Law in no case deprives a state of its capacity for action, for instance on account of its size, age, or the like. A state may, however, be deprived of its

---

[1] Here and in the sequel we often speak, *pars pro toto*, of a "state" as the equivalent of a "subject of International Law".

power of action by virtue of existing special arrangements, and it does not matter whether these have been fixed by treaty or by constitution. In that case we have a relationship which is analogous to the condition of *minority*. The state concerned acquires rights or incurs duties by the acts of others. But if it has retained its self-government it is itself the subject bound and alone capable of fulfilling the duties.

In this instance too the arrangement which deprives a state of its capacity for action, either totally or merely in certain relations may be based either on equality or inequality.

A. Total or partial abrogation of the capacity for action on the basis of equality: *states in a confederation.*

The arrangement is based on equality if the capacity for action has been consigned to a federal organ created by representatives of two or more states. We have then a *confederation of states.* Whether this has been established by treaty or constitution is of no consequence. Thus the confederation of states is not, like the federal state, a new state, since no limitations are made in the self-government of the confederated states. The confederation exists merely by means of a common organ which on behalf of the confederated states exercises their international legal capacity for action, either fully or to a certain extent. Hence the confederation itself is not subject to international legal duties.

A confederation may occur in the pure form or in association with a federal state, that is to say, in such a way that the government in internal affairs also to a certain extent is transferred to the federal organ.

B. Total or partial abrogation of the capacity for action on the basis of *inequality: protectorate.*

Inequality, on the other hand, is the basis of the arrangement if another state also functions as a federal organ exercising the power of action on behalf of the "minor" state. The superior state is then called the *protector state,* the subordinate state the *protected state,* or briefly: protectorate, and the relation between them a relation of protectorate. Whether the relation has been established by treaty or constitution is still of no consequence whatever.

A relation of protectorate may occur in a pure form or in

connection with a relation of vassalage, that is to say in such a form that the protector state also to a certain extent governs the internal affairs of the subordinate state.

The various possibilities in respect of limitations in the capacity for duty and action may by tabulated as follows:

	pure forms		mixed forms
	part abrogation of self-government and thus of the capacity for duty*	total or partial abrogation of the capacity for action	
equality:	pure federal state	pure confederation	federal state + confederation
inequality:	pure vassalage	pure protectorate relation	vassalage + protectorate relation

* But not the capacity for action beyond the self-evident limitation that the latter never extends beyond self-government.

Concerning their occurance in practice it should be noted that

1. *The pure federal state* is a phenomenon that probably does not occur at all in practice.

2. *The pure confederation.* As historical examples may probably be mentioned the Netherlands Confederacy (the Utrecht Union of 1579), the American Confederation 1781—1789, the German Confederation 1815—1866, the North German Confederation 1866—1871, the Swiss Confederation 1815—1848, and the League of Nations (with but slight capability of action).

3. *The pure vassal state* is presumably also a phenomenon that does not occur in practice.

4. *The pure protectorate relation.* As this relationship has not come under the notice of the traditional theory it is difficult to decide, without thoroughgoing special investigations, whether those relations which are generally called relations of protectorate are pure or mixed with vassalage. Incidentally, the protectorate relation has so far mostly come into play between the European colonial powers and various weaker, previously independent, Asiatic and African states which through the relation of protectorate have been drawn within the sphere of influence of the superior state without being reduced to the status of vassal states or colonies. Under France, for instance, we

have Tunis, Morocco, and Franch Indo-China (Annam and Cambodia); under England, for instance, the Indian native states, the Malay states, the sultanate Zanzibar, British Borneo etc.

A distinction is drawn between *complete* and *incomplete* protectorate relations. The former are present when the capacity for action is exercised directly by the organs of the protecting state, the latter when the protecting state confines itself to controlling the protegé state's exercise of its power of action by means of its own organs.

The protectorate relation implies not only that the leading state acts on behalf of the other state, but also that the leading state acts *on its own judgment in its own interest.* (In return for this the leading state has generally undertaken the duty of protecting, in a military respect too, the protectorate and the interests of its citizens. For easily understandable ideological reasons it is this protection which is emphasised in the current terminology). Politically, therefore, the protectorate relation is characterised by *dependence and leadership* and is sharply marked off from that representation which has only the character of a transaction of business that takes place according to the directions of the represented state and in the interests of that state. Thus according to the Danish-Icelandic Act of Union § 7 Denmark took charge on behalf of Iceland (" umboði þess") of the foreign affairs of that country, whereby it was implied that this charge was exercised in the interests and according to the directions of Iceland.

5. *A federal state in connection with a confederation of states.* It is in reality this combination which is present in those situations which are normally designated merely as federal states, the member states being to a greater or less extent deprived of their capacity for acting in foreign affairs. While, on the one hand, the member states in the German state after the constitution of 1871 still possessed considerable independence externally, there are, conversely, cases in which the member states have been deprived of all capacity for action, for example Brazil (constitution of 1892) and Venezuela (constitution of 1904). Sometimes the member states have been granted power to conclude certain minor, non-political agreements with the consent of the federal state, as for instance in Switzerland (const. 1874), the

U. S. A. (const. 1789), Argentina (const. 1860), and the German Reich after the Weimar constitution.[2]

6. *Vassalage in connection with a relation of protectorate.* Possibly some or all of the examples mentioned under 4 must be referred to this type.

It is no real objection to this system that some of the pure types do not actually occur. Only by segregating the pure elements is it possible to carry out a satisfactory analysis of the combined forms existing in reality. The natural reason why the pure federal state and the pure vassal state hardly occur in practice is that it would be politically absurd to establish a fellowship or a leadership with respect to the internal government of a state without at the same time entirely abolishing the independence of the state in foreign policy. On the other hand, the reverse may very well be conceived; a fellowship or leadership in respect of foreign affairs (pure confederation of states, pure relation of protectorate) is from a political point of view the minor thing, which may exist without comprising the internal government as well. Experience has shown, however, that these forms are not stable. They have a tendency to dissolve or to develop into the corresponding mixed forms which also comprise the internal government.

From a political point of view there is a gulf between the equality and the inequality types respectively. The partial abrogation of self-government and/or capacity for action which takes place in a federal state and a confederation of states and their combinations does not, we know, from a political point of view express any dependence but merely *a fellowship* with others on an equal footing. Otherwise in the relations of vassalage and protectorate which from a political point of view express a relation of *dependence and leadership*.

This is the reason why from political discretion and tact these cases are not always given their real names. The political leadership underlying the relations of vassalage and protectorate may exist and have the intended effect without its being necessary to establish the relation in an offensive way by formal legal rules. In these situations the creation of new organs is not

---

[2] Mexico, Canada, Australia, and Austria 1920—38 may likewise be mentioned as examples of federal states in connection with federations of states.

required — as in the case of confederations. We speak of *quasi-protectorates* (dollar protectorates). The term is especially used about various Central American republics which as a result of financial difficulties have become politically dependent on the United States. Ecconomic or military power may of course in numerous ways more or less undermine the formal independence of a state. Friendly protection (occupation for the purpose of protection) is often a form that covers a real dependence. Sometimes independence is a mere fiction which only subserves political ends (Manchukuo). Ultimately, only the states that have power to carry through an independent foreign policy are really independent. But then we have entirely left the legal forms which it is the task of a book on International Law to present.

So far confederations of states and relations of protectorate have only played a subordinate part in the interrelationship between the old civilised states. Under the influence of the ideology of political sovereignty the independence of the individual states has been the lodestar. But much would seem to indicate that this cannot remain the watchword of the future. If continued war is to be avoided, a co-ordination of the foreign policy of the states seems inevitable. The fortunate issue of the recent war affords security that this will be carried through in democratic forms founded on principles of equality and fellowship and not in the form of a dictatorship based on the supremacy of a single state.

§ 16
THE CAPACITY FOR INTERNATIONAL RIGHTS

As previously explained (§ 2, IV), according to the concept of International Law there is nothing to prevent anybody whatever, private individuals included, from possessing international rights. To what extent this is the case depends solely on the content of the international duties incumbent on the states; for a right is nothing but a duty viewed under a certain aspect. Here we have especially to consider its relation to the person who is directly interested in the fulfilment of the duty (the subject of the interest) and to the person who can take action (the subject of disposition or action).

A. As *subjects of interest* private individuals, societies, subordinate legal communities, and the like come largely into consideration according to current International Law. Many of the general rules of International Law, for instance in the law concerning aliens, and especially many provisions of treaties, directly safeguard private interests.

B. On the other hand, it is the normal rule that not individuals, but states alone have *the right to take action* in international affairs. Thus the Statute of the International Court of Justice, Article 34, expressly excludes other than states from being parties in cases before the Court. This attitude is presumably connected with the metaphysical conception that rights, as an independent legal quality, are co-ordinate with duties (§ 2, III). It is then supposed that just as the states (the self-governing communities) are alone subject to international legal duties, they must also be the real possessors of the international legal rights. The practical consideration that, as long as an obligatory interstate administration of justice has not been created, with an organised compulsory executive, only a demand upheld by the political authority of a state will have any chance of being carried through, does not go so far as to exclude a private individual from bringing a claim before the court. It could only lead to the necessity for the state to intervene, if a judicial decision in favour of the private individual were not complied with. And the consideration that private proceedings against foreign states may be conceived to lead to complications of foreign policy can at most cause private proceedings to be dependent on the consent of the home state.

That private action is by no means impracticable will appear from the few exceptional instances in which such action has been recognised. We may mention the Central American Court of Justice at Carthago 1907—17 (the Washington Treaty of 1907 between five Central American states) and the mixed arbitration courts in accordance with Article 297 of the Versailles Treaty, as well as the projected international Prize Court according to the non-ratified Hague Convention of 1907.[1]

In recent times a praiseworthy tendency has made itself felt

---

[1] In this case the home state might, however, forbid the proceedings or undertake them itself, see XII. Conc. Art. 4.

within the literature on International Law, a tendency to assert the individual's direct subjection to the law. That this tendency occasionally changes into a dogmatic assertion to the effect that the individual is the only real subject of International Law has been mentioned above in § 2, IV.

§ 17

THE TRADITIONAL DOCTRINE OF STATES
AND UNIONS OF STATES

It is hardly too much to say that the traditional doctrine of states and the relations between states is in an unequalled condition of chaotic confusion. The reason for this is to be found in the deficient theoretical foundation on which the doctrine has been based.

A. In the first place the task, as usually approached, is not conceived to be the development of the International Law of Persons, the rules concerning the ordinary conditions for being subject to International Law in various relations, but as a description of various *types of states* (sovereign, half-sovereign, non-sovereign states, independent states, composite and non-composite states etc.). The advantage which can here be gained in the description of historical varieties, is won at the expense of the essential thing, viz, the working out of *the rules of the law of persons*. For that reason it has not been observed, for instance, that what is usually called a federal state is in reality two quite heterogeneous legal phenomena which, as has been done here, should be segregated in the types "federal state" and "confederation of states".

Partly the types traditionally described are of no interest at all for the position of the state under the law of persons. An example is the stock section on "neutralised" states, i. e. states that have bound themselves by treaty to a lasting neutrality. This obligation by treaty neither affects the self-government of the state nor its capacity for action, but is a simple restriction on its liberty of conduct, in principle on a line with every other kind of obligation.

B. This would be of minor importance if the description of types was valuable in other respects. But that is far from being the case. For the basis of the description is the highly confused *concept of sovereignty.*

It follows, firstly that the various real legal functions lurking under this concept, especially self-government and the capability of action, are jumbled together. Under the designation half-sovereign states are brought together for instance the entirely different legal phenomena where self-government and capability of action respectively are restricted (member states in a federal state, protectorates) without, on the other hand, referring to this concept the states in a confederation of states, the capability of action of which is also restricted.

Owing to the connection of the concept of sovereignty with the theories of will and the doctrine dependent thereon of the fundamental importance of the basis of validity ("treaty" versus "constitution", "sole subjection to International Law", cf. above § 1, V and § 3, IV)it likewise follows that *in a quite untenable way the description of types becomes connected with the distinction between treaty and constitution.* "Sovereignty" is preserved if only the restrictions limiting the self-government, capacity for action, and liberty of conduct of the state have been undertaken by treaty, then it does not otherwise matter how crucial, destructive, and humiliating are the obligations undertaken. Conversely, as soon as the state is subject to a constitution, it loses its "sovereignty"—even though the purport of this constitution may be to give very far-reaching independence to the state. In this way the description of types loses all connection with reality, or else it is smoothed into normal patterns from which there then constantly occur deviations (member-states have no sovereignty and therefore cannot act in external affairs, though it may happen . . . etc. etc.).

C. The current doctrine is further bungled by the fact that it is quite without analytical understanding of the *various forms of legal subjectivity* (capacity for duties, action, rights). By uncritically combining these in one concept essential differences have been passed over at the outset. This is especially of importance for the distinction between federal states and confederations of states (as pure forms) and with respect to the status of individuals under International Law. The reason why the latter problem seems to become stuck between two radically opposed views is that the distinction between the status of the individual as subject to duties and as entitled to rights has not been sufficiently noticed.

D. Notably *the doctrine of unions of states* suffers not only from the mysticism of the concept of sovereignty, but also from the traditional notion that the types: personal union, real union, confederation of states, and federal state determine a series *with increasing unity* of the states. This is quite misleading.

Personal and *real unions* must be kept entirely distinct from the genuine unions of states. These concepts are generally understood to mean unions (by treaty) between states with a common head but without common international legal organs. The line between a personal and a real union is drawn in different ways, for instance either according as the identity of the monarch is "accidental" or "purposive"; or according as the fact that they have something in common is confined to the person of the king or extends further. In all cases it is decisive that these unions never possess real organs of their own and therefore never have in any way abolished or restricted the independence of the states united either in internal or in external affairs. Thus the status of the members under the law of persons is not affected in any way whatsoever. There is *no legal community* at all, but only the factual community arising out of the fact that it is one and the same person who is the head of the states. The relation is exactly like the factual union created between two or more joint stock companies by the fact that some of the the same human individuals appear on the board of directors or management committee of the respective companies. Incidentally there is no reason to stop at a common element confined to the person of the head of the state. The stressing of this element, like the distinction between a personal and a real union, has only a historical motive. These concepts should be abolished and be replaced by the concept of *mere personal unions* as a term for all such unions as are based solely on identity of persons occupying organic positions. Nor can it, therefore, be contended that the union in these cases is of a weaker character than in confederations of states and federal states. It is of quite a different character. It is factual, personal, not legally organised. But according to the circumstances there is nothing to prevent the factual, personal link from being of greater importance than the legal one. We need only think for instance of a personal union of two countries under the same dictator.

§ 18.
RECOGNITION OF STATES AND INSURGENT PARTIES

I. *The legal significance of recognition.*

In § 14, I it was explained that International Law is valid for a certain individually delimited circle of states, which is called the society of nations and which at present comprises almost the whole civilised world. Within this circle of civilised states it must, conversely, be supposed that International Law applies to each state without regard to its individuality, merely by virtue of its general character as a stabilised self-governing community on a territorial basis. Hence, if it should happen that a new state should arise within the cultural circle of the society of nations this too of course will come under the norms of International Law. Exactly like an individual in a state, the newly created state is born into a community and is automatically ranged under its law without any question of its own or others' consent. It must respect the duties which International Law imposes on the members of its society and, conversely, may itself demand that these duties are respected by others. Such a new formation of a state may especially take place by the breaking away of part of an older state, e. g. a. colony, but may also occur by the division of a state into several, or by the joining of two or more older states into a whole. Such events are typical in connection with insurrections (civil wars) or wars.

Hence the fact that there exists an *effective stabilised government* within a certain territory is decisive for the existence of the new state and also for its subjection to International Law. An organised state system must have been created which is able to assert its power regularly and effectively within the territory and thus to carry out the normal functions of a state, whereas it is of no consequence under what constitutional forms it takes place. It may of course, especially if the new state comes to birth during a struggle with the older state, be difficult in practice to establish definitely the moment when this demand has been complied with. A special consequence of the demand for the stabilised character of the system is that the new state in the case in question cannot be considered to have come into existence before the fight against the old government has practically come to an end, so that there is no longer any appreciable probability that the insurrection may be put down. On the other hand, isolated local resistance of minor importance is no obstacle to considering the new state as formed.

From this main point of view it follows, on the one hand, that the mere *declaration of independence* with appeal to the right of self-determination is not sufficient to establish a state; and on the other hand, that the *legitimacy* of the new state, understood as its legal validity according to the laws of the mother country, is without any importance.

As previously mentioned, when according to these views a new state has come into existence it enters automatically into all the rights and duties of a state under International Law. It is bound to respect the life and property of alien citizens and may demand the same respect for its own citizens etc., etc. But this does not include any mutual obligation to enter into normal diplomatic relations, for according to International Law that is a voluntary matter. It is therefore usual, partly in order to establish such relations, and partly that the new condition of affairs may be acknowledged, that the newly formed state applies to other states, especially those nearest (geographically, economically, politically) with a request for *recognition* as a state.

But if such recognition is given this means in the first place that a *new legal basis* is created for the relation between the two states. The vague international rule about effectiveness, which will often give rise to doubt, is superseded by the recognition, the recognising state being thus debarred from contesting the existence of the new state at the moment of recognition, unless it would dispute the validity of the recognition itself as given on erroneous assumptions as to the actual facts. The recognition must be supposed to have the same effect as the declaration by which a person in civil law admits the existence of a debt, and may be termed a novation. In practice the acknowledgement is made without indication of the time from which the new state is regarded as having effectively established itself. This point is left to be decided by the general rule of International Law with the qualification that at any rate it is admitted that the new state existed at the moment of recognition.

Simultaneously with the recognition and as a natural consequence of it, it is usual for the two states to enter into normal
diplomatic relations. But, strictly, this cannot be said to be an
effect of the recognition. Theoretically, there is nothing to
prevent a state from recognising another and yet refusing to
enter into diplomatic relations with it. This merely corresponds
to the well-known fact that a state may at any time break off
its diplomatic relations with another state without, of course, its
being implied that it no longer recognises the existence of the
other state.

The theory here set forth, according to which the non-recognised state is eo ipso a subject of International Law, is generally
expressed by saying that the recognition merely has a *declaratory, not a constitutive* effect. This does not exclude, however,
the possibility that the rules of International Law in certain
cases may draw a distinction between the legal status of
recognised and non-recognised states respectively. The recognition may to that extent be said to be constitutive in relation to
these effects, though not in relation to the subjection to law as a
whole. Whether such discriminating rules can be shown to
exist is doubtful. In the practice of several states a non-recognised
state is refused admission to the courts as a plaintiff, just as the
courts refuse to show the usual consideration for the legal acts
of a non-recognised state. But since this practice, which seems
to be in course of being abandoned, is based on the act-of-state
doctrine, it is doubtful to what extent international legal rules
may be derived from it, cf. below IV. E. In addition it is not
clear what claims can be made by a recognised state in these
respects, according to International Law.

II. *The political significance of recognition.*

That the question of recognition or non-recognition plays so
conspicuous a part in the practice of the states and arouses such
a fervent interest is not, as will easily be understood, due to
the above-mentioned renewal of the legal relation between the
two states. If non-recognition rests not only on the purely
technical view that there is actually nothing to recognise, that
is to say, if recognition is *refused* in cases where it might quite
well have been given, non-recognition will, politically, assume
the same significance as breaking off diplomatic relations with a

state: a protest and an inimical act, which may in addition contain a more or less grave threat of political countermoves. Refusal of recognition means, more precisely defined:

1. Refusal to make a novation.
2. Refusal to enter into the usual diplomatic relations.
3. Further, an unfriendly, politically discouraging attitude towards the new state, which may especially manifest itself in the refusal to admit it to the courts as plaintiff, in the courts declining to consider the legal acts of the newly formed state, cf. below IV. E., and in obstacles being interposed to economic intercourse with the new state or with its subjects. Especially if there is a highly developed state regulation of foreign commerce, such an attitude will have far-reaching economic consequences.

On the other hand, non-recognition does not mean that the state may disregard normal international obligations towards the new state. If non-recognition manifests itself in this way, cf. IV. D., it also involves

4. a breach of International Law.

As long as the new constellation of power is not yet finally consolidated, but is still struggling with the difficulties of the transition period, the recognition or non-recognition of other states, on account of the political and economic consequences involved, may be one of the factors that decide whether or not the consolidation will be successful. If, on the other hand, this aspect of the matter be regarded as definitely settled, the refusal of recognition will assume the character of a protest against the new state of affairs. One cannot however, oust injustice from the world merely by closing one's eyes. Facts may be fought, but not denied. A non-recognition of a firmly established position which is not followed by political instruments of power for an effective struggle against that which is considered unjust cannot fail to look slightly comical. In this connection *Fischer Williams* recalls an old English ballad. On each side of a castle gate hung a sword and a horn, and the gate would open to him who chose rightly between the two. A knight rode up and blew the horn. The gate did not open, but from the interior of the castle a voice was heard, saying:

"Cursed be the fool or ever he was borne
who feared to draw the sword, before he blew the horn."[1]

Non-recognition of this type is not only a vain gesture which in the course of time must be rendered futile in the face of the facts, but also a violation of the interests of innocent private individuals, in so far as according to internal law the courts are bound to ignore the acts of state of the non-recognised state (IV. E).

In recent times especially, non-recognition has been widely applied as a political instrument, often with a colouring of an idealistic protest against illegal encroachments. On the occasion of the Japanese invasion of the Chinese province of Manchuria the American foreign secretary Stimson in 1932 declared in a note to Japan and China that the U. S. A. did not intend to recognise any situation, treaty or agreement brought about by means in conflict with the Briand-Kellogg Pact of 1928 (the *Stimson* doctrine). And shortly after the League of Nations passed a resolution that it is incumbent on the members of the League not to recognise any situation, treaty or agreement brought about by instruments in conflict with the Covenant of the League or the Briand-Kellogg Pact of 1928.

III. *The speculative theory of the constitutive effect of recognition.*

The view here put forward, according to which the non-recognised state (the *"de facto* state") too is a subject of International Law and the recognition has only a *declaratory* significance, has hardly been seriously disputed in practice.[2] It would not occur to any statesman that such a state could be outside the law. Nevertheless the literature contains a very widespread view according to which recognition is said to have a *constitutive* effect, that is to say, be itself the law-creating fact which first makes the new state a member of the society of nations, entitled to rights and subject to obligations. This practically absurd

---

[1] *John. Fischer Williams*, Recognition in International Law, Harv. Law Rev. 1933—34 (47) 790. Cf. an excellent article by *B. M. Telders*, La reconnaissance de l'empire Italien et le droit international, N. T. 1938 apprendix, 3.

[2] Note especially that the Anglo-American practice mentioned in IV. E, as stated there, is not based on international legal rules conflicting herewith.

theory is an imaginative lucubration which would never have seen the light of day if it had not originated as a purely constructive consequence of the false theory of International Law as a conventional law (§ 1, V). For if we take for granted that all International Law must necessarily depend on an agreement between the states bound we must accept the consequence that the new state, which has not concluded any agreement with any one, is outside International Law. Hence something was sought which could function as a constitutive agreement creating a common obligation under the rules of International Law and it was found in the phenomenon of recognition. It will easily be seen that this theory is practically absurd as well as theoretically impossible.

A. It may often happen that a long time passes between the actual coming into existence of a new state and its legal recognition. As an example may be mentioned that Spain did not recognise the independence of Portugal until 1688, though it had already seceded in 1640. Greece was recognised by the guarantors in 1827, by Turkey not until 1832. Spain and Portugal only recognised the South American States, the former colonies, many years after their actual secession and their recognition by America and Great Britain. Belgium was not recognised by Holland until 1839. The Austrian Republic came into existence on the 30th October 1918 and was recognised by the Entente on the 29th May 1919. According to the constitutive theory these states would in the *interval* be outside International Law. They would be without any international legal remedy against encroachments and themselves be able to perform any act without responsibility. Since there is not supposed to exist any duty of recognition, this state of affairs might, then, be prolonged at will. This idea is entirely without connection with reality.

B. Since the recognition is not binding on other states, the strange situation would supervene that in relation to *some* states the new state must be regarded as a member of the family of nations, but not in relation to others.

C. It is evidently a *fiction* to see in the recognition an agreement for the states to be mutually bound by International Law.

D. Theoretically the assumption of a constitutive agreement lands us in *difficulties*. How can the new state, before it becomes a subject of International Law, effectively conclude agreements with other states?

IV. *The conditions, forms, and varieties of recognition.*

After this account of the principle of recognition and its effect we shall describe some rules concerning the conditions, forms, and varieties of recognition which have become established in the practice of states. The most important material in this respect is France's recognition of North America in 1778 and the U. S. A.'s recognition of the South American states after the secession from Spain (about 1822). Here it is important to keep in mind that the usual act of recognition, as already pointed out, includes, besides the actual recognition (as a novation) the assumption of diplomatic intercourse.

A. The recognition may, according to its form, be either *explicit* (for instance in a note) or *implicit,* i. e. take place through conclusive acts which plainly give expression to the will to recognise, for instance the interchange of envoys, the granting of consular exequatur, the formal conclusion of treaties, but not, on the other hand, relations through unofficial agents.

B. Recognition may be granted either *individually* or *collectively,* that is to say, it may be granted simultaneously by a number of states *en bloc.* The latter form of recognition will especially be given by allied powers after a war.

C. In diplomatic usage a distinction is made between *de jure* and *de facto* recognition. This distinction has hardly any legal significance. It has been thought that *de facto* recognition was distinguished by being temporary, revocable. However, diplomatic relations can always be freely broken off, and as far as the actual recognition is concerned it must always, but also only, be capable of being challenged or withdrawn if the recognition is based on erroneous assumptions as to the factual conditions, or these conditions change later on. The significance of the distinction is political: *de facto* recognition takes place in an atmosphere of reservation with respect to the further development (settlement of boundary lines, form of state, and the like), or of actual ill-will (in spite of which certain relations with the new state are practically necessary, for instance for the safeguarding of the interests of the citizens). It is therefore emphasised that relations are only temporary and less cordial, for instance by the fact that they are not kept up through the usual envoys, but by means of extraordinary (though nevertheless official) agents.

D. There is no *obligation* to recognise a new state. This applies unconditionally to the assumption of diplomatic relations. As far as the actual recognition is concerned, it is true that there is no obligation of express recognition, but the duty to respect a new state in deed may entail a duty to perform acts involving tacit recognition. A legal claim, for instance, cannot be dismissed as a legal nullity, reprisals are not admissible until an appeal for reparation has been made, etc.

Conversely, in case of a revolutionary secession from the mother country there exists a duty not to recognise the secession until the above-mentioned objective conditions are present, hence especially not until the struggle has practically been brought to a victorious end. Premature recognition, as for instance France's recognition as early as 1778 of the United States, is a violation of the law in regard to the mother state.

E. According to a deeply rooted Anglo-American legal practice it is not for the courts to pronounce an independent opinion on the question whether or not a new state has been born (the question may occur preliminary, § 6. II C). For recognition is regarded as an act of state which the government alone is competent to carry out without judicial control (*act of state doctrine*). In such cases the courts simply enquire of the foreign office whether or not the state in question is recognised, and base their decision thereon. If recognition has not been granted the foreign state will not be admitted as plaintiff before the courts and the foreign acts of state will be regarded as nullities. If recognition has been granted it is given *retroactive* effect, that is to say, it is made effective from the date when the new state had effectively established itself. This practice then rests in the first place on an internal distribution of competence, and does not necessarily imply that respect is not due to the non-recognised state in these cases. Since it is further extremely uncertain what legal claims a recognised state may make in these respects, it is doubtful whether an international legal rule can be deduced from this practice. The greater the part played by non-recognition as a political instrument, the longer the time that passes between the birth of a state and its recognition, the greater becomes the inconviniences of this practice which as a matter of fact seems to have been abandoned in the U. S. A. in recent times under the pressure of circumstances.

The case *Luther v. Sagor & Co.* furnishes a good example of the importance of recognition in earlier English practice, (Court of Appeal, 1921, Scott 61). The prosecuting company had carried on business in Russia since 1899, and in 1919 was in possession of a consignment of timber there which was expropriated without compensation by the Soviet Russian government, who later sold the consignment to Sagor & Co. After the timber had been imported into England, the original owner claimed its surrender. In the first instance judgment was passed in his favour, with a reference to the fact that the British government had not recognised the Soviet government, and consequently the court could not do so either, or acknowledge that the Soviet government had been able to deprive the plaintiff of his proprietary right. The court of appeal adopted the same view. But in the meanwhile the Russian government had been recognised by Great Britain. In consequence of this, the decision of the lower court was set aside, since the expropriation must now — in accordance with the retroactive force of the recognition — be regarded as a legitimate act af state which must be respected in other countries.[8]

V. *Recognition of the local insurgent party as belligerent.*

When an insurgent party has succeeded in consolidating itself on a certain territory by the establishment of a local *de facto government* (§ 14. II) it has acquired such a state-like character that there is good reason for International Law to recognise it as a subject with certain rights and duties and a corresponding responsibility. It would lead to obviously offensive results if the insurrection were regarded from a purely individualist, internal angle and the insurgents looked upon as a group of criminals:

---

[8] For more recent judgments which show a tendency to give up the act of state doctrine when it leads to absurd results, see *Boris N. Sokoloff v. The National City Bank of New York* (1922) 199 N. Y. Supp. 355 cf. 196 N. Y. Supp, 364; *Russian Reinsurance Company and Paul Rasor v. Francis and the Bankers Trust Co.* (1925) 240 N. Y. 149; 147 N. E. 703; *Salinoff & Co. v. Standard Oil Co.* 262 N. Y. Supp. 693.

traitors in relation to the mother state, pirates or guerilla bands in relation to a third state; in any case liable to unlimited punishment.

No doubt it is also generally agreed that it would be in accordance with the claims of humanity and the sense of justice of civilised nations if International Law granted the local insurgent party rights and duties as a belligerent state. But according to the almost unanimous conception of the doctrine,[4] this is not the case; according to this the insurgent party has not *ipso jure* an internationally legal status, but only when and in so far as it is *recognised* as a belligerent. Thus the recognition has a constitutive effect. It is always voluntary and is only effective in relation to the recognising state.

Against this doctrine the same objections may be raised as were mentioned under III. It is due to speculative prejudices and a confusion of the political and legal significance of recognition, and its consequences, offensive to all sense of justice, have not, as is generally contended, any safe warrant in the practice of the states.

A. A survey of the practice of the states since the American war of independence[5] shows that in many and important cases the legitimate government has treated the insurgents as belligerents. And even if a number of cases can be cited in which it has treated them as lawless criminals, it does not follow that that was done because such a course was conceived to be in accordance with the law, acknowledged by the opponent too and by other states. In the nature of the case it will be difficult for the views of the insurgents to assert themselves and be heard. As far as is known, there is no judicial decision concerning the question. The legal position is not clear, but I should think that a possible judicial decision in accordance with the claims of humanity and a general sense of justice would tend to impose the duty on the legitimate government of conducting the war according to the laws of war, especially of treating overpowered participants in the fight as prisoners of war. Only a narrow positivism could lead to another result.

B. As regards the relation to a third state, it is true that there are some few cases in which such a state has treated insurgents

---

[4] Also maintained by authors who otherwise oppose the theory of the constitutive effect of recognition, see e. g. *Kunz*, Die Anerkennung von Staaten und Regierungen im Völkerrecht, 169 f. 207. Opposed by *Vattel*, Le droit des gens, t. III, ch. XVIII, § 294.

[5] See *Kunz*, l. c. 174—77.

who have carried out hostile actions at sea as pirates.[6] But such decisions have met with severe criticism, and recently the prevalent attitude seems to go in the opposite direction, at any rate when the insurgents do not direct actions against a third state.[7] This does not mean, however, that the third state acknowledges that in relation to itself the insurgent party has the same rights of control of navigation as a belligerent state. On this point it is often contended that such rights are only acquired by recognition of the insurgents as belligerents.[8] But this does not necessarily imply that the insurgent party is not a subject of International Law, and that an attempt to arrogate such control can be treated as piracy,[9] but only that the legal position as between the insurgent party and a third state is different from the situation according to the law of neutrality.

Nor does it seem to be acknowledged that a third state, in case of direct hostile complications with the insurgent party, has a right to treat these as guerilla bands. During encounters with de Gaulle's fighting forces in Africa in 1942 the Germans threatened to do so, but probably gave up this idea upon protest and threats of reprisals on the part of Britain.

Summing up, it may probably be said that it is not possible to interpret the practice of states as an expression of an unambiguous and consistent view of the position of an insurgent party. But in conformity with the claims of humanity the idea seems to have gained ground, though not undisputed, that the

---

[6] The case of *The United States v. The Ambrose Light*, 1885 (25 Fed. 408; Scott, 544) which gave rise to much criticism, even in the U. S. A., *Wharton*, III, 465—69. (On the other hand, the case of *"The Huascar"* (1877) cannot be quoted since in this case the insurgents evidently had no organised government, cf. *Pitt-Cobbett*, 300).

[7] See *Pitt-Cobbett*, 301, who quotes the cases of *"The Montezuma"* (1887) and *"Kniaz-Potemkin"* (1905). During the Spanish civil war too the states refused to regard the insurrectionist cruiser *"Almirante Cervera"* as a pirate ship, cf. *Castberg*, Folkerettslige Spörsmål omkring den spanske Borgerkrig, N. T. 1937, 168. — Occasionally the third state takes the way of recognising the rebels as insurgents without recognising them as belligerents, see *Kunz*, Die Anerkennung von Staaten, 212 f.

[8] Thus the U. S. A. in the case of numerous Central American and South American revolts, see e. g. *Williams v. Bruffy* (1877, Scott, 40) and President McKinley's message, 1897, on the occasion of the Cuban revolt, *Moore*, I, 198. England and other states took up the same attitude during the Spanish civil war 1936—39, cf. *Castberg*, l. c. 167, whereas U. S. A. during the civil war 1860—65 assumed the right to declare a blockade.

[9] This standpoint was however taken by England in 1873 in an instruction relating to the Spanish revolt in Carthagena. Likewise Germany (1902) in the affair *"Crête à Pierrot"*, see *Pitt-Cobbett*, 301—02.

insurgents cannot be regarded as a gang of criminals who are each of them separately responsible under the criminal law, but that the responsibility must be placed collectively on the organised group, in principle on the analogy of the international legal rules concerning war. This is enough to prove that the insurgent party is *ipso jure* a subject of International Law. Hence it is of no consequence that, according to the general practice, it seems very doubtful to what extent the rules of International Law concerning war and neutrality may be applied and especially whether the insurgents and the mother state are granted rights as belligerents in relation to a third state. Technical reasons favour the assumption that a third state must respect this consequence of the situation.

§ 19
SUCCESSION OF STATES

I. *Systematic survey and leading ideas.*

We speak of a succession of states in those cases where a certain territory T passes from the supremacy of one state under that of another. The first state will in the sequel be called the predecessor state or A, and the succeeding state the successor state or B. The international legal problems arising in this connection must — in contrast with the usual practice in the current doctrine — be sharply distinguished from each other and placed in two groups.

The very circumstance that T is now regarded as belonging to B, not to A, immediately gives rise to legal changes. These are simply subject to the rules applying to the relation of a state to its territory and the persons inhabiting it (Chapters VI—VII). Hence in so far it is not necessary to lay down special rules attaching legal effects to succession as such (*pseudo-succession*).

In addition to this the question arises whether the successor state, by virtue of the territorial succession, also to a certain extent enters into the predecessor's international legal duties and rights. The question to be considered here is a legal status for B which does not follow directly from the general rules concerning a state's relation to its territory, but is a result of the territorial succession (*genuine succession*). Genuine succession is treated under II, pseudo-succession under III.

To begin with it is necessary to gain a systematic view of the various cases which may here come under consideration, based on such criteria as must *prima facie* be supposed to be of importance for the formulation of the legal rules. Common to all the cases is the feature that a territory T passes from the supremacy of a state A to that of a state B:

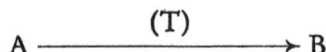

$$A \xrightarrow{\quad (T) \quad} B$$

Now the following three sets of possibilities may be imagined, each of which must be supposed to be of a certain importance:

    1. T constituted part of A's territory.

        T constituted the whole of A's territory.

    2. A still exists after the succession.

        A has ceased to exist after the succession.

    3. B existed before the succession.

        B did not exist before the succession.

Combining these factors we get the following scheme:

	A exists after the succession.	A is extinguished by the succession.
T = part of A	1) cession (B "old") 2) secession, (B "new")	3) division (B "old") 4) dismemberment (B "new")
T = the whole of A	does not occur	5) incorporation (B "old") 6) merger (B "new")

If considerable parts of a state break off from the mother state it is difficult to separate this case from the breaking up of the state into several independent new states (e. g. the fate of Austria-Hungary after the first world var).

If an incorporated state is of a considerable size in proportion to the absorbing state it is difficult to separate this case from a merging of two states into a new state.

Leading ideas: Even if a certain territory with a certain population is indeed a prerequisite for the international duties and rights of a state, these are nevertheless in the first place attached to the state as a political legal unit. Normally it would therefore be absurd to regard them as belonging to the territory and to let them accompany this *pro rata* at a territorial succession. This is most plainly seen in cases of purely political obligations, as for instance obligations of alliance. It would be absurd to let such an obligation wholly or partly devolve on the successor state. But the same must apply as a main rule to any other obligation or right which a state has created for itself. Exceptions to this rule can only be recognised when the obligation or right either has a very *special local association* with the territory in question (specially localised legal conditions) or when territorial possession *generally and quantitatively* is the natural prerequisite of a certain obligation (debts).

II. *Genuine succession.*

A. *Treaty obligations.* — In accordance with the leading ideas the main rule is that no succession to these takes place. This applies whether the predecessor continues to exist or has become extinct (in which case the obligation lapses); whether it is its whole territory or only part of it that is transferred; and whether or not the successor state is a new state. With special reference to the case of cession we speak of *the principle of the movable treaty boundaries.* If A for instance has made a commercial contract with C this contract does not become valid as between B and C. Conversely, a commercial agreement which B may have concluded with C, is automatically extended to be valid for the acquired territory. It is quite another matter that on general principles the territorial change may cancel or modify A's and B's legal relation to a third state. The territorial reduction of A may possibly cause an assumed guarantee to fall to the ground or reduce stipulated quantities in commercial treaties.

An exception to this, that is to say, a succession of B to A's legal status, is recognised to a certain extent in the case of treaty obligations with a *special local connection* with the territory in question. That at any rate applies to treaties in which the boundaries of the territory towards a third state are established. Thus in a judgment of 1891 the German Reichgericht took it for granted that the boundary treaty of 1840 concluded between the grand-duchy of Baden and France had remained valid even after the border country Alsace-Lorraine had been ceded to Germany by France.[1] Whether the exception can also be extended to other treaties especially concerned with territory, as for instance neutralisation and demilitarisation treaties, river treaties, fishery treaties, etc. is controversial.

---

[1] *Bruns,* Fontes (Reichgericht), 116 (No. 37).

Sometimes it is considered possible to solve this problem by positing the concept *state servitudes*. Usually this refers to treaty obligations by which a state's territory, or parts thereof, within certain limits but permanently, *serves the interests of another state* — either positively by giving access to a certain control for the foreign state or its citizens (right of occupation, bases, transit, fisheries etc.); or negatively by the state itself being excluded from a certain control of the territory (e. g. demilitarisation duty). The inference is then drawn that since the right in these cases according to its content concerns control over a thing (the territory) it is of the nature of a *jus in rem*, and consequently protected against a third party, that is to say, the obligation must be respected by the successor state. Such reasoning is jurisprudence of mere empty concepts. It is an arbitrary postulate based on a dogmatic prejudice that there must necessarily be a connection between the content of a right and its protection against a third party. The question must be decided on the basis of positive legal experience, and according to this the maxim cannot possibly have this general application. Numerous treaty obligations, for instance under an ordinary settlement treaty, would come under this definition though no warrant for their passing over to the successor state can be demonstrated in the practice of the states.

It is indeed at the outset a mistake to transfer the distinction drawn in private law between real and personal rights to international conditions. For the essential feature in this distinction is whether the right according to its content refers to a particular thing or to a mass of property, a point of view not applicable to International Law.[2]

If a fundamental distinction were to be made in International Law which would be of significance for the protection against a third party, it would more probably turn upon whether or not the right is manifested in an *actual exercise of power* on foreign territory, as when a state has been given the right to establish a customhouse, military bases, and the like on the territory of another. There would then be something to favour the idea that a third state — both a third state in general and the successor state — would be bound to respect the established actual condition which includes an extension of the sphere of influence of the entitled state. But whether this can be asserted to be International Law is not quite certain.

An exception must perhaps also be recognised when the treaty obligation has come into existence by a *collective treaty*,

---

[2] *Ross*, Towards a Realistic Jurisprudence, chapters IX and X.

and later on one of the contracting parties acquires the territory concerned.

On the other hand, there is no genuine succession in cases where the charge is imposed by a collective treaty which has become established as generally binding law (*"droit public européen"*). The obligation here follows directly from the generally recognised order and therefore it is of no consequence whether or not the successor state was originally one of the contracting parties. On such views it was asserted unanimously by the powers in the London conferences of 1830 and 1831 that the new state Belgium, founded by secession from Holland, was bound by the "European" treaty obligations incumbent on Holland, and on the same basis the committee of jurists came to the result that Finland, after acquiring the Åland Islands, was bound by the treaty of 1856 concerning their demilitarisation as *"droit public européen"*.

B. *The debts of the state.* With respect to the financial obligations of the state the case is essentially different. On the one hand these, owing to their abstract character, are not very closely associated with the state as a political unit; on the other hand, the financiel ability of the state as a presupposition for its financial obligations is quantitatively dependent on the territory and its population. Finally the financial burdens are, according to their nature, divisible. There is much therefore to favour the practice of letting the debt accompany the territory. This applies especially to those cases where the predecessor ceases to exist and the creditors therefore in the opposite case would be entirely without any possibility of covering their claims. It also agrees with generally recognised principles of law that the person who takes over the assets of an estate as a whole can only do so by also respecting the liabilities incumbent on it.

Nevertheless according to current International Law it cannot be stated as a general maxim that the successor state must to a certain extent take over the debts of the predecessor. It is true that numerous examples can be mentioned of *special treaties* concluded in connection with territorial succession, according to which an arrangement has been made about the simultaneous transfer of a pro rata part of the general national debt. Thus at the Vienna Congress in 1815 arrangements were made with respect to the national debts of Poland, Saxony, and the former grand-duchy of Frankfurt. After Greece had achieved independence, the country agreed to pay certain amounts to Turkey as a compensation for its part of the national debt. Arrangements with respect to national debts were also made in the two treaties of 1864 by which respectively Denmark ceded the duchies, and England renounced its protectorate of the Ionian Isles and agreed to their union with Greece. According to Art. 254 of the Treaty of Versailles those states to which German territory was ceded were to take over part of the amount that the German national debt, (debt of the Reich as a whole and debt of the individual states), constituted on the 1st August 1914. But the various above-mentioned arrangements are based on special agreements, and examples to the contrary can also be found. Thus in 1871 Germany took over no part of the French national debt and on the strength of this fact Art. 255 of the Treaty of Versailles exempted France from any obligation consequent on Art. 254 with respect to the acquisition of Alsace-Lorraine.

On the other hand, more detailed rules can be laid down concerning the assumption of debts. In the first place it is recognised in practice that the successor state is liable for *local debt,* that is to say, debts contracted within the financial autonomy of a ceded part of a state *(special debts, dettes speciales);* or which have been incurred by the general administration but exclusively in the interest of the ceded part of the state *(relative debts, dettes hypothéquées).* The rule is particularly clear and applicable in the first case. It was applied in a large number of cases in the relation between Spain and the seceding South American colonies. It is true that a special agreement was made in connection with Spain's recognition of their independence. But that a generally recognised legal principle was here concerned appears from an elaborate exchange of notes between Spain and the United States of America concerning the Cuban debts. After the United States had in 1898 supported the revolt of Cuba and compelled its independence (under American protection) she refused to take over any part of the Cuban debt. But the refusal was based on the view that the Cuban debt was not really a local debt but a debt contracted by the Spanish state for general national purposes, even chiefly for fighting through many years the Cuban efforts to gain independence. Both parties recognised as general law the rule that local debts devolve on the successor state.[3] Finally it was also recognised as a matter of course, in an exchange of notes between the Entente and the Reich in 1919 in connection with the peace negotiations, that the local debts of Alsace-Lorraine were to be assumed by France, so that — irrespectively of the provision in Article 255 — it was unnecessary to embody any provision to that effect in the peace treaty.[4]

On the other hand, it seems not to be recognised that the circumstance that security for national debt is given in local values or revenues, (land, taxes, customs duties), causes the successor state to be liable. The United States disputed this in the above-mentioned case concerning the debt of Cuba.[5]

If the predecessor *ceases to exist* at the succession there is a tendency, out of regard for the creditors, to an extended liability for the whole national debt. A rule to that effect can most easily be enforced where the territory of the predecessor passes undivided into the same hands, that is to say, in *incorporation* and *merger,* and is probably also recognised in those cases,[6] whereas the rule meets with difficulties in cases where the territory is divided and passes to a multiplicity of successors, that is to say, upon *division* and *dismemberment.* For here a further rule is required concerning the *pro rata* shares of the various successors in the national debt. If a voluntary agreement cannot be arrived at, the decision must be made by arbitration.

The rules concerning the assumption of debts are, however, limited by the fact that the successor state is never liable for debts contracted for the financing of wars or other similar hostile undertakings against itself.[7]

---

[3] See *Moore,* Intern. Law, I, 351 f.

[4] Quoted by *Verdross,* Völkerrecht, 243, note 3.

[5] See also the case of Chile's assumption in 1883 of the *guano deposits in Tarapaco,* formerly belonging to Peru. The proceeds thereof had been pledged by Peru to her creditors. Chile recognised these liens but emphasised that it was under no obligation to do so. On the part of the U. S. A. too, only a moral obligation for Chile to acknowledge the rights of the creditors was mentioned. See *Moore,* International Law, I, 334—36.

[6] Several decisions in this direction cited in *Verdross,* Völkerrecht 244, note 2. Against it may be cited that England at the annexation of the Fiji Islands did not admit any legal obligation to take over the debts of the islands. See *Moore,* Intern. Law I, 347 f. especially 350.

[7] This rule was assumed to be valid in the dispute about the Cuban debt, see especially the American memorandum of Oct. 27 1898 and the Spanish

Again, it follows from the fundamental limits of International Law that — without a treaty — there is never any responsibility to creditors who, after the succession, belong as citizens to the successor state. To its own citizens the state according to general International Law has no obligations. It follows that normally the successor state has no international obligation as far as the internal national debts of the predecessor are concerned.

C. *The state property.* Similar rules apply to this. If the predecessor state continues to exist (cession, secession) it loses its claim to the *local* property of the administration, that is to say, the buildings, fortifications, plants etc.

If, on the other hand, the predecessor state ceases to exist all state funds, including such as are invested abroad, devolve on the successor state. In case of division and dismemberment a norm of distribution is required. No general rule for this distribution exists. If agreement between the states concerned cannot be obtained the question remains open.

III. *Pseudo-succession.*

The very circumstance that the territory passing over to the successor now constitutes part of the territory of that state involves certain direct legal consequences by virtue of the general rules of International Law concerning territory and population. B does not follow A in a certain legal status according to special rules of succession; the position of B is directly determined by the territorial fact of succession in connection with the general rules of International Law.

A. *Nationality.* — That the inhabitants of the territory passing over to the successor state normally become citizens of that state is not a concequence of B succeeding to A's "right" to these people. The new legal status is a simple consequence of the fact that B in accordance with the general rules of International Law is now free by its own legislation to increase its circle of citizens by including the population of the territory taken over.

reply of Nov. 16 of the same year, *Moore*, Intern. Law I 367 and 377. See also Entsch. des Reichsgerichts 3 Juni 1924 (*Bruns*, Fontes, 121). In art. 254 of the Treaty of Versailles it was only required that the successor states should take over a part of what the German national debt amounted to on Aug. 1 1914 — i. e. any part of the debt contracted during the war.

The limits of the nationality legislation of the state are determined by the existence of certain relations between the individual
and the state. If these principles were to be strictly observed in
this situation, B would be able to appeal to the following facts
as grounds for nationality:

1. Birth in T.
2. Descent from persons belonging to group 1, and
3. Marriage to men under groups 1 and 2.

An application of these rules would, however, not only be
beset with great practical difficulties but would also lead to
undesired and absurd results. Usually there will be a special
treaty arrangement between A and B. But in the absence of this,
and as far as the relation to a third state is concerned, the rule
holds good that B can appropriate the inhabitants *domiciled on
the territory who were previously citizens in the predecessor
state.* Citizens of a third state domiciled on the territory, on the
other hand, preserve their nationality. In case of incorporation,
when the whole of A's territory is absorbed by B, the successor
state can, however, acquire alle the citizens of the predecessor
since no opposed interests assert themselves here.

Often special provisions as to *option* have been made by
treaty, that is to say, a right for the individual, irrespectively of
the general rules of the transfer of the state citizens, to reserve
for themselves their original nationality by a declaration of will.
This right of option, which is often made subject to special conditions, limits the successor state's general liberty under International Law of conferring citizenship on these persons.

B. *The proprietary rights of the population,* for example *concessions.* — It is usually said that the successor state is bound to
respect the private rights acquired. The succession it is said, is
merely an assumption of the public rights of "sovereignty", not
of private proprietary rights. On this point, however, there is
no succession, there is merely the simple fact that the inhabitants
of the transferred territory are now subject to the sovereignty of the successor state. If they — as normally happens
— have likewise become citizens in the new state, they are —
apart from special treaty provisions[8] — entirely without inter-

---

[8] A large number of treaties contain explicit provisions relating to the
successor state's obligation to recognise contracts and concessions. See
Moore, Intern. Law I. 385.

national legal protection against it. Only towards *aliens* has the successor state certain duties determined by the general principles of international law (§ 28. III). According to this the successor state is bound to respect such rights as an alien has acquired under a foreign legal order. In the case under consideration this principle (with certain reservations) obliges the successor state to respect rights which before the succession were legitimately conferred by the predecessor.[9] The question is of most practical importance in the case of concessions.[10] Further it must be borne in mind that even if the successor state is bound by the concession, the legal rights are, henceforth, subject to the state's own legislative competence, and may therefore, if necessary, be further regulated, modified, or entirely cancelled — all within the limits of the law relating to aliens.

C. Further, all the general international obligations and rights in one way or another connected with the territory are incumbent upon the successor state. If the successor state is new the obligations also arise as new. If the successor state was already in existence, there merely occurs an increase in the area to which the legal conditions apply.

§ 20
REVOLUTION

It is generally acknowledged that an internal revolution in the government of a state does not involve any change in the international status of the state. If this is accepted it is of no consequence whether we say with the prevailing doctrine that the state in spite of the internal revolution preserves international identity *(the principle of the continuity of the state)* or whether we prefer to say that a new state has come into existence which

---

[9] See the report of the *Transvaal Concessions Commission* (1901), *Moore*, Intern. Law I 411.

[10] In the case of the *Manila Railway Co. (Moore* 1. c. 395) the United States refused to respect a concession on the ground that it had not been contracted in the interest of the ceded terriory but for the benefit of the Spanish central government for the easier control of the colony. There is here presumably an unwarranted application of succession principles to this problem.

succeeds universally to the legal status of the former state (Kelsen).

The principle has been recognised in a series of arbitral awards and national judicial decisions, as well as generally by writers.[1] It acquires special importance in cases where the constitution of a state at the outset declares acts performed in violation of the constitution (*coups d'état,* revolutions) to be invalid. Such provisions occur in several South American constitutions (Chile, Peru, Venezuela).[2] As a typical example of the application of the principle may be mentioned the *Peru-Dreyfus* affair which was settled by arbitration in 1921. On the strength of a contract of 1869 the French firm Dreyfus raised certain claims against the government of Peru which, however, would not recognise them. But after Pierola had made himself dictator in 1879 he recognised the French claims up to a certain amount. Before this amount had been paid Pierola was overthrown and the congress of Peru, appealing to the constitution, refused to abide by the recognition of the dictator. After lengthy negotiations the case was decided in 1921 by a court of arbitration which rejected the view of Peru and declared that Pierola as the head of the republic recognised as such by foreign powers had acted on behalf of the nation and bound it.

The principle was likewise recognised by the democratic provisional Russian government in 1917. It was rejected by the succeeding Soviet government which categorically refused to assume the international obligations of Czardom. The consequence was that a great number of foreign states refused to recognise the Soviet Russian government. Gradually, however, it obtained recognition from an increasing number of states in return for renouncing all the rights of the former Russian state. Thus a complete breach with the principle of the continuity of the state was carried through. This, however, has not caused any change in the international legal view of this point.

---

[1] Cf. *Mirkine-Guetzevitch,* Droit constitutionnel international, 42 f.
[2] See l. c. 67 f.

Chapter IV
THE DELIMITATION OF THE SPHERES OF DOMINION OF STATES: THE TERRITORY

§ 21
TERRITORY AND POPULATION AS PRELIMINARY CONCEPTS

In the current textbooks great obscurity prevails as to the systematic placing and development of the rules concerning the territory and population of states. Usually these are dealt with in the chapter on the subjects of International Law, the territory and population being regarded as natural elements of the state, which is there mentioned and described as the subject of International Law *par excellence.*

This arrangement is mistaken. Even if the territory and the population should be natural parts of the state it cannot be the task of the International Law of persons to describe these any more than it is the task of the municipal law of persons to describe the anatomy of man. The science of the Law of Nations is an exposition of law and neither a general doctrine of states nor geography or ethnography. A systematic rearrangement is therefore necessary.

It is the object of International Law to present legal rules for the relations between self-governing communities, primarily states. The first section of the central international legal rules (see table p. 76) deals with the mutual delimitation of the spheres of dominion of the states (Chapters VI—VII), especially the rules for their jurisdictional competence and the territorial integrity. These rules are based on two fundamental concepts, namely a state's territory and its population. It is necessary, therefore, before they can be presented, to know exactly what is meant by these concepts in the rules in question. On this point International Law itself gives a more detailed explanation in other rules intended to establish what areas belong to the territory of a state and what persons to its population. But these rules are not really independent international rules but merely fragments of such. The exposition of the rules concerning territory and population must therefore be regarded as *preliminary in relation to the complete rules concerning the mutual delimitation of the spheres of dominion of the states.*

The *territory* of a state can then be defined as the area which under International Law (in preliminary rules) is attributed to the state concerned as its territory. Its legal significance appears from the various complete international rules in which the word territory or its synonyms occur. These are primarily the rules concerning the delimitation of the spheres of dominion of the states.

Similarly, the *population* of a state may be defined as the group of persons which under International Law (in preliminary rules) is regarded as belonging to the state concerned as its population. Its legal significance appears from the various complete international legal rules in which the word population or its synonyms occur. These are in the first place the rules relating to the delimitation of the spheres of dominion of the states.

§ 22
THE LEGAL SIGNIFICANCE IN GENERAL OF THE TERRITORY AND THE POPULATION

It is a historical fact that the various states are separated from each other and bounded territorially. This of course is not fortuitous but deeply rooted in the nature of the case. The states are primarily an organisation of power. Each of them claims to be, within a certain territory separated from others, the supreme power in relation to its subjects (a self-governing community). The simplest principle, almost a matter of course, for the individualisation and separation of these competing instruments of power is the spacial or territorial. This of course is not an invention of International Law. Already before any International Law existed the separate states did in fact, grow up round a centre of power territorially determined. It is not until we have a multiplicity of states facing each other and each of them claiming respect for its actual territorial possessions that what was originally a mere fact develops into a legally recognised delimitation. Here as on other fundamental points International Law can only defer to the facts and invest them with legal validity *(the maxim of effectiveness)*.

In conformity herewith the *fundamental international legal norm of the distribution of competence* is to the effect that every state is competent, and exclusively competent, within its own territory to perform acts which — actually or potentially — consist in the working of the compulsory apparatus of the state *(the maxim of territorial supremacy)*.

Intercourse between states without such an actual legal territorial delimitation would in practice be inconceivable. On the other hand, a delimitation on this basis alone would be quite conceivable. But such is not the actual state of affairs. An unlimited territorial compulsory authority over every person present on the territory would conflict with that bond of sympathy binding some of these persons to foreign states. Certain restrictions in territorial competence are therefore recognised for the benefit of individuals with foreign ties. It is here that the concept "population" or "citizens" becomes of importance. For, according to the general International Law these restrictions are solely dependent on the formal status as citizens in a foreign state. They may be classed in three groups:

1. The rules concerning exterritoriality (§ 27).
2. The general law relating to aliens (§ 28).
3. Special rules concerning ships in foreign territorial waters (§ 29).

Further, by way of extension, it has been recognised that in rare cases the state can exercise jurisdiction on foreign state territory, namely over foreign ships on the open sea (§ 30).

De lege ferenda it is questionable whether it is desirable that International Law should associate protection for foreigners solely with formal citizenship. The actual feeling of being foreigners and, conversely, a foreign state's actual bond of interest with certain individuals, may be connected with other criteria, especially ethnographic: e. g. national minorities. And on the other hand, the citizen relation, after several generations' domicile abroad, may have worn so thin that it is doubtful whether it should be a ground for privileges according to the law relating to aliens. The great advantage of the criterion of citizenship lies in its technical legal sharpness. It will presumably be the task of the International Law of future times to create a better rapprochement on this point between the law and the actual interests concerned.

§ 23
WHAT AREA IS REGARDED BY INTERNATIONAL LAW AS THE TERRITORY BELONGING TO A PARTICULAR STATE?

I. *The principle of effectiveness.*

As already stated it is not within the competence of International Law to give arbitrary rules for the area to be attributed to a particular state as its territory. International Law must in the main defer to political facts. The attribution therefore takes place in accordance with the principle, that area being attributed to a particular state in which *the organs of power of that state assert themselves effectively and continually.* It may also be expressed thus. Just as International Law may contain general references to national law (§ 6), so it here contains a general reference to facts.

It may seem doubtful whether a principle that blindly submits to the force of facts can be regarded as a legal principle at all. For it would seem that in this way every possibility of a divergence between the claims of law and actual conditions would be excluded at the outset. That is not the case, however. It is only the continual actual assertion of power which the law cannot disregard. This does not preclude that an isolated action may be regarded as conflicting with the law (e. g. if the police cross frontiers in order to take people into custody); or that legal regulation of many details is possible (e. g. the fixing of boundaries, rules concerning ships etc.)

The principle of effectiveness determines both the *static* description of the area which at a given time is regarded as the territory of a state (II—V) and the *dynamic* rules concerning the acquisition and loss of territory (VI).

II. *Land territory.*

The *geographical* territory of a state is usually divided into three parts: the land territory, the territorial waters, and the national waters. To this may be added as accessories the air space over and the subsoil under the territory.

The extent of the land territory does not normally give rise to doubt. It is especially on land that the state organs of power regularly display their activities. By the sea or other waters the boundaries are determined by the natural coast or shore line and their precise determination (high water mark, low water mark) is of no interest. Towards the land territory of another state the boundary will normally be distinctly marked by boundary signs. In case the boundary is indicated by natural geographical formations (rivers, lakes, mountain ranges) International Law contains some declaratory rules concerning its accurate determination, into which we shall not enter here.

III. *The territorial waters.*

The territorial waters are the belt of sea extending along the land territory of a state. Here too the principle of effectiveness acts as the basis for its extent. It is true that, as a matter of course, the state does not here display such a regular activity that its extent can be established by merely considering the facts at a given moment. The principle of effectiveness therefore acquires a *historical* character. The maritime belt extends as far as the state in the course of history has asserted its power in action against other states.

On the one hand this implies that *there is no rule of International Law* directly determining the extent of the territorial waters. Even though most states nowadays have accepted the nautical three-mile boundary there are nevertheless a considerable number which operate with other distances and different distances in different relations (fisheries, neutrality etc.). It is another matter that *historically* the now prevalent standard of 3 miles has developed under the influence of international ideas of the extent of the territorial waters. While in earlier times leading naval powers often made very far-reaching claims of "sovereignty" over the sea the maxim advanced by *Bynkershoek* that *potestas terrae finitur ubi finitur armorum vis* gained more and more ground in the course of the 18th century. In 1872 the Italian *Galiani* suggested that the longest range of gun-shot should once for all be fixed at 3 nautical miles.[1] This

---

[1] At that time, however, the effective range was far short of 3 nautical miles or 5556 km. Up to about the middle of the last century muzzle loader ordnance were in use which hardly had a wider range than 1000 paces

rule was already accepted in practice during the Napoleonic wars by the U. S. A. and Great Britain, and in the 19th century the other states gradually followed suit. In our day the rule of the range of gun-shot must be regarded as without significance.

On the other hand it also implies that a state *cannot itself arbitrarily* decide upon the extent of its territorial waters — not even within the maximum range of gunfire. A one-sided outward displacement of the boundary would be a violation of the time-honoured prescriptive rights of other states to the area in question as open sea, whereas the state can of course waive its claims to territorial waters to which it has hitherto asserted its right. It may be doubtful when the mere non-exercise of rights, or the mere onesided restriction can be regarded as a binding relinquishment. The question is of importance for Denmark which from the old days has asserted its rights to a distance of four nautical miles but has in recent times actually and legally only maintained its claim to three nautical miles.

At the codification conference at the Hague in 1930 an attempt was made to agree upon a common distance with the only result of registering disagreement, even though states representing about 80 p. c. of the world's tonnage proclaimed their adherence to the three-mile zone. Not a few of these, however, attached to this a claim for the recognition of a so-called "contiguous zone" for the protection of certain interests. The negative result of the conference was presumably in the first place due to the fact that the wrong purpose was aimed at. Owing to the geographical conditions and the great dissimilarity of interests a general arrangement must probably be considered unattainable. The object should rather be an individual settlement and regulation by the marking of the boundaries of the territorial waters for each country on charts in which account should be taken of the necessity for establishing different boundaries in connection with the different protected interests (fisheries, sanitation, customs, neutrality etc.).

The exact determination of the territorial waters requires the marking of two boundaries, the outer boundary towards the open sea, and the inner boundary towards the land territory or the national waters.

(800 m) at a normal elevation of 5—6°. The distance fixed even exceeds the theoretically calculated maximal range at an elevation of 45°, which is stated to be 4000—5000 m.

A. *The outer boundary*. — On account of the technical difficulties the boundary of the territorial waters towards the open
sea is not — like that of the land territory towards a foreign
country — visibly marked off by means of buoys or the like, but
is determined only by means of certain calculations. These
comprise two elements 1) indication of a base line, 2) indication
of a distance from this. Then the outer limit is constructed as
the line which at the said distance runs approximately parallel
to the base line indicated.

As to 1. If continents and islands were formed by the hand
of nature as regular geometrical figures bounded by straight
lines or arcs of circles it would be natural to chose the natural
coast line as a base. As matters stand such a procedure would not
only be technically very difficult or impossible but would also
conflict with practical interests. *The base line* therefore is determined as the *conventional coast-line* (at low water mark), the
natural irregularities being to a certain extent eliminated by
*drawing the base line round the outward side of islands, islets
and reefs, and across bays, fiords, and mouths or rivers.*

To what extent this is done cannot be fixed by general rules.
The geographical conditions and the actual interests are too
dissimilar for this to be done. This applies especially to the
question as to what islands, islets, and reefs are to be enclosed
behind the base lines (see e. g. the coast of Norway). As far as
bays, fiords, and river mouths are concerned the rule is often
adhered to that a base line is drawn right across the opening at
a place nearest the inlet where the width does not exceed a
certain measure, often, as in Denmark, 10 nautical miles. But
beyond this several countries, especially England, have from
olden times base lines across bays of considerable width without
taking account of any rules for distances. Such bays are usually
called "*historical*".[1]

As to 2. The distance determining the outer limit in relation

---

[1] Norway e. g. asserts that Varanger Fiord is territorial, though its mouth
is 32 nautical miles wide. Previously England maintained the territorial
character of the so-called King's Chambers, which include those parts of the
sea that come within lines drawn from headland to headland, but it is not
probable that this claim will be maintained, cf. the attitude taken by the
English government in the case *Mortensen v. Peters* and the Trawling in
Prohibited Areas Prevention Act, 1909 (§ 6, II with Note 6). See also
Oppenheim, International Law, § 191.

to the base (the conventional coast-line) is usually indicated in nautical miles (1 nautical mile $= \frac{1}{60}$ of a latitudinal degree or 1852 m). As already stated, a distance of 3 nautical miles (5,556 km) is the commonest, but distances of 4, 5, 6, 10, 12, and 20 nautical miles and combinations hereof in various relations also occur.

B. *The inner limit.* — In so far as the base is formed by the natural coast line there can be no doubt that this is also the inner limit of the territorial waters. But doubt arises in the cases where the base is determined by artificially drawn lines; is the base line then the inner limit or not? Is the water situated between the coast and base line national water or territorial water? The practical interest of the question is whether the restrictions on the supremacy of the state that apply to territorial waters (the right to peaceful passage) will also apply to these waters or not. Where special considerations do not favour the contrary it must be assumed that the base line is likewise the inner limit and the intermediate waters (bays, fiords, sounds) are then national waters.

From *Eduard von Waldkirch* und *Ernst Vanselow*, Neutralitetsrecht, we borrow the following survey of the claims made by the various states with regard to the extent of their territorial waters.

	Supremacy					
	outside free coasts n. m.	in bays up to a width of n. m.	neutrality n m.	fishery[1]) n m.	customs[1]) n. m	Notes
Germany	3	6	3	3		
Argentine	5			10		
Belgium	3	6	3	3	10 km	
Bolivia	5					
Brazil	3		3			
Chile	3		3			
China	3		3			
Denmark	3	10	3	4 (3)		
Danzig	3		3	3		
England	3	6	3	3	3 (12)	historic bays
Ecuador	3	12	6			
Esthonia	3	10	3			
France	6	10	3	3	20 km	

	Supremacy					
	outside free coasts n. m.	in bays up to a width of n m.	neutrality n. m.	fishery[1] n. m.	customs[1] n. m.	Notes
Finland	4		3		10.6 km (12 km)	
Greece	6		6	3	6	
Italy	6	20	6		12	
Japan	3	10	3			
Yugoslavia						
Cuba	3		3			
Colombia		12				
Latvia	3	12	3		6 (12)	
			3		12	
Netherlands	3	10	3			
Norway	4	all fiords	3	4	10	
Panama	3		3			
Poland	3	12	3			
Portugal	18 (?)		6	3 (6)	6	
Russia	4[2]				12	
Roumania	3	10	10			
Sweden	4	12	4	4 (3)	4	
Spain	6	12	3	6	6	
Turkey	5	12	6		12	historic bays
U. S. A.	3		3			
Uruguay	5		5			

[1] The figures in brackets denote that these deviations occur in treaty law or state law.

[2] Outside the Baltic 12 n. m.

IV. *The national waters*

are the waters, fresh or salt, which are situated inside the territorial waters, such as lakes, rivers, canals, harbours, roadsteads, as also such sounds, fiords and bays as are situated inside the base lines of the territorial waters, when these (as a rule) form the inner limit of the territorial waters.

V. *The floating territorry.*

As the territory of the state are also reckoned *certain ships* viz. on the open sea all national ships, in foreign territory national men-of-war and other ships that serve to exercise the imperial power of the state (e. g. police vessels, customs vessels). This territory is not, as has often been supposed, fictional. This idea is based on the unfounded implication that the term "territory" necessarily denotes a geographical concept in International Law. The floating territory merely differs from the geographical in that the atmospheric space over it is not included in the territory nor has it any territorial water belonging to it.

VI. *Acquisition and loss of territory.*

It follows from the effectivity principle that *the only fact which can prove the acquisition of territory is the lasting, effective taking possession of it*. The application of the principle acquires a somewhat different aspect according as the territory concerned has previously been subject to the supremacy of another state or not.

A. In the former case there will occur *cession, incorporation* (or one of the other forms of succession). In both cases the transfer may have taken place by virtue of agreement, transfer, or by military force, by conquest.

In case of a peaceful *transfer* there will hardly be any doubt about the point of time and extent of the territorial acquisition which are both determined by the actual assumption of administration.

In the case of a *conquest* by war the transition does not take place until the hostile resistance — from the enemy himself or his allies — has practically been finally put down. Remaining scattered resistance therefore is no hindrance. On the other hand, mere *invasion* or provisional *hostile occupation* does not involve the actual transfer of the territory. Hostile occupation, however, does involve, as an intermediate condition, that within certain limits the territorial supremacy passes to the occupant. That it is only exercised *on behalf of the opponent* appears, however, from a series of international rules concerning hostile occupation the chief tenor of which is that the occupant takes over the political and economic power, but — with a reservation with respect to its military interests — is bound to exercise this for the preservation of the *status quo* and the protection of the private, economic and cultural life of the population on the basis of the extant law.[2]

---

[2] See the 4. Hague Conv. 1907 Arts. 43 and 46. The German occupations during the recent war often meant the grossest breaches of this principle, in itself so clear and reasonable.

B. The question grows much more difficult when the territory has not previously been subject to the dominion of a state. We then speak of seizure or *occupation,* more precisely civil occupation in contradistinction to military occupation (which again may be either by war or peaceful, according as a state of war prevails between the parties or not). Since we are here concerned with establishing a state-like administration in uncivilised regions, often uninhabited from the start, it is by the nature of the case far more difficult to fix both the time for and the extent of the territorial acquisition. It is clear that an organisation of similar intensity to that common in civilised countries cannot be demanded. No more can be demanded than is sufficient for colonial government according to the international standard, when geographical, ethnographical, traffic and other conditions are taken into consideration *(the maxim of the international standard).*

From various judicial decisions, most recently the judgment of the Permanent Court in the case about the *legal status of Eastern Greenland,* it would seem that the demands that can be made according to this principle concerning the exercise of "sovereignty" are very small, especially in sparsely populated countries and in countries with no fixed settlements.[3] Though Denmark had actually never exercised authority on the eastern coast of Greenland the Court yet recognised that in the course of time, especially because various Danish acts and treaties had assumed validity for the whole Greenland area, Denmark had exercised sufficient authority over the non-colonised part to create a valid title of "sovereignty".[4] The Court refers to the fact that legislation is one of the most obvious forms of the exercise of sovereign power.[5] This is a fresh example of how the terminology of "sovereignty" may obscure a clear understanding. To legislate for a certain territory is merely a vain pretention when there

---

[3] "It is impossible to read the records of the decisions in cases as to territorial sovereignty without observing that in many cases the tribunal has been satisfied with very little in the way of the actual exercise of sovereign rights, provided that the other State could not make out a superior claim. This is particularly true in the case of claims of sovereignty over areas in thinly populated or unsettled countries," Permanent Court of International Justice, Serie A/B No. 53, p. 46.

[4] L. c. 54.

[5] L. c. 48.

are no authorities to enforce the laws.[6] In reality the standpoint of the Court means that it has *relinquished all demands of effectivity and recognised* that in connection with a lasting and effective occupation which takes place within a certain large naturally rounded-off region within which no other state has planted colonies, the mere will to extend the occupation to the whole region is sufficient to create a legal claim which must be respected by other states *(the theory of geographical unity).* But instead of making a straightforward statement to that effect the Court has by undermining the effectivity concept tried to make the result harmonise with the fundamental norm of occupation. This veiling of the actual state of affairs is unfortunate since it will easily give rise to technically unfounded conclusions with respect to what is generally required for an effective occupation.

From the above it will appear that the mere *discovery* of new territory is not in itself sufficient to bring about acquisition of territory. The same applies to symbolic seizure (hoisting of the flag etc.). An exception to this has however been recognised by an arbitral award of 1931 with respect to desert islands.[7] On the other hand, a formal *declaration of occupation* or notification is not required, but of course is often to be recommended by way of proof. The demand, often advanced in theory and expressly stated in the Greenland award,[8] that occupation, besides the objective exercise of "sovereignty", also subjectively requires the "will to act as sovereign", is an empty phantom, a rudiment of the Roman animus possidendi which had itself sprung from a primitive animistic mysticsm.[9]

VII. *The current theory of acquisition and loss of territory.*

In contradistinction to the present exposition which only (in accordance with *Kelsen*[10]) knows one fact that can afford grounds for territorial acquisition, the prevalent doctrine posits a number of different modes of acquisition. In accordance with the Roman doctrine of the acquisition of proprietary rights, it

---

[6] This is emphasised by *Anzilotti* in his dissentient opinion, l. c. 83.

[7] Pronounced by the King of Italy in a dispute between France and Mexico about the island of *Clipperton*.

[8] In note 3 l. c. 46.

[9] See *Axel Hägerström,* Der römische Obligationsbegriff, I 236—95.

[10] *Hans Kelsen,* Théorie générale du Droit international public 88 f.

is usual to distinguish between original and derivative acquisition. In the former category must be reckoned accretion, occupation, and conquest; in the latter, cession.

It is not difficult to see, however, that the original acquisitions are only variants of an effective seizure under different circumstances. The same applies to cession. For it is never an agreement as such which entails acquisition of territory but only the actual taking over of the territory.[11] If the ceding state opposes this, its action is indeed in conflict with the law, but no transfer of territory takes place. The prevailing doctrine is due to a confusion of the territorial transfer itself with a legal obligation to tolerate and respect the transfer.

A similar situation may occur in the case of occupation. A state may have bound itself by agreement not to occupy an area within a certain territory (for instance Norway in relation to Denmark, with respect to Greenland). If nevertheless the state in question occupies the said area, the occupation is indeed in conflict with the law, but none the less, if it is maintained, it entails acquisition of the territory.

Further, it has been thought that seizure might in certain cases under International Law be *reserved* for a particular state, and so would conflict with the law if undertaken by others. According to a widespread view *discovery* creates such a prior right within a reasonable space of time. There is a similar tendency in the so-called contiguity theory, or the theory of *geographical unity* according to which the state which has occupied a certain area acquires a prior right to further occupation of such areas as together with the occupied area constitute a natural geographical unit. A special application is the so-called *sector theory*, according to which in polar regions the contiguous states have a prior right to occupation in the sector determined by the boundary and the parallels of longitude to the pole. It is extremely doubtful how far these rules of priority can really be regarded as current International Law. As stated above, the decision of the Permanent Court of International Justice in the Greenland case would seem to imply a recognition of the theory of geographical unity.

---

[11] It is another matter that agreement concerning cession has the effect that the acquiring state after the territory has been taken over need not respect such acts on the part of the ceding state as have been carried out after the agreement or with a view to it to the detriment of the acquiring state e. g. alienation of state property, conferring of concessions etc.

Chapter V
DELIMITATION OF THE SPHERES OF DOMINION OF STATES: THE POPULATION

§ 24
WHAT BODY OF PERSONS IS REGARDED BY INTERNATIONAL LAW AS THE POPULATION OF A PARTICULAR STATE?

As previously stated, the population or the citizens of a state may be defined as the body of persons which is regarded by International Law (in preliminary rules) as belonging to that state as its population. The significance of the concept lies in the fact that it is decisive of certain restrictions on the territorial competence of other states. The legal claims resulting therefrom cannot, according to current International Law, be asserted directly by the private individuals concerned but only by the state whose citizens they are. The concept therefore will also determine the competence of the home state to maintain the protected interests of the persons concerned against other states.

Now, what body of persons is regarded by International Law as citizens of a particular state? No direct reply to this question can be found in International Law. International Law leaves it to each separate state to decide through its own laws who are its citizens. But — as correctly expressed in the Hague Convention of 1930 on certain questions of nationality — those laws are only to be respected by other states in so far as they accord with international conventions, international custom, and the generally recognised legal principles concerning nationality. The widespread view that according to International Law the state has unlimited freedom to give whatever content it likes to its laws of nationality is not correct.[1] This is at once evident from the

---

[1] It is, however, held by the Permanent Court which, in an opinion No. 4 1923 *corcerning certain nationality decrees in Tunis and Morocco*, says that questions of nationality are among the questions not in principle regulated by

fact that all international rules regarding aliens would then in principle be dependent on the discretion of the state. By bestowing citizenship on all persons staying on its territory it might set aside all obligations. That this has been overlooked is presumably due to the fact that transgression of what is permissible in this domain is actually rare. That renders it more difficult to discover the legal principles which must be recognised. In recent times there have been several arbitral awards which have disallowed the conferring of citizenship in certain cases as conflicting with International Law.

Since a state, owing to the rules of territorial supremacy and double nationality, cf. §§ 25 and 26, will not be able to obtain results of any great practical value by conferring citizenship on persons residing outside its territory, the problem centres round those instances in which the person concerned is staying within the state's own territory. As International Law permits nationality to be conferred on any person born on the territory, the problem further becomes limited to the naturalisation (in the widest sense) of aliens resident on the territory of the state.

For a distinction can be drawn between:

A. The acquisition of citizenship by *birth*, or the case of native citizens. Birth of course is the chief ground for acquisition. In most instances the nationality of a person is decided by his birth without subsequently undergoing any change. According to the fixed practice of states it is recognised that it is permitted to associate acquisition of citizenship both with birth on the territory (*jus soli, original territorial principle*) and with birth of national parents (*jus sanguinis, original personal principle* or *principle of descent*). Most countries base their laws on a combination of these two principles. On the other hand, it would no doubt be regarded as conflicting with International Law to go beyond the lines drawn by these principles and, for instance, associate citizenship with birth of foreign parents belonging to national minorities in a foreign state.

B. Acquisition of citizenship by a *subsequent* event or the case of naturalised citizens (in the widest sense).

International Law (at its present stage of development) and so fall within the "reserved domain", if the question has not been settled by special agreement (Perm. Court Publ. Series B. No. 4, pp. 23—24).

According to the practice of states subsequent acquisition of citizenship may have the following grounds:

(1) Close *family relationship* to a person who is or becomes a citizen, especially the relation of a wife to her husband, and of children (adopted children) to their parents *(subsequent personal principle)*. Usually a woman acquires citizenship by marrying a national, and as a rule a man's acquisition of citizenship is extended to his wife and legitimate children, a woman's acquisition of citizenship to her illegitimate children; in case of marriage, however, only to those whom she had by her husband before marriage and who thus become legitimate by the marriage.

(2) To a certain extent also a *fixed domicile*[2] in the state *(subsequent territorial principle)*, viz. in connection either with territorial succession (§ 19. III) or with an application for its acquisition (naturalisation in the narrower sense). On the other hand, the state can hardly enforce naturalisation on the basis of the domicile alone.

Beyond these two groups of facts — which express a close objective connection with the population of the state and its territory respectively — the subsequent conferring of citizenship must no doubt be regarded as conflicting with International Law. Thus for instance an entirely subjective criterion can hardly be recognised as a basis for naturalisation, that is to say, naturalisation can hardly be given merely because of an application.[3] It may further be mentioned that the Mexican Aliens Act of 1886 — which provides that any foreigner who acquires real estate in Mexico thereby *ipso jure* becomes a Mexican citizen if he does not expressly declare that he desires to retain his original nationality — was declared to be in conflict with International Law by the German-Mexican Claims Commission. The

---

[2] The laws of states usually require a fixed domicile for a number of years as a condition of naturalisation, but there is no warrant for laying down any general international requirement in that respect. (On the *Bancroft Treaties* see § 25). The sole safeguard against abuse is the strictness of the demands made by International Law in order that the domicile may be recognised as fixed.

[3] When in practice non-resident persons are sometimes naturalised, it is presumably only persons whose naturalisation might be due to one of the abovementioned principles who are concerned.

same view was held by the French-Mexican Claims Commission.[4]
Similarly it must be supposed that an acquisition of citizenship
conditioned solely for instance by sojourn on the territory of the
state, the pursuit of some occupation on the territory or the like,
would also be deemed in conflict with International Law.

At first sight it may seem strange that the feature conflicting
with International Law in a certain law of citizenship is solely
that the state confers citizenship on too *many* persons. It must
be kept in mind that the privileges which may attach to citizenship according to the National Law have nothing to do with
International Law. From the point of view of International
Law, i. e. in relation to the interests of other states, the sole relevance of citizenship is that it withdraws the persons concerned
from the protection of the international law regarding aliens and
thus prevents other states from diplomatic intervention for the
benefit of the person in question, even if the other state regards
that person as a citizen, cf. § 25.

Summing up, it would seem then that the following rules may
be laid down. Within certain limits International Law leaves it
to each state itself to decide by its legislation what persons are
its citizens. It never conflicts with International Law to omit
to confer citizenship on certain persons or to deprive them of
citizenship. The condition essential to a certain person being
regarded by the state as a citizen is that this person is either
originally connected with the territory and/or population of
this state by birth (original territorial or personal principle); or
that he subsequently obtains such connection by settlement or
through a family relationship (subsequent territorial and personal principle).

§ 25
RULES CONCERNING DOUBLE NATIONALITY
(sujets mixtes).

Since International Law does not itself unambiguously define
what body of citizens belongs to each separate state but
within certain limits leaves this to be determined by the municipal laws, it is inevitable that the national arrangements must
in certain cases clash, either by the same person possessing citi-

---

[4] See *Verdross*, Völkerrecht, § 34.

zenship in two or more states *(double nationality, sujets mixtes)*, or by a person not being recognised as a citizen of any state *(statelessness, apatrides)*. Both cases are a calamity for the individual, which may entail the direst consequences, especially in times of international unrest.

General International Law has laid down two rules concerning double citizenship.

One is that in the relation between two states which both (legitimately) claim the same person as a citizen, each of the states is excluded from giving diplomatic protection against the other to the person concerned. That is to say, the latter is without legal protection against either of the states under International Law.

The other is that a third state is only bound to recognise one of the two home states as competent to protect its national, namely either the one in which the person is resident or the one with which he must be supposed to be actually most closely connected. The choice lies with the state against which a legal claim is put forward, not with the person himself or his home states.

Both these rules have been confirmed by the Hague Convention of 1930 on Certain Questions Relating to the Conflict of Nationality Laws. At the same time it was attempted in some degree to mitigate the disadvantages of double nationality and statelessness. The convention with three appended protocols has, however, only been ratified by a small number of states.

It has also been attempted to solve conflicts between nationality laws by special treaties. At a certain time in the 19th century there was some disagreement between the United States of America and the European countries from which immigrants came. America then sought to promote immigration by rapid naturalisation, while the home countries on their part were disinclined to give up the emigrants as citizens. To do away with the disadvantages resulting from double citizenship a series of treaties, the so-called *Bancroft Treaties,* were concluded between the United States and the European countries about the year 1870. Their main provisions were that America bound herself not to naturalise immigrants until after 5 years' sojourn while in return the European states agreed, subject to that condition, to recognise the naturalisation as involving loss of previous nationality. In case the person returned to his homeland, he should have easy access to regain his original citizenship with the effect of losing his citizenship in America. Later on the changed attitude of America towards the question of immigration has deprived these treaties of their practical value, and at the same time it has become usual for states to recognise that any subsequent acquisition, legitimate under International Law, of alien citizenship entails loss of the previous nationality.

Chapter VI
DELIMITATION OF THE SPHERES OF DOMINION
OF THE STATES: COMPETENCE OF JURISDICTION

§ 26
THE MAXIM OF TERRITORIAL COMPETENCE
OF JURISDICTION

In § 22 it was mentioned that the fundamental rule concerning the distribution of competence according to International Law is to the effect that each state is competent, and exclusively competent, within its own territory to perform actions which — actually or potentially — consist in the use of the state's instrument of power (*the maxim of territorial supremacy*). Here an account will be given of this maxim and its material limitations in so far as the competence of jurisdiction is concerned, that is to say, the competence of the state to use force *against individuals* to give effect to the law.

As already mentioned, the maxim has not been invented by International Law but is merely a legal confirmation of the historical fact, grounded in nature, that the instruments of power of the various states have developed and asserted themselves on a territorial basis, separated in space from each other. Within its territory each state (as self-governing) claims to be the supreme judicial power in relation to its citizens, and these claims would of course lead to constant clashes if the executive organs were not kept spatially separated.

It follows that the maxim is a rule which restricts *the territorial freedom of movement of the executive organs, and nothing else.*

Notably it may be mentioned that

(1) the maxim does *not* restrict the *legislative competence* of the state, that is to say, it does not cut off the state from attaching legal consequences to conditioning facts which have taken place

outside the territory. Every state, in fact, to a certain extent attributes exterritorial validity to its legislation. It is another question that often such legislation cannot become very effective, seeing that it can only be enforced within the state's own boundaries. The principle is clearly stated by the Permanent Court in the Lotus judgment in which it says:

Now the first and foremost restriction imposed by international law upon a State is that — failing the existence of a permissive rule to the contrary — it may not exercise its power in any form in the territory of another State. In this sense jurisdiction is certainly territorial; it cannot be exercised by a State outside its territory except by virtue of a permissive rule derived from international custom or from a convention.

It does not, however, follow that international law prohibits a State from exercising jurisdiction in its own territory, in respect of any case which relates to acts which have taken place abroad, and in which it cannot rely on some permissive rule of international law.[1]

This applies especially, as stated in the judgment, to ships on the open sea.

(2) the maxim does *not* restrict the free movement of *other state organs* in the exercise of their functions. It is true that the matter is often represented as if International Law in principle forbids every state organ from functioning on foreign territory and only in certain particular cases makes exceptions to this rule (the heads of states, ambassadors, consuls). But this cannot be right. There is — for International Law, be it said — no sensible reason to forbid, for instance, a clergyman from performing a marriage service, or a chief constable from issuing a licence, abroad. Nor can it be said to affect the interests of another state should a British judge pass a sentence during a stay on its territory, or should the Parliament assemble there. All these acts are just as harmless in relation to another state as the King's signature to a law which is generally recognised to be internationally allowed.

It is another matter that the state of sojourn by virtue of its territorial competence can either forbid foreign state organs to operate on its territory, or at any rate for its own part refuse to acknowledge the validity of these actions.

---

[1] Perm. Court Publications Series A No. 10, pp. 18—19.

It is also another thing that the home state for various obvious reasons does not ordinarily wish its organs to function during a stay in a foreign country, where they are as a rule subject to the police authority of the foreign state. The question, therefore, is hardly of much practical importance. A sentence passed abroad for instance would lack the unimpeachability resulting from the complete personal independence of the judge protected by the laws and police of his home state. Moreover, 'for reasons of honour alone it would be regarded as offensive that a supreme state organ during the exercise of its authority should be subject to the supremacy of another state. In most cases there is therefore a tacit but self-evident presumption that the organs of the state — apart from quite extraordinary situations — can only function within the state's own territory, or at any rate not on foreign territory. Such considerations will explain that the voting that took place after the German annexation of Austria (1938) among German and Austria citizens resident in Denmark was assigned to a German vessel outside the three-mile zone in Køge Bay.

Material restrictions in the maxim of a state's territorial competence of jurisdiction are made in three sets of rules.

    a. The rules of exterritoriality (§ 27).

    b. The general law relating to aliens (§ 28).

    c. Special rules relating to ships (§ 29).

§ 27
EXTERRITORIALITY

I. *Leading ideas.*

From the old days it has been recognised that certain foreigners, who in a special degree represent a foreign power, occupy the privileged position of being in principle entirely withdrawn from the territorial jurisdiction of the state of residence. Hence no form of state compulsion can be exercised towards them. This does not mean that they need not comply with the decrees of law and justice, but it is taken for granted, on the strength of their responsible position, that they will voluntarily fulfil their obligations. The reason for this privilege is in general to be found in the consideration due to the honour of the state they represent. In certain cases, for instance as regards diplomatic envoys who have an office to fulfil in the foreign state, the motive must be added that the persons concerned may be able to feel entirely unaffected by foreign influence in the performance of their functions. In so far, then, exterritoriality is a natural counterpart to the above-mentioned reluctance to have the functionaries of the state carrying out their duties under the supremacy of a foreign state.

II. *What persons are exterritorial?*

Exterritorial persons are:

1. The heads of states, their deputies and wives.
2. Armed forces under command.
3. Diplomatic envoys and their staffs, not only the head of the legation but also
   a. the other members of the legation (appointed by the state by which they have been sent out), such as various secretaries, attachés, interpreters, chaplains etc.
   b. the members of their families and the servants living with them or the head of the legation, in so far as they are not nationals of the state of residence.
   c. the subordinate personnel of the legation (appointed by the head of the legation), in so far as they are not nationals of the state of residence, and
   d. couriers.
4. By special treaty: the members of the Permanent Court at the Hague and some few other persons.

The personal exterritoriality here dealt with as well as that to which state ships are entitled (§ 23, V cf. § 33, D) may be regarded as offshoots of the privileged position accorded in principle to foreign states in relation to the tribunals of the country, cf. § 33, D.

III. *The content of exterritoriality.*

Exterritoriality consists in the exemption of the persons concerned from any form of compulsion exercised by the state. They cannot be charged with crimes or sued in order to compel them to fulfil their civil obligations. Their possessions cannot be distrained upon, their persons cannot be placed under arrest. Notably no form of administrative compulsion on the part of the police can be exercised against them, just as they cannot be compelled to give evidence and no public office can be forced upon them.

There are, however, the following exceptions to the rule:

1. The home state of the exterritorial person may forego the privilege.
2. Actions in respect of real estate on the territory of the state of residence are allowed.
-3. In an action brought by the exterritorial person the defendant may set up a counter claim. It is controversial whether he can also obtain an independent judgment if the amount of the counter claim exceeds that of the claim against him.
4. It may probably be assumed that an exterritorial person may be sued for claims arising from some commercial transaction carried on by him.

On the other hand, as we have already mentioned, exterritoriality does not mean that the person concerned is above the laws of the land. The significance of this only comes out clearly through the fact that he can be sued before the courts of his home state, just as he can be charged and prosecuted in the state of residence when his exterritoriality has lapsed. Further, the state of residence can through diplomatic channels make the home state responsible, in so far as the latter is responsible for a breach of the law according to the general rules (§ 52). Finally conflicts with the law acquire importance as a presupposition for the estimation of the acts or responsibilities of another person: self-defence is lawful and a liability insurance covers actions of exterritorial persons which cause damage.

§ 28
THE GENERAL LAW RELATING TO ALIENS

I. *Leading ideas.*

By the law relating to aliens is meant partly the internal legal rules regulating the legal status of aliens in particular states; partly the international legal rules which in relation to other nations bind a state to a certain treatment of foreign citizens and thus constitute a restriction on the territorial jurisdictional competence of the state of residence. It is only with the law of aliens in the latter sense that an exposition of International Law is concerned. Further we shall here only present the rules following from general International Law. For beyond this the legal status of foreigners is to a large extent fixed by special commercial treaties and treaties relating to residence.

The internal law of modern civilised states to a very great extent gives foreigners a legal status that in an improvement on the minimum demands of the international rules. Broadly speaking the evolution has been from an originally complete lack of legal protection towards a status equalling that of the country's own citizens. This development has taken place partly through internal legislation implying reciprocity, partly through bilateral treaties, the clause of the most favoured nation having contributed to give these a wider application. Since the first world war, however, the marked nationalist attitude in economics and politics has brought about a distinct reaction.

The law of aliens is one of the domains which, especially in relation to backward states, constantly gives rise to a great many disputes. On the other hand, these may often be adjusted by negotiation or by judicial decisions, since state interests are not directly involved.

A congress convened expressly for the purpose of codifying the International Law of aliens met at Paris in 1929 but did not lead to any result. The rules must be deduced from the ample international practice.

The international law of aliens is based in the first place on the idea that *the natural home and field of activity of every human being is his home state.* He cannot claim any right to be admitted to or settle in foreign states. If admitted, he is merely a *guest* who must put up with the conditions offered him. He must obey the general laws of the land — do in Rome as the Romans do — and being a stranger he must put up with the lack of many advantages conferred on the natives. If he is not satisfied, he can leave the country. Hence the main rule, in legal parlance, is that the foreigner is subject to the territorial competence of the state in which he resides. There are, however, *certain fundamental considerations* due to the stranger on the part of the state in which he is resident, when it has once granted him access to its territory. But these have the character of special exceptions.

First, the state of residence, as a member of the family of civilised nations, must respect a certain *minimum standard of human rights.* It must respect a fellow man even in the person of a foreigner and not subject him to treatment conflicting with the elementary ideas of common civilisation (II).

Second, the state of residence must respect the alien as the *citizen of another state.* By his citizenship he is still, in spite of his stay in a foreign country, connected with another human community which to a certain extent must be able to count upon his obedience and loyalty to the home state. These ties and claims must in some degree be respected by the state where he is a resident, and thus another restriction on the territorial competence will arise (III).

Finally the state of residence must in the person of the alien to a certain extent respect the *legal system of other states* in estimating the concrete legal standing of the alien. That is to say, the international claims upon the rules of national law relating to conflict of laws constitute the third section of the law of aliens (IV).

II. *The minimum standards of civilisation.*

International Law demands — without regard to the status of the natives — that the treatment of aliens should not fall below the *standards of international civilisation as the objective goal.* This was admirably expressed by the American-Mexican Claims Commission in the *Neer case* (1926), as follows:

"that the treatment of an alien, in order to constitute an international delinquency, should amount to an outrage, to bad faith, to wilful neglect of duty, or to an insufficiency of governmental action so far short of international standards that every reasonable and impartial man would recognize its insufficiency . Whether the insufficiency proceeds from the deficient execution of an intelligent law, or from the fact that the laws of the country do not empower the authorities to measure up to international standards, is immaterial."[1]

In this it is implied, in the first place that the state of residence is allowed to discriminate between natives and aliens, as long as the position of the latter does not fall below the lowest standards of civilisation. Such discrimination is in fact widely practised, especially since the nationalist reaction against free trade policy.

Conversely it follows from the above that a state cannot

---

[1] Quoted from *Eagleton*, Responsibility of States, 84.

justify its conduct merely by referring to the fact that its own citizens are not better off than the aliens.[2]

It is not possible, however, to give an exhaustive systematic exposition of the requirements following from this maxim. But they can be illustrated by a number of examples.

A. Aliens have *no right to enter a state* or to stay there. Actually states do in our time keep stringent control of the admission of aliens through their immigration and permit legislation. The question of immigration is included in the "reserved domain" (§ 3. VI), although it is one of the problems which may give rise to a serious international conflict of interests. Discriminations according to national and racial criteria occur (America).

Since an alien has no international legal claim to residence in a state the latter may at any time, if the laws of the land do not prevent it, send him out of the country. This may happen not only in cases already regulated by law or treaty (usually upon *the ruling of a court* owing to some crime committed; by *extradition* for prosecution; or by *sending home* for maintenance), but also at discretion by *expulsion*. The state however must not arbitrarily abuse this right and upon request is bound to state the reason for the expulsion.

B. Conversely, it must be supposed that a state in which an alien is domiciled cannot forbid him to *leave* the country if he has fulfilled his local obligations, for example, if he has served his punishment.[3]

C. In private law the state is bound to allow an alien the ordinary *capacity of rights and action*. Slavery is incompatible with the demands of civilisation. It is permitted, however, to introduce restrictions so that an alien for instance cannot hold real property on the territory, or own ships, aircraft, and the like. The limit must be that aliens must be allowed such an ordinary capacity of rights and action under private law as is

---

[2] Recognised in the Permanent Court judgment No. 7 concerning certain German interests in Polish Upper Silesia, 33.

[3] This does not exclude that leaving the country under extraordinary circumstances, is made dependent on a visa. But the refusal to grant a visa without sufficient reason will presumably be illegal.

the necessary prerequisite for a normal private life, hence especially the right to own and acquire the common necessaries of life; the normal personal and family rights and the rights and capacities of inheritance; as well as the capacity of making the ordinary contracts of everyday life. Thus it would be in conflict with International Law to refuse aliens the right to enter into marriage or to inherit. It is in fact the general rule that in this sphere aliens are on the same footing as the inhabitants of the country, so for that reason it is difficult as well as unimportant to establish minimum international demands.

D. In *public law,* on the other hand, it is usual for aliens to be less favoured than citizens.

As a matter of course they have no political rights, and public offices are reserved for the native population. In addition a series of posts or functions that imply a certain confidence on the part of the public are reserved for the country's own inhabitants, e. g. positions as barristers, notaries, authorised auditors, physicians, money changers, authorised brokers, pilots and others. On the other hand, aliens can claim certain elementary human rights, especially protection against arbitrary deprivation of liberty or dispossession of property, and the right to religious liberty, but hardly to unrestricted freedom of printing, association, and assembly, owing to the derived political character of these rights, or to public worship.[4]

It is of special importance that an alien has no right to economic activity by practising a profession or following a trade on the territory. Nowadays any form of occupation usually requires a special *working permission.* But beyond this the national laws often exclude aliens from participation in various special occupations or make it dependent on particular conditions; this applies especially to the exploitation of the natural wealth of the country (mining, fishing in territorial waters, certain industries) and to coastal navigation and peddling; membership of the board and management of joint stock companies, insurance activities etc. An attempt made at the Conference in Paris in 1929 to establish economic equality in principle in accord with free trade ideas failed and was perhaps

---

[4] The liberties to which Danish subjects are entitled by the Danish constitution are all supposed to be applicable to aliens who are lawfully sojourning in the country.

bound to fail, considering the general trend of the times. Finally, an alien has no claim to support in the state where he is domiciled.

E. As a necessary supplement to the material rights International Law claims for aliens the right to institute *judicial proceedings*. In this respect it is an international duty to see that aliens are offered a fair trial complying with the elementary requirements of judicial procedure. Violation of this right is termed denial of justice in a wide sense.

Denial of justice in a narrower sense occurs when an alien is either absolutely refused as party to a lawsuit or when his case is unduly delayed. The South American States on the whole assert that the international responsibility of the state does not go beyond what is implied by this requirement.

According to a more advanced view the state is also responsible for *distortion of justice* (manifest injustice), that is to say, for all cases of corrupt administration of law, a procedure which is only in form a trial but in reality is a veiled arbitrary exercise of force. This is so, for instance, if the judge owing to manifest partiality passes an arbitrary sentence (prejudice in the case in question, bribery, political dependence) or if the alien party or accused is denied the production of witnesses, documentation, and defence in accord with the common rules of the administration of justice; likewise if he is unnecessarily imprisoned, or while in prison subjected to inhuman treatment, and finally, if the judgment in his favour in a civil case is not duly carried out.

The *Cutting* case[5] affords a good illustration of these matters (America-Mexico 1886). According to the American report Cutting — due to a simple case of libel — was summarily imprisoned by a court whose partiality became clear from its proceedings. He was refused counsel for defence and an interpreter to explain the charge against him. Evidence against him was not brought forward in due order and he was given no opportunity to defend himself. After a trial that thus offended against the most elementary claims of justice he was cast into a filthy cell with 6—8 fellow prisoners. Bail was refused him. The only ventilation in the cell was by the door; he was given no bedclothes, not even a sheet etc.

In cases of distortion of justice it may be the legislative measures

---

[5] *Moore*, International Law, § 201.

themselves which do not satisfy the claims of justice (direct violation of International Law), cf. § 6. III. But more frequently the legislative measures will be adequate, but their administrators may *mala fide* not allow justice to be done to the foreigner according to the law of the land (indirect violation of International Law.). On the other hand, a state has no responsibility merely because a decision is wrong according to the law in force. A state cannot be bound to have infallible judges. *Errare humanum est.* It is another matter that the decision may conflict with International Law from other points of view than those treated here.

F. The state of residence is further bound to *protect* the alien against assaults on his person and property.

For that purpose the requisite *penal rules* are of course necessary. This requirement is met by the simple fact that the penal code is valid for assaults on natives and aliens alike. A differentiation with less severe penal sentences for assaults on aliens would conflict with the general sense of justice, nor does it in fact exist.

But besides this the state is bound to provide reasonable *police measures* for the protection of threatened aliens and for the effective *prosecution* and *punishment* of the criminals, should crime occur in spite of all. The state is responsible if it does not show due diligence and care in any of these respects (the *culpa* rule).

The responsibility of the state in cases of internal dissension, or civil war is especially controversial. Rightly conceived the above maxims hold good unaltered in both of these situations, but according to the circumstances they lead, in practice, to responsibility in the former, but freedom from responsibility in the latter case.

In case of *internal disturbances* — lynching, racial and national persecution, riotous labour unrest etc. — the authorities will often be subject to the same wave of feeling that runs high among the mob. A typical example from the classical country of lynching, America, is presented by the aforementioned *Abbagnato* case (p. 72 above) in which, incidentally, the United States for the first time admitted responsibility towards a foreign state in connection with outrages of this kind.

During a *civil war*, on the other hand, the state, itself fighting for existence, will often, in spite of good intentions, be unable to extend effective protection to aliens. If the insurgents have consolidated themselves as a local insurrectionist party the legitimate government must presumably be free from all responsibility for the actions of that party. (According to the common view, on condition that the party has been recognised as belligerent, cf. § 18. V). Attempts to impose responsibility on states without fault from the point of view of the risk incurred have sometimes been made good in the case af weaker states, but have hardly gained legal recognition.[6]

G. Just as the state must protect the property of aliens against assault it must also itself refrain from assault. Hence *expropriation* can only take place if compensation is paid.

It is extremely doubtful, however, how far this obligation goes.

It is clear that the state must be held responsible for an arbitrary dispossession of property (confiscation) as well as for expropriation directed solely against the property of aliens, or in which compensation is paid to the state's own citizens but nôt to aliens.

Doubt can only arise in cases in which the surrender of property takes place for public purposes, and in which according to the municipal law no compensation is given to natives. Can the alien claim to be in a more favourable position here, and obtain compensation in all cases?

The view generally prevalent among writers answers this question in the affirmative, and many decisions and authoritative pronouncements to that effect can indeed be adduced, especially from the last century.[7]

Nevertheless, after the development that has now taken place the question is anything but clear. The great problem in International as well as in National Law arises when there is a case of expropriation in which the state is liable to pay compensation, and when there is a socially conditioned restriction in the proprietary rights which does not involve compensation. After the social evolution that has taken place since the noontide of liberalism and capitalism there can be no doubt that this limit has been shifted to the damage of the protection of property.

---

[6] Cf. *Eagleton*, Responsibility of States, 140, 144.

[7] See *Verdross*, Traitement des étrangers, Rec. 37 (1931) 364 f.

Even in America it has been recognised by the doctrine of "public power" that despite the guarantee of the 14th amendment, the state can to a great extent abolish ownership without compensation. Can International Law stand aside from this development and still assert the liberal dogma that all surrender of property demands compensation? In my opinion it cannot. The international rule must keep abreast of the social development. International Law must leave it to national law to judge of what is actually "expropriation". It is absurd to speak about a "minimum standard of civilisation" in this connection. It is impossible to maintain that the states which have greatly limited the protection of proprietary rights represent a backward civilisation which cannot be tolerated by their fellow states in the society of civilised nations. The situation would be patently absurd if International Law were to claim compensation for an interference for which no state would be held liable for compensation by its internal law.

The current contention of International Law that expropriation always involves liability for compensation to aliens is at any rate a very rough formulation which cannot fail to invite closer analysis. For it is obvious that it is not every compulsory surrender of proprietary rights which can be termed "expropriation". In that case not only taxes, imposts, and fines but also a large number of social restrictions in the law of property (building laws, sanitation laws etc.) would require compensation. Thus International Law cannot avoid *defining* "expropriation" in a narrower sense, i. e. expropriation involving compensation. As far as I know, however, the theory of International Law has made no attempt to do so. And as a matter of fact the decision must be left to national law as it develops. The current unanalysed dogma that "expropriation" entails the obligation of compensation in fact only means that the liberalist legal views of earlier times are allowed to prevail, instead of the legal ideas now governing the law. In the 19th century the international legal doctrine could be valid because it harmonised with the ideas of national law. Today it is a cultural rudiment.

As shown by *Fischer Williams*, the recent adjudications of International Law do not seem, either, to have decisively established liability to compensation in cases where nationals

---

[8] *Fischer Williams*, Chapters on Current International Law, chapt. VII.

had no claim to it.[8] This applies especially to the oft-quoted judgment No. 7 of the Permanent Court on *certain German interests in Polish Silesia*. The award only *obiter dictum* implies that International Law contains a principle of respect for acquired rights, and in addition recognises that "expropriation for reasons of public utility" falls outside this. That leaves the question open.[9]

III. *Aliens as citizens of other states.*

Beyond the minimum standard of civilisation which follows from the nature of the alien as a fellow-creature, further duties arise for the state where he is domiciled, duties determined by the character of the alien as *a citizen* of another state. The home state has a potential unlimited power over its citizens abroad — that is to say, if they return — which it can use to influence their actions already during their stay in the foreign country.[10] Thus the alien is subject to *a double supremacy:* actually to that of the state where he resides, potentially to that of his home state. He serves two masters and may easily find himself in painful situations of conflict if the demands of the two states do not agree. It is the task of International Law to try to bring about harmony by a delimitation of the competence of the competing states.

There can be no doubt that the competence of the state where the alien is domiciled must come first, so that consideration for the home state can only give rise to a few special restrictions in it.

Thus *liability for military service*, the duty which in the very highest degree depends on the solidarity of the individual with the state, the duty to lay down one's life in the defence of one's country, can only, according to the general opinion, be imposed on the state's own citizens. Conversely, the home state can at any time call home its citizens abroad for military service. The former rule has an ancient prescriptive standing in the theory of International Law and also seems to be generally recognised in the practice of states. It is expressly included in a large number of bilateral treaties and has in addition received general

---

[9] Public. of the Permanent Court Series A No. 7 p. 22.

[10] The home state has also a certain indirect power, if the citizen has property at home that can be made subject to sanctions.

recognition on several occasions.[11] The result remains the same even if Denmark by the Conscription Act of the 8th June 1912 in principle imposes military service on foreigners residing in that country. In so far this Act is in conflict with International Law.[12]

The exemption applies not only to actual military service but also to civil service for war purposes on the home front, but not to compulsory guard duty or protective service for the fighting of various internal dangers or damages (gendarme service, fire guard service, corps for aid in natural catastrophes, social corps for the combating of labour disturbances, air defence police etc.).

In return the home state must not try to prevent its citizens abroad from obeying the laws of the land in which they are domiciled, or influence them to perform acts to the detriment of the security and interests of the state whose guests they are (espionage, political undermining activities, illegal propaganda and the like).

IV. *Respect for foreign law and acts of law.*

If the state in which an alien is domiciled has to decide a case in which an alien is a party it cannot simply make the decision on the basis of its own law and entirely neglect all foreign law. To a certain extent it is bound to consider the fact that there exist other organised legal communities, and to base its decision on foreign law. That is to say, every single state must be guided in the formulation of its rules relating to conflict of laws by certain demands of International Law (§ 7). In regard to the state's own citizens, however, this is never so. If in a lawsuit between two citizens the preliminary question arises whether foreign law shall be applied — cf. the case *Luther v. Sagor* (p. 122) — the courts have a free hand as far as Interna-

---

[11] The pan-American Convention (Havanna 1928) on the codification of the Aliens Law, Art. 3. The draft of the Legue of Nations for a codification of the Aliens Law (1928) Art. 11, cf. *Verdross*, Rec. 37 (1931) 379—80.

[12] The conclusion of exemption treaties with a great number of states (see the Danish Home Office Circular No. 15 of Jan. 10 1928) in connection with a lenient interpretation of § 2 of the Conscription Act has made the question as to the conscription of aliens unimportant in practice.

tional Law is concerned. The international demands therefore constitute part of the international law of aliens.[13]

These demands are very moderate. In the main it is left to each state to shape its rules relating to conflict of laws as it likes. Occasionally it is supposed that unlimited freedom prevails in this sphere. This is a mistake, however. But here, as in other spheres where the demands of International Law are elementary, it may be difficult to evolve the maxims for the very reason that owing to their elementary character they are rarely violated and therefore seldom come under our notice. That there must be certain limits to freedom will best be realised if one tries to imagine the results that must otherwise be accepted. A few examples[14] will illustrate our contention. If a state was quite free to act as it liked, it could for instance, if a foreigner bought a trunk abroad, refuse to recognise the acquisition as legal and consider the object as derelict; or, if he had made a legitimate arrest abroad, it might punish him for depriving another party of his liberty etc.

In this connection it is important to note (a fact as a rule overlooked), that unlimited freedom would mean not only that in all cases the state had a free choice with respect to the basis of its judgments, but also that it might give its own legal system a limited application and refuse to recognise other systems outside it. Law-creating facts that took place outside the range of the state's own system would then have to be regarded as having taken place in a space devoid of law and so be entirely without effect. Rights acquired abroad under circumstances where the law of the adjudicating state did not apply would then be null and void. This would evidently be at variance with the fundamental ideas of civilised intercourse expressed in the international law of aliens. It can therefore be laid down as the *first maxim* that the judgment of a case must always be based on *some legal system*. Spaces devoid of law must not occur. Acquired rights must be respected even if the adjudicating state has a wide choice with respect to the system according to which it chooses to decide whether or not a right is acquired.

---

[13] To this extent, however, they go beyond the law of aliens in the sense indicated above that they have a bearing on every case in which an alien is a party whether or not he is domiciled on the territory.

[14] *Verdross*, Völkerrecht, § 35, II.

As regards this choice we may presumably with *Verdross, Makarov*[15] and others lay down the *second* maxim that the condition essential to the application of a particular national system, especially that of the state in which the alien is domiciled, as the basis of judgment is that *the case concerned at least in one respect shall have actual contact* with the state in question — in addition of course to the proceedings being instituted in the courts of that state. It follows more particularly that a state cannot base its judgment on its own legal system in a case that has not in any of its elements an association with that state, and that in a case which in all its elements is associated with one and the same state judgment must also be based on the law of that state.

Makarov thinks that beyond this it is not possible to establish more precisely what can come into consideration in International Law as a legitimate "association"; in that respect the states must have a free hand. This cannot possibly be right. It would be the same as abolishing every restriction — by the introduction of quite arbitrary criteria of association. The proper thing here is to fall back on the same criteria that apply to the legislation concerning nationality: the association must be an association either with the persons of the state (the personal principle) or with its territory (the territorial principle).

By the nature of the case *personal* association only occurs through the medium of the *parties* in the case by one or both of them being citizens of the state.

Territorial association, on the other hand, may be through several of the factors in the case:

In the first place through the *parties* in the case by the fact that one or both of them are domiciled in the state, whereas a mere visit cannot be regarded as sufficient to establish a territorial association through one of the parties, any more than the fact that a party owns real estate in the country, follows a trade, or the like.

Further, through *judicial facts* when these have taken place on the territory.

Finally, through the *object of the case*, by the fact that it is present there.

---

[15] *Verdross*, l. c.; *Makarov*, Völkerrecht und internationales Privatrecht ("Mélanges Streit", Athens 1939), 552—53.

If a case judged according to these criteria is associated with several states International Law offers a choice between the legal systems of these states as a basis for the judgment. If for instance a case concerning a purchase deed concluded in France between an Englishman (domiciled in America) and a German (domiciled in Italy) concerning real estate in Denmark is brought before a British court the court has the option, under International Law, of basing its judgment on French, English, American, German, Italian, or Danish Law.

If, on the other hand, the case has reference to a dispute between two Frenchmen domiciled in France concerning a contract of purchace relating to a parcel of goods which is present there, British courts are obliged to base their decision on French law. For by all relevant criteria the case points back to France.

The duty of using foreign law, however, only applies with the reservation that it is not in conflict with fundamental national legal principles *(ordre public)*. Great Britain, for instance, would not be bound to recognise a double marriage or relation of slavery lawfully contracted in a foreign country.

Similar principles involve that the *validity* of foreign *acts of state* — which may be of importance for a case preliminary — must always be judged on the basis of the foreign legal system concerned. To place a person under arrest for instance cannot be regarded as an illegal deprivation of liberty because it would not be legal under the law of the adjudicating state, expropriation under similar circumstances could not be regarded as robbery etc. But this does not mean that the adjudicating state is bound to admit that the foreign act of state has the *legal effects* intended by it. This is especially of importance for *foreign judgments*. Here it is generally admitted that the adjudicating state is not bound to ascribe legal force to foreign judgments (a binding effect on the parties in the case), not to speak of executive force. The question has been largely settled by treaties.

It is especially the international *penal law*, which has given rise to international debate and award.

The question is not, however, what law is to be applied — a state does not usually apply any penal law but its own — but whether and to what extent the state can include foreigners under its right of punishment, cf. § 7, Note 1.

If, first, we consider the principles actually applied in the practice of the states we can distinguish between the following groups:

Least far-reaching is the *territorial principle* which is acted upon in Anglo-American practice. According to this principle only such delinquencies are punished as have been committed within the territory of the state. In practice the principle has, however, been considerably extended in that not only physical but also "constructive" presence is recognised as a ground for punishment, that is to say, cases in which, though the delinquent at the moment of the act was physically outside the territory, the direct effects of the act developed within it. As typical examples are usually mentioned disharge of a fatal shot across the frontier or the sending of a libellous letter from abroad.

Of wider application is the *qualified principle* of *protection* according to which actions are punished which are directed aaginst the security or credit of the state, or other qualified legal benefits. This principle has been adopted in modern times by most states.

The principle of the widest application is the *unqualified principle* of *protection,* which further punishes any act directed against a citizen. Thus for instance in Turkey and Italy. According to this the citizens abroad are not confined to the protection that the state in which they are domiciled affords them as aliens in accordance with the provisions of the aliens law, but they enjoy, in addition, the protection of their national penal law, in so far as the delinquent is later arrested on the territory of the home state.

From the point of view of International Law there cannot be any doubt, however, that both the territorial principle (even with "constructive" presence) and the qualified principle of protection must be recognised as permissible. On the other hand, the unqualified protection principle presumably goes beyond what would be recognised as lawful. The question came up before the Permanent Court in the *Lotus* case (1927). On the 2nd of August 1926 a collision took place on the open sea between the French ship *Lotus* and the Turkish ship *Boz-Kourt*. The latter foundered and eight Turkish citizens perished. The *Lotus* continued its voyage to Constantinople where Lieutenant Demons, the officer on duty at the moment of collision, was charged with manslaughter, sentenced to 80 days' imprisonment, and fined £22. France disputed the competence of the Turkish state to punish, and the case was brought before the court at the Hague. But the Court failed to express any opinion on the problem as to the international validity of the unqualified protection principle, the penal competence of the Turkish state being considered warranted already by the territorial principle with "constructive" presence.[16] For the direct effect had occurred onboard the Turkish ship which constitutes part of the Turkish territory. In this connection it was considered without importance that the prosecution was based on a clause in the Turkish penal law which rested on the unqualified protection principle.[17] See also the *Cutting* case in which[18] the United States protested energetically because an American citizen in Mexico was prosecuted for a publication in the United States.

To all international law of aliens the reservation applies which is implied in the rule of local remedies. Since that rule is of a procedural nature the reader is referred for this question to the exposition below in § 56. III.

§ 29.
SPECIAL RULES FOR SHIPS

I. *Right of passage.*

It was stated above that aliens have usually no right to stay on or pass through the territory of a state. It would be patently unreasonable, however, if foreign vessels should for that reason be obliged to lay their course outside the territorial waters instead of taking the route most convenient for navigation. From the old days it has therefore been generally recognised that ships have a right to pass through foreign territorial waters when due consideration is shown for the interests of the littoral state (passage inoffensif), whereas a similar right for aircraft to pass over any part of a state's territory is not recognised, cf. § 43.

Thus only a right of passage comes into question, not a

---

[16] Public. of the Permanent Court Series, A No. 10, p. 22—23.
[17] L. c. 24.
[18] *Moore*, Intern. Law, § 201.

right to stay (except in cases of emergency or common nautical usage), nor to fish or pursue other activities on the territory. In accord with the leading interest it cannot be supposed, either, that there exists any right to cross territorial waters in order to penetrate into the inner waters. For the same reason the right of passage can hardly be supposed to extend to those parts of the sea that lie within the base lines of the territorial waters. (§ 23. III). The right of passage implies that the littoral state must not forbid or hinder the traffic nor make it dependent on duties imposed merely for the passage (as e. g. the Sound Dues down to 1857). On the other hand, the littoral state may exact dues for services rendered to the ship.

Further, the passage must take place with due consideration for the interests of the littoral state (it must be *"inoffensive"*). That is to say, no actions must be performed which interfere with the security, public order, or fiscal interests of the littoral state. Notably, the foreign ship is to observe the laws and regulations enacted by the littoral state in accord with custom and usage for the safety of navigation (sailing rules, pilotage), the protection of the water from pollution, the maintenance of the natural products of the sea, the protection of fishery rights, sanitary protection, or the combating of smuggling.

It is often taught that according to customary International Law there exists a similar right of passage with respect to certain rivers, viz. the so-called *international rivers,* that is to say those that flow either through or between two or more states. It is, indeed, clear that there is a strong general interest in such traffic, in the first place for the riparian states communicating with the open sea by the river. The principle of free navigation on rivers has in fact been asserted in the literature on International Law since *Grotius,* and established by several general treaties especially by the Vienna Congress Act of 1815 and the Barcelona Convention of 1921. Nevertheless it is difficult to infer a common right of navigation from general International Law. For the fact is that the traffic on rivers, in a much higher degree than the traffic in territorial waters, directly concerns the riparian states and implies the use of their devices for traffic (piers, locks, and the like). The right of passage must therefore similarly be dependent on the observance of a series of regulations. Conditions are moreover so different from one river to another that a special arrangement is necessary in each separate case. And as a matter of fact, for nearly all the more important international rivers, *special arrangements* have been made by treaty, often in connection with a highly developed international apparatus of administration (the Danube Commission). Under these circumstances we can hardly speak of a direct right of traffic warranted by general International Law, but only of a certain duty for the riparian states to co-operate in making treaty arrangements on the basis of the general principle of free and equal traffic for the ships of all states.[1]

The principle of free river traffic was first established at the Vienna Congress in 1815; it was left to the parties to apply the principle in the individual instances by means of special arrangements. In accord herewith a number of European rivers were opened to traffic in the years that followed, though provisionally only for the riparian states. The Paris Treaty of 1856 initiated a new departure. It introduced general freedom of traffic on the Danube and created a special international organ, the so-called *European Danube Commission,* equipped with considerable legal powers to regulate and administer matters relating to the river. The Commission was able to reduce to order the previously chaotic sailing conditions on the Danube. Later a number of other important rivers have been opened to general traffic. By the peace treaties of 1919 various international commissions were created for the most important central European rivers, but these have later lost their importance. At the instance of the League of Nations a general transit conference was convened at Barcelona in 1921, resulting in a treaty which establishes a series of general principles concerning free and general traffic as a basis for special arrangements.

For *international straits,* i. e. such as connect parts of the open sea, the same rules apply in principle as for other territorial waters. Only here the interest on both sides is intensified. On the one hand, the desire for intercourse is especially marked since blockading of the strait if it is so narrow that no part of it is open sea would either entirely prevent the connection between two parts of the open sea or at any rate make it more difficult. On the other hand, the narrowness of the fairway makes it of increased interest for the littoral state to protect its territory, especially during a war. The conditions relating to straits ap-

---

[1] Thus also *Brierly,* Law of Nations, 155.

proximate to those relating to rivers. Since here the right of passage takes the shape of a special restriction on the littoral state's normal unlimited supremacy over the territorial waters, and moreover it is recognised as a mere inoffensive right of use with consideration for the interests of the littoral state (cf. above), it seems natural — in the absence of a positive warrant to the contrary — to assume that during a war the littoral state must be able to blockade an international strait to protect its neutrality or as a war measure, for instance by the laying of mines.[2]

The right of passage through the territorial waters holds good not only for merchant vessels but also for men-of-war, at any rate in time of peace. It is true that men-of-war are exterritorial, and compulsion is therefore excluded if only for that reason. Nevertheless the rule is of importance since exterritorial units, too, are bound to respect the law.

On the same view it must be supposed that the right of passage is merely a right in so far as there is a passage-way, while no claim can be made that a way should be kept open against the interests of the littoral state, if it makes other arrangements in the territorial waters, for instance by reclaiming land and building dams or bridges which hinder the passage of ships. In that case there is no longer any strait and accordingly no right of passage. The opposite view would lead to the littoral state being bound to re-establish the passage even if it was stopped by natural events (such as silting up, landslips and the like). This would be quite unreasonable.

As a natural consequence of the fact that the conditions of a strait approximate to those of rivers positive *special arrange-*

---

[2] This view was held and consistently maintained by Denmark without protest during the first world war. The decision to lay mines in the Belts on Aug. 5, 1914, was communicated to the English government in a note of Aug. 8, in which it was pointed out that the steps taken were "not in conflict with International Law", nor did the English government enter any protest against it. Since there would have been reasonable cause for England to protest if it did not agree in this view, it must be possible in this case to regard the passivity as approbation (§ 10, Note 3). — When Turkey closed the Turkish straits during the war in Tripoli 1911—12 Russia and France did indeed protest, but England recognised Turkey's right to the temporary closing of the straits as a precaution which was reasonable and necessary to defend its security. See *Brüel*, The Danish Straits A. S. I. G. in N. T. 1940 p. 63 and The Turkish Straits, A. S. I. G. in N. T. 1943, p. 49—53.

ments have been made in the case of certain straits (the Danish belts, the Bosphorus and Dardanelles, the Strait of Gibraltar and the Strait of Magellan).

II. *Other restrictions on territorial competence?*

Another question is whether foreign ships in territorial or national waters are subject to the civil and criminal jurisdiction of the littoral state.

The question must be divided into two. One is whether the courts of the state are competent with respect to acts committed on board the foreign vessels. The question is of special significance in its criminal aspect and is in fact a ramification of the problems of the international penal law.

In English law the competence of the littoral state is expressly established by *The Territorial Waters Jurisdiction Act* of 1878, a result of the *Franconia case* (p. 66). This point of view has, however, been criticised in theory as unduly extreme, and the only reason why the law has not caused international protest is perhaps that in practice it has been very tolerantly administered.

A contrast to this is French practice, established by a decision of the highest administrative court, the *Conseil d'Etat*, of 1806. According to this, French courts are only to a very limited extent regarded as competent, particularly when either the interests of the state are concerned, its police regulations transgressed, the peace of its ports disturbed, or its aid invoked. These rules have since with more or less modification spread to a number of other countries, but there are also those who follow the English line.

The second question is whether the authorities of the littoral state can take immediate action with respect to the foreign ship, e. g. stop it to arrest a person or seize goods. It is beyond doubt that the littoral state is competent to do so provided that its courts, from an international point of view — especially under the rules just quoted — are competent to pass judgment in the case of which the coercive measure is part.

It cannot be denied that unrestricted jurisdiction over foreign ships, especially in our day when even a brief delay of a large vessel may involve considerable economic losses, conflicts with the right of traffic. On this view an attempt was made at the Codification Conference at the Hague in 1930 to put reasonable limits to the jurisdiction, but as is well known, these efforts were futile.

It follows from the exterritoriality of foreign state-owned vessels that they are not subject to the jurisdiction of the littoral state, cf. § 23. V and § 33. D.

§ 30
THE FREEDOM OF THE SEA

It is usual to lay down the maxim of the freedom of the open sea as an independent international principle. This means

a. that no state can carry out jurisdictional acts directly against foreign ships on the open sea;

b. that ships of all nationalities have a right freely to sail the seas and also use them for every purpose (fisheries, whaling etc.) and that consequently no state even on its own territory can subsequently exercise jurisdiction on account of such actions performed on the open sea.

On the other hand, as established by the judgment in the *Lotus* case, this does not imply that it is otherwise forbidden for a state to exercise subsequent jurisdiction on its own territory because of actions, for instance manslaughter, committed on board a foreign ship on the open sea. The limits of a state's competence in that respect are determined by the general rules of the international penal law. (§ 28, IV).

It is, however, *superfluous* to lay down any independent rule concerning the freedom of the sea. The above-mentioned results follow quite automatically from the already recognised rules concerning the extent of the territorial waters and the character of ships as floating parts of the territory of the home state, in connection with the rules concerning the limits to the jurisdictional competence of states, especially the rules of the international penal law.

There are, however, some few exceptions to the principle of the freedom of the sea — and that even in the strict form that compulsion may be used directly against a ship on the open sea. When the ship and its passage on the sea is employed for committing palpable gross delinquencies against other ships it is in the interest of the security of traffic to make an ex-

12*

ception. From the old days it has therefore been recognised that *pirates* can be seized by any one on the open sea and be brought home to the captor's own port for trial. By piracy is understood every unauthorised act of violence against persons or goods committed on the open sea either by a private vessel against another vessel or by the mutinous crew or passengers against their own vessel (Oppenheim). Acts carried out by state authority or on the authorisation of a local insurgent party therefore are not piracy. In this connection it may be noted that the Paris Maritime Law Declaration of 1856 has abolished privateering, i. e. authorisation for private individuals to take part in naval wars. Similar considerations would seem to favour the seizure of smuggling vessels too on the open sea, but this has not won general recognition.

If a ship has committed a transgression in territorial waters and is pursued for that reason but escapes to the open sea, the littoral state is allowed to continue the pursuit without interruption (pursuit *in continenti* or hot pursuit).

Finally it follows from the general principles of the right of self-defence and self-preservation (§ 51, II and IV) that in *self-defence* a state may capture a vessel on its way to support a rising against that state and thus to commit an act directed against the security of the same state.[1] The competence to punish in these cases follows from the general rules concerning international penal law. The special feature resides in the fact that the jurisdiction can be exercised directly over the ship on the open sea. Likewise, in case of *imminent distress*, states can capture a ship to secure a cargo of foodstuffs.[2]

In addition extraordinary jurisdiction over the ships of co-contractors has been granted to parties by various treaties, as, for instance, by the North Sea Fishery Treaty of 1882 and by various treaties for the combating of the slave trade and the protection of deep sea cables.

---

[1] Cf. the case of the *Virginius*, a steamer flying the American flag, which in 1873 during the Cuban rebellion against Spain (1868—78) tried to supply the rebels with weapons and stores. The ship was, however, captured on the open sea by the Spaniards and the crew executed. The U. S. entered a protest but did not proceed further in the matter since it turned out that the ship had had no right to fly the American flag.

[2] Cf. the *Neptune* case, § 51, IV.

Chapter VII
DELIMITATION OF THE SPHERES OF DOMINION OF THE STATES: THE "FUNDAMENTAL RIGHTS" OF STATES

§ 31
GENERAL CONSIDERATIONS

In principle the delimitation of the spheres of dominion of the states is based on the maxim of territorial supremacy.

In the preceding chapter this maxim and its material limitations were — for practical reasons — discussed in particular with respect to jurisdictional competence, that is to say, the competence of a state to exercise compulsion for the purpose of giving effect to the law directly against individuals.

In the present chapter I come to the further development of the maxim, and especially to the delimitation of the spheres of power of the states in relation to the interests of other states. By way of introduction I premise some remarks for the general characterisation of the whole group of problems relating to the delimitation of the dominion of states.

We are here concerned with the most important norms of intercourse in International Law. Adopting to some extent an earlier terminology we may say that they determine the fundamental rights and duties of states. But in contradistinction to the origin of the terminology from Natural Law this only means that they follow directly from the rules of general International Law and unconditionally apply to any member of the family of nations. In that respect they contrast with the duties and rights which are conditioned by special circumstances or founded on special treaties. Hence the expression by no means implies that these norms are not as "positive" as other International Law. Like other general rules of International Law they are justified by the conception of the law which is implied in the practice of the states, formulated in general treaties or otherwise recognised by the civilised states.

Corresponding to this, in internal law, we find the great mass of material norms regulating and co-ordinating the intercourse of individuals by — within certain limits — protecting their life, liberty, and property. Through the rules concerning compensation and punishment and the manifold regulations and decrees of public law a social balance is created which, on the one hand, secures for the individual a certain liberty and a sphere within which he can dispose, but on the other hand at the same time sets limits to that sphere out of consideration for the interests of others and the promotion of public undertakings. In this way the law becomes something else and more than a mere delimitation of the "living space" of individuals. It also becomes a social co-ordination, a union for the common welfare which is the prerequisite for all true social life.

Unfortunately things are quite different in the domain of International Law. In order fully to understand the difference and the peculiarity of International Law it is necessary first to consider more closely the technique of the social function of Internal Law.

Let us for example consider property law. By the fact that the community recognises a proprietary right for individuals in relation to certain things, an external direct delimitation of the spheres in which individuals can dispose is, in the first place, created. If, provisionally, we imagine that a proprietary right left the owner full liberty to dispose directly in any way he liked of a thing, the result would be that no one would have security for the most effective utilisation of his goods. The right would certainly mean that other people's direct control of my things would be excluded but would not ensure that other people's control of their own things did not *indirectly* spoil my chances of utilisation. If a person owning a revolver were at liberty to discharge it in any direction he liked it would mean danger and damage to other people's life and property. If my neighbour is quite free to use the plot of ground he owns as he likes it must necessarily encroach on the pleasure I take in my own plot. That is to say, a proprietary right with unrestricted liberty actually cancels itself, because the corresponding liberty of other people indirectly prevents the utilisation of it. The result of such a state of affairs would be a *formal liberty* but no *real security*. All would fight against all to obtain the greatest advantages.

In order to give real value to a proprietary right it must therefore be socially delimited, freedom of action being restricted owing to the *indirect bearing any action has on the interests of others*. The liberty to use a revolver must be restricted because of the consequences to the life and property of other people, and the liberty to dispose of a plot of ground owing to the interests of other ground landlords. The individual loses some formal liberty thereby but in reality wins more, as the same restriction applies to everybody else. Technically this means that the external delimitation of the sphere of control in regard to certain things must be supplemented by rules restricting the extent of the control owing to its indirect bearing on the interests of others. Thus within the rules relating to property rights two sets of norms may be distinguished: those which establish who has control of particular objects, i. e. the *formal norms of competence,* and those which define more precisely the extent and limit of the control in relation to the interests of others, the *material co-ordination norms.* It is the latter which change the proprietary right from an individualistic living space in a struggle of all against all, into a socially conditioned position in a community.

As stated above, conditions are quite different in the sphere of International Law. The general international rules concerning the intercourse of states are principally confined to a *formal delimitation of their living space.* The fundamental duty of states is therefore in the main only the duty not to interfere directly in this living space and, conversely, the fundamental right is the right to demand that this living space be respected (*territorial supremacy,* § 32). Beyond this International Law contains few and narrowly limited material norms of co-ordination, that is to say, such as socially delimit freedom within a certain living space out of consideration for the interests of other states (the *material limits* of territorial supremacy, § 33). In other words, in the main general International Law gives expression to an unscrupulous individualism, according to which each state can behave as it likes within its formal sphere of competence without considering the consequences for the interests of other states, the social co-ordination of interests being in the main left to be regulated by special treaty arrangements (Chapt. X). In reality it is a struggle of all against all. Even peace is no real peace but a war by other than military means. If only a state keeps formally within its own living space it can there with unrestricted liberty settle questions concerning immigration and emigration, imports and exports, raw materials and other items of trade policy, national minorities, political and racial ideologies, rearmament and fortification, problems of exchange and labour conditions, traffic conditions and many other problems, and all this though these are questions that vitally affect the interests of other states.

§ 32
THE FORMAL DELIMITATION OF THE LIVING SPACE OF STATES
(TERRITORIAL SUPREMACY)

As previously mentioned, it follows from the principle of effectivity that the living space of a state is its territory; within this the state alone is competent to exercise compulsion and thus effective state authority. This can also be expressed thus: *respect for territory* is the *formal* fundamental right and duty of states.

On the one hand, it is a main rule that within its own territory the state has liberty to exercise its power as it likes without considering the indirect consequences to the interests of other states. The few social restrictions on the territorial sovereignty of states will be mentioned in the next section.

On the other hand, a state is bound to refrain from any exercise of compulsion directly on *foreign* territory. This applies not only to the jurisdictional compulsion mentioned in the last chapter but to any form of state compulsion, more especially military coercion.

This rule applies not only to the actual exercise of compulsion but also to preparation or support for it. Therefore the mere presence on a state's territory of alien units of force is prohibited — unless permission has been given or there is a warrant under International Law (the passage of men-of-war through territorial waters) — just as it is prohibited to use the territory as a base for military operations.

Territorial supremacy is also violated by a symbolical or secret exercise of supreme power, for instance by hoisting flags, wearing uniforms, or by the activity of secret agents.

Intervention means the dictatorial interference of a state in the internal or external affairs of another state. Mere friendly advice or general political influence do not therefore come under this term, which implies that the interference should take place by the use of violence or — at least — a threat to use violence. Since such violent interference as a rule cannot come about without encroachment on foreign territory, the question of intervention must be discussed in this connection.

Since the threat of an evil conflicting with the law must conflict just as much with the law as the evil itself it is presumably clear that intervention — as a potential violation of territorial supremacy — conflicts with International Law, unless circumstances are present which, as an exception, exclude conflict with the law. Nevertheless it will be wisest to let the chapter on intervention disappear entirely from International Law, at any rate for the present. For here we have passed the limit of what has a reasonable chance of being respected as law. In principle, intervention is violence as part of the policy of states. To stretch expectation too far on this point by pretending that the law can forbid any such thing is merely to undermine the confidence in International Law in a sphere where it might really mean something. The hopelessness of forbidding intervention by law will also appear clearly when we consider the fluid "upward" and "downward" limits of intervention.

"Upwardly" intervention borders on *war* which is the most radical form of violent interference. Since International Law has not in practice until quite recently (the League of Nations, the Briand-Kellogg Pact) made any attempt to distinguish between lawful and unlawful wars, and since hitherto all attempts at prohibiting war must be regarded as a failure, the strange result would be that International Law prohibited the threat of intervention but not its materialisation. Therefore, before an effective organ of power has been developed among the community of nations which in the name of the law can counteract and overcome the outrages of individual states it is too early to introduce legal prohibitions on war and intervention.

"Downwardly" intervention borders on the general political *influence* which accompanies the instruments of force of the great powers and often makes the independence and voluntary adherence of small states a mere semblance. A threat need not appear brutally as a threat. It is often the mission of diplomacy to express the matter in a veiled form, yet unambiguously. Nay, what is the whole political game and tug of war but a fight with latent threats? It is still beyond the ability of the law to substitute a legal procedure for this struggle.

Intervention must therefore be regarded as an entirely *political phenomenon* and its value must be measured by a political measure, according to the circumstances. Often, for the very want of an international coercive force, the collective intervention of the great powers or the dominant influence of a single power within a certain "space" may be substituted for a legally organised system of peace. The classical example is the *pax romana*. From recent times we may mention the policy of the Holy Alliance in the first half of the 19th century. The allied powers frequently intervened in European affairs in support of the legitimacy principle and the maintenance of peace. The Covenant of the League of Nations (especially Art. 17) also seems to rest on the implication that the members would arrogate to themselves the right to intervene in the affairs of other states for the preservation of peace.

As there was a possibility that the Holy Alliance upon the secession of the Spanish colonies (c. 1810—20) would extend its policy of intervention to the American Continent it was opposed by the United States. In 1823, shortly after the states had recognised the secession, President Monroe propounded the famous Doctrine which has been named after him. In this two principles are enunciated. First — with respect to the above-mentioned affair — that just as the United States will refrain from interference in European affairs and wars, they will, conversely, regard any interference on the part of Europe in the affairs of the American states as an unfriendly act. Further — with special reference to Russia and conditions in the north-western part of the Continent — that the American continents could no longer be considered as subjects for colonisation by European powers.

The *Monroe Doctrine* has since played a decisive part as a guiding star in American policy. Its historical evolution is part of America's political history. In the course of time it has developed, besides its original negative content — the prohibition of European intervention — a corresponding positive side, a demand from the United States for the right to intervention in every conflict between an American and a non-American state. This policy has in recent times been increasingly contested on the part of South America. Conversely, Great Britain, Germany, and Japan have lately put forward political claims to certain spheres of interest, claims which are reminiscent of the ideas of the Monroe Doctrine.

§ 33
THE MATERIAL LIMITS OF TERRITORIAL SOVEREIGNTY

It was stated above that general International Law contains few material co-ordination rules. As a main rule it may be said that within its territorially defined living space a state can display its power with unlimited liberty. Certain social limits to the exercise of power in its own territory may, however, be demonstrated. And consequently a corresponding number of *material* fundamental duties and rights are established.

A. Fundamental duties and rights with respect to *alien* citizens. For these the reader is referred to Chapter VI.

B. Even though a state is at liberty to pursue an internal and external policy which in a military and economic respect threatens other states with ruin, still every *direct plot* against the *security* of foreign states i. e. against the internal order, especially the constitution, is forbidden. States must therefore refrain from instigating or supporting revolutionary movements in other countries by propaganda or financial contributions. When in 1933 America recognised the Soviet Russian government the latter undertook carefully to respect the undisputed right of the United States to organise living conditions on its own territory in its own way, just as it undertook to refrain from all interference in American internal affairs, and to prevent such interference on the part of persons in the service of the Russian government, under its control, or receiving financial support from it. It would likewise be in conflict with the law if a state by technical manipulations or financial operations tried to undermine the credit of another nation.

A state is also bound, to the best of its ability, to prevent *private* individuals, native or foreign, from making similar plots against foreign governments on or from its territory. The state, it is true, incurs no responsibility because a few persons cross the frontier to support a rising but it must not tolerate that corps are formed on its territory or that any organised activity whatever is undertaken on its territory for this purpose, nor that its territory is in any way used as a base for the revolutionary movement. Thus in the above-mentioned declaration the Russian government further undertook not to tolerate that any group or organisation should be formed or take up its abode on its territory whose object was a revolution or a preparation for a revolution of the social or political system in the United States or any of its parts.

On the whole it may be said that the obligations of a state to foreign states with respect to revolutionary movements are analogous to the duties incumbent on a neutral state in relation to belligerent states, cf. especially the 5th and 13th Hague Conventions of 1907. If the revolutionary movement consolidates itself as a local insurgent party the state has presumably corresponding obligations towards it, cf. § 18. V.

C. In the same way a state is also bound to respect the *dignity* of other states. The state itself must naturally refrain from offending other states, their heads, institutions, or symbols, by word or deed. But presumably it is also bound to prevent its citizens and others staying on its territory from similar designs and to punish them in case of transgression.[1] It is clear however that there must be real insults, imputations or expressions of contempt, and not merely criticism, historical research, political or moral verdicts — whether or not the foreign government tolerates such freedom of speech within its own boundaries. Nevertheless, it is inevitable that the views as to the limit to the freedom of speech must vary with the different

---

[1] Cf. § 52. When rioters in New York harbour on July 26, 1935 insulted the German flag on the S. S. Bremen, the German government demanded that the demonstrators should be punished.

political systems. Notably the responsibility of a state for statements in the press may give rise to delicate problems. Moreover, it is a condition that the insult should be aimed directly at the foreign state or persons or symbols representing the state, perhaps also at the nation as such — not only at a party, a group, or private individuals abroad.[2] Here also doubtful questions may arise when a party in some measure is representative of the state.

Most states have incorporated special provisions in their penal codes concerning punishments for insulting a foreign state, the head or the envoy of a foreign state, its flag or other recognised national symbols.

D. Nearly related to the respect demanded for the honour of foreign states is the rule that a state cannot be sued before the courts of another state. Thus foreign states enjoy "exemption from jurisdiction" or have the right of *"exterritoriality"*. For it would be felt as offensive to the dignity of a state if its legal status could be established onesidedly by the organs of another co-ordinate state. Even if the judgment pronounced would often be without effect — namely, in so far as the foreign state and its possessions are actually out of reach of the executive organs of the adjudicating state — still the mere pronouncement of the judgment is felt as the exercise of a "sovereignty" which one state does not possess over another: *par in parem non habet imperium.* Therefore the person who thinks he has a claim on another state must either sue it before its own courts or prefer his claim through diplomatic channels.

The exemption is due not only to the foreign state itself but also to various persons who especially represent the state (§ 27). To these persons, therefore, exterritoriality only acquires special importance in so far as their non-official actions are

---

[2] Cf. a Danish Judgment U. f. R. 1934, 589, according to which a communist member of the Folketing, charged with transgressing § 108 of the Penal Code, who at a meeting held in the harbour of Aabenraa on Aug. 7, 1933 had spoken of the German hooked cross flag as a "murderer's flag", and in full view of all had torn to pieces a ship's pennant marked with the hooked cross, was acquitted. Evidence had been brought forward during the trial that the hooked cross had been denoted as a symbol of national sovereignty in a German decree of July 6, 1933 concerning the flags of aircraft, but not until Sept. 22 1933 did the German ambassador state officially that the hooked cross flag was the German national flag, this statement being published in the official gazette on the 29th of that month.

concerned. For by the actions of the official organs only the foreign state, not the representative himself, is bound. The distinction is significant by the fact that immunity for official acts as associated with the state persists even after the representative has lost his official standing.

Concerning the content of the immunity and the exceptions to it the reader is referred to § 27. III above, with the modifications following from the nature of the case in direct proceedings against a state.

It should especially be noted that according to the earlier view exemption includes proceedings concerning acts by which the foreign state has exercised supreme power as well as proceedings for acts falling under civil law especially *industrial activities*. Most states probably still follow this rule, but it must probably now be admitted that a change has taken place in the international view, the duty now only applying to the former cases. Some few countries, as for instance Belgium and Italy, have based their practice on this view without it giving rise to international protest. And there is reason to believe that this practice will gradually find adherents in other countries, too. For the fact is that while state enterprise was previously an exceptional phenomenon, the total or partial nationalisation of industries which has taken place as a permanent or provisional measure in various countries has given a marked practical significance to the problem. To allow foreign states immunity in ordinary commercial concerns is felt to be an unreasonable favour to the detriment of the co-contractor. When the state places itself on an equal footing with private individuals it must also share their fortunes. In accord herewith a clause has been inserted in several commercial treaties with the Soviet Union to the effect that the Soviet government at the outset recognises the foreign courts as competent — in conformity with the general rules of the *forum competens* within the limits of international procedural law — in proceedings concerning trade relations.

But even if the foreign state is subject to the competence of the courts, either by special agreement or because the immunity is not in general assumed to apply to relations in civil law, it does not follow that the judgment can also be *given effect* in the case of state property situated on the territory of the adjudicating state. The general view seems to favour the reverse.

The question is of special importance with respect to *state-owned ships* used for ordinary commercial traffic. Thus English practice still recognises that ships owned by foreign states or chartered as a whole by them cannot be seized or subjected to other proceedings. The rule has caused much discontent in commercial and shipping circles and at a conference in Brussels in 1926 a number of states concluded a treaty according to which such ships are withdrawn from the protection of ex-territoriality.[8]

§ 34
THE TRADITIONAL DOCTRINE OF THE FUNDAMENTAL RIGHTS OF STATES

From the old days it has been customary to lay down five fundamental rights, namely: the rights of independence, of selv-preservation, of equality, of intercourse, and of dignity. But often several others are mentioned, such as the rights of existence, development, defence, internal and external "sovereignty", etc. Great difference of opinion prevails about the number and formulation of these rights. Nearly every author has a new way of presenting them.

The doctrine of fundamental rights is rooted in Natural Law. Just as the law between individuals was thought to be based on certain innate rights inherent in the nature or reason of man, the positive legal system being merely a more detailed recognition and development of these, so also states were supposed to be equipped with natural fundamental rights as the basis for the development of positive International Law. The markedly positivist authors have therefore rejected the doctrine of fundamental rights. But of recent years the doctrine has again won popularity on the view that we are here concerned with rights expressing the fundamental conditions for all inter-course between states, which must, therefore, necessarily be implied in International Law.[1]

The current doctrine of fundamental rights presents a sorry picture of methodical and systematic confusion. Marked by its

---

[8] The treaty was ratified by Belgium, Brazil, Chile, Esthonia, Germany, Holland, Hungary, Italy, Poland and Sweden (1937).

[1] Thus *Verdross*, Völkerrecht, § 47.

derivation from Natural Law it consists mostly of speculative postulates which either are directly at variance with the evidence of experience or are formulated in such a way that they are really unmeaning even though solemn phrases cloak the emptiness of thought.

In general it may be said on this subject:

1. The fundamental rights are not fundamental in any other sense than that indicated above. They are warranted directly and unconditionally by general International Law but are otherwise *just as positive* as other international arrangements.

2. They are in part based on a misunderstanding of the conception of "rights". A right, as we have seen (§ 2. III), is the expression of a favourable position created and protected by the legal system as a counterpart to the duties imposed on others. My proprietary right, for instance, only exists legally by virtue of the duties incumbent on all others not to disturb me in my enjoyment of a certain benefit. If, on the other hand, the legal system in a certain domain does not create such preferences through restraints imposed on others, but lets every individual be free to do as he likes, we speak of *liberties*. Thus e. g. in trade in so far as there is free competition. Every one, then, is at liberty to conquer the whole market, but has no legal claim to any part of it. What is given out as fundamental rights in International Law — especially the right to existence, free activity, independence, and the like — is in great part merely liberties, that is to say, simply manifestations of the absence of a legal regulation. The value of such a liberty is dependent on the right of the more mighty and does not involve any legal claim.

3. The fundamental rights are often formulated in such a way that they presuppose the legal limit which they were meant to define. The right of independence, for instance, is the right freely to arrange *one's own* affairs, but limited by the claim of other states to respect for *their* affairs and rights. A transgression would be an illegal intervention. But this says nothing as to which affairs are "one's own" and which "those of others". The right of independence and the interdiction against intervention are thus merely tautological expressions showing that there is a certain limit — not defined — to the liberty of states. In the same way the "right" of existence is limited by the same right for other states.

4. Finally, some of the rights indicated — for instance the right of self-preservation, of defence, and the like — are not independent rights but (at most) common *limitations* to any international duty and therefore belong to another place in the system, viz. to the general doctrine of breaches of international law (circumstances excluding normal illegality, § 51).

About some few of the fundamental rights the following may especially be stated:

A. The right of *independence.* As already stated, this "right" in connection with the interdiction against intervention is quite futile. It implies a rule which states what are the state's *own* affairs. It will appear from the above that this rule is the formal rule of respect for foreign territory (§ 32).

B. The right of *self-preservation,* self-assertion, existence, and the like. There is here no real right but either merely an unregulated liberty or certain common limits to all conflicts with the law (self-defence, self-preservation in emergencies, etc.). As a main rule the state has liberty to act as it likes on its own territory. One might then enumerate an infinite number of "rights", named for the various objects of state activity such as the right of having a constitution, of legislation, of defence, of a foreign policy etc.

C. The right of *equality.* It is not clear what is meant by this. The states are actually extremely unequal in many respects. Hence the claim to equality cannot mean that all should have the same legal status. Just as no one would hold that equality had been violated in a society where there was a different law for married and unmarried people, it cannot, either, be a violation of equality between states that a differing legal status is associated with different criteria. There can be no objection to the legal status being different for neutralised and belligerent states, for states that have concluded and states that have not concluded a certain treaty, for allied and non-allied states, for states with and without a maritime belt, etc. etc. *Formally,* therefore, the demand for equality says nothing but that the legal status is to be defined by *general rules* and not arbitrarily associated with the subject as a single individuality. *Any* rule as such will then satisfy the demand for equality. If anything beyond this is to be implied in the demand it must further *materially* be stated that the rule must not contain certain *criteria* discriminating between rights. If for instance equality with men is claimed for women, this means that the legal rules must not contain the criterion "sex".

If, therefore, the claim to equality is to mean anything in International Law but the self-evident fact that International Law must consist of general rules — or it would not be law at all — it must further be stated what discriminations are excluded. This has not been done in the doctrine of fundamental rights. But it might be supposed that the intention was that International Law must not discriminate on the basis of the *size* of the states. Small powers as such must have the same rights as great powers as such. According to current International Law this is probably the case, as a general rule. But there are exceptions — in the League of Nations, for instance, the great powers were given a certain privileged position — and in any case there are no grounds for raising equality in this respect to a fundamental right, if this were to mean something that would be binding for the development of International Law. Incidentally, it must be admitted that the dogma of equality is a consequence of the political jealousy and inferiority complexes of the small states and, strictly observed, would merely tend to prevent an appropriate development of International Law. International Law cannot, any more than other law, shut its eyes to important political facts. The law would then merely become an illusion. It is absurd and inconceivable that a Lilliput state should in every respect have the same right to co-operation and influence as a great power. Such a "right" would be a mere piece of finery. As an example of the dire consequences of the dogma of equality may be mentioned that the excellent plan of establishing an International Court of Arbitration in 1907 was wrecked on the circumstance alone that the small states insisted on being represented in the tribunal on an equal footing with the great powers (§ 61, I). On account of the shortsighted vanity of the small states it must be a task of the future as far as possible to camouflage the dominant position of the great powers through other criteria of selection.[2]

Anyhow, the conclusions attempted to be drawn from the

---

[2] Cf. on the composition of the Permanent Court § 61, II.

right of equality have nothing to do with equality or inequality at all.

In the first place it is pointed out that a state is only bound by the decisions to which it agrees itself. Every one has a right of veto (*the principle of unanimity* v. the principle of majority). Even if this is true as a general rule (§ 1, V and § 10, I), equality would be satisfied no less under the principle of majority; no one sees any violation of equality in this principle in the case of the law between individuals. No discrimination between the voting states is introduced by this principle.

Further, the *exterritoriality* of a state is generally deduced from the maxim of equality. In this, too, there is no sense. Equality would not be less if the rule held good that a state — like everybody else — was subject to the jurisdiction of foreign courts.

D. *The right of intercourse.* It is often maintained that as a fundamental condition of all social life there exists a fundamental right and duty of mutual intercourse; what is meant must be partly the access of foreigners to stay and settle in a state, partly the diplomatic relations between states. The evidence of experience, however, is entirely against the existence of such a right in both these domains, cf. § 28, II and § 18, I. This is merely a postulate of natural law, not positive International Law.

E. *The right of dignity.* This right can be recognised, cf. § 33.

§ 35
PACTA SUNT SERVANDA

Perhaps in addition to the fundamental duties previously mentioned one more might be named, namely the duty of keeping agreements once entered upon — within certain limits. It may then further be said that the whole international doctrine of treaties (Chapt. IX) is merely a more detailed development and definition of this duty, expressed in the sentence *pacta sunt servanda.*

Chapter VIII

THE ORGANS OF INTERNATIONAL INTERCOURSE

§ 36
THE ORGANS OF INTERNATIONAL INTERCOURSE

Here we shall briefly mention the organs created by the states to regulate international intercourse. Most of the rules concerning their appointment, functions, and legal position have the character of national law, however, and therefore do not concern International Law.

I. *Central organs.*

The general competence to deal with the foreign affairs of a state is usually deputed to the *head of the state,* that is to say, the supreme representative of the executive power. But the power to conclude treaties may also be assigned to the legislative body.

The head of the state may be a monarch, a president or — as in Switzerland and the U. S. S. R. — a collective organ (the Federal Council, the Presidency of the supreme Soviet).

As the representative of the state par excellence the head of the state is according to the general rules entitled to exterritoriality, increased protection by law, and exemption from certain laws while staying abroad, cf. the rules for envoys in III. Further a number of special marks of honour are conferred on the heads of states. As a quaint manifestation of the mysticism attaching to "sovereignty" it may be mentioned that in this respect it has been attempted to draw a distinction between kings and presidents on the assumption that "sovereignty" is inherent in the monarch himself whereas in a republic the "sovereignty" lies with the people, and the president is merely the first citizen of the state.

A prince travelling *incognito* is also entitled to these prerogatives though of course he can only claim them if he gives up secrecy.

The same privileges are enjoyed by a person who governs the state as regent on behalf of the king, but not by former heads of states.

In constitutional states the head of the state exercises his power through ministers, in international questions *through the minister for foreign affairs,* who is the responsible leader of the foreign policy and supreme chief over the diplomatic corps. Beyond this it is established in practice that the competence of the head of the state may to a certain extent be exercised by *ministers independently,* either by the minister for foreign affairs or by the prime minister on behalf of the government (government agreements), or by other ministers within their special departments (departmental agreements).

Ministers as such do not enjoy diplomatic privileges when staying abroad.

II. *Recognition of governments.*

The government which can bind the state by its declarations (and impose responsibility on it by its actions) is simply that which has actually asserted itself as the *effective* government of the country. As for the rest, it does not matter whether the government has come to power in conformity with the rules of the constitutional law in force or, for instance, by a *coup d'état* or a revolution. In the former case the government is generally called a *de jure* government, in the latter a *de facto* government. It is clear that these designations are not fundamental. In the last instance any government is based directly or indirectly on power, just as a *de facto* government in the course of time by imperceptible degrees becomes a *de jure* government.

The same reasons which have led to the practice called the recognition of states, have led to a similar procedure in cases of revolutionary changes in the government of a state. We then speak of a *recognition* of governments.

In principle exactly the same rules apply to this case as those set forth in § 18. Actual power alone determines the international competence of the new government. The struggle against the old government must have come to an end.

The legal significance of the recognition, therefore, lies solely in a novation of the legal relation, in connection with which there is generally a renewal of the diplomatic relations between the states, the ambassadors being regarded as the representatives of the government. Therefore either the old ambassadors are recalled, or they are furnished with new credentials.

Recognition and non-recognition are, as in the case of states, predominantly of political importance. The *principle of legitimacy* asserted by the Holy Alliance, according to which every attempt on the part of the people to abolish or restrict the legitimate rule of the existing dynasties would be regarded as conflicting with the divine rights of these and therefore would not be tolerated by or recognised by the Holy Alliance, have of course long since disappeared from the practice of states as incompatible with the later political evolution. On the other hand, in more recent times a *principle of legality*[1] has developed within a limited sphere, based on the democratic ideology of "the sovereignty of the people", just as the earlier principle was based on the ideology of the "sovereignty of princes". According to this, it is a condition of the recognition of a revolutionary government that it has won the approbation of the "popular will" in democratic forms. This doctrine, first formulated by *Tobar*, the sometime foreign minister of Ecuador, (the *Tobar Doctrine*), has been recognised by two conventions between the Central American States, dated 1907 and 1923. According to these the contracting parties bind themselves not to recognise any government which has come into power as a consequence of a *coup d'état* or a revolution in any of the five republics, as long as freely elected representatives of the people have not constitutionally organised the government. These treaties are only valid between the Central American states. But on the plea that the treaties had been brought about by the intervention of the United States, the latter have arrogated to themselves the power to pursue the same non-recognition policy in relation to the Central American States (the *Wilson Doctrine*, since 1913). Behind the democratic ideology there is in reality, on the part of the United States, a political endeavour to establish control over Central America.

As to explicit and implicit, individual and collective, *de facto*

---

[1] Cf. *Kunz*, Die Anmerkennung von Staaten und Regierungen im Völkerrecht, 145 f.

and *de jure* recognition, and as to the duty of recognition and the effects of such under internal law, the reader is referred to the preceding exposition.

The diplomatic envoys of the former government lose all international competence from the moment the old government has actually ceased to exist. The actions they may carry out are from that moment without significance and the receiving state is guilty of a breach of law in relation to the new government if it continues to attribute a representative character to the former ambassadors when they are not approved by the new government. Nevertheless, the United States still for a long time after the Russian revolution continued to regard the former Russian ambassador as the lawful plenipotentiary.

Finally, we recall the maxim that the state preserves its international identity regardless of inner revolutions (§ 20).

III. *Decentralised organs.*

The competent central organs as a rule carry on negotiations with foreign states by local representatives who are permanently accredited to the foreign state in question. These are called *envoys.* They differ from the central organs in the first place by having no competence — in spite of their often very grand titles — to act on behalf of the state. They cannot enter upon agreements and cannot bind the state by declarations on behalf of the state. They are only organs of negotiation. Expressed in terms of private law their position is simply that of a *messenger,* not of an agent.

Further they differ from the central organs by the fact that their functions are locally limited to the particular foreign state to which they are accredited.

Envoys for the purpose of negotiation have been employed as far back as history goes. But standing legations did not become common in Europe until after the Westphalian Peace in 1648. *Grotius* still held that permanent embassies were superfluous. It was the Italian city republics which were the pioneers for permanent missions in various states. The first permanent legation dates from 1455 when a Venetian embassy was established at Genoa.

On the whole the diplomatic corps has lost some of its independent political value with the recent development. This is due partly to the change from absolutism to constitutional government, in which the more important foreign affairs are under democratic control, partly to the development of the modern means of communication which have made it easier to give the diplomatic representatives effective instructions.

Since there exists no duty of intercourse a state is not bound either to send out or to receive ambassadors. By the nature of things, however, no state can in our day entirely shut itself off from regular intercourse with all the others. Conversely, of course any state which can agree thereon with others can send and receive envoys. The only prerequisite is that the state at any rate possesses a certain international capacity of action, which again is dependent on the legal system to which the state is subject — either by constitution or treaty (§ 15). Thus the states of the former German empire possessed the right of legation but such a right does not belong to the cantons of Switzerland, or to the member states of the United States.

The question as to the order of precedence of envoys was at one time the subject of much dispute. This led to the adoption of a classification at the Vienna Congress 1815 (with an appendix in 1818). According to this four categories are distinguished:

1. Ambassadors.
2. Ministers plenipotentiary and envoys exstraordinary.
3. Ministers resident.
4. Chargés d'affaires.

The distinction is only of importance with regard to various honorary rights. The original idea was that — in accord with the claim for the equality of states — each state should normally have the right to use all categories. Before the second World War, however, the practice had developed that ambassadors were exchanged between the great powers only. During the war the Allied Nations agreed to send and receive ambassadors irrespectively of the size of the state.

The appointment to the post of envoy is of course an entirely internal affair. But the *reception* of envoys has an international aspect. For a state can — even without the wish to break off diplomatic relations — refuse a particular person. It need not give any reason for this, much less justify its rejection. Since a refusal is in any case of a painful nature the practice has developed that the state sending the envoy secures approval beforehand of the envoy-to-be as *persona grata*. This approval is called in diplomatic parlance the assignment of *agrément*.

After the approval the envoy is furnished with a letter of credence *(lettre de créance)* which at the reception is handed to the head of the foreign state or — in the case of a chargé d'affaires — to the foreign minister.

As to the function of the envoys there is only reason to mention that as far as International Law is concerned they are *instruments of negotiation* for the competent authorities in their home state. That in addition they practice various activities in the service of their nationals in the state to which they are accredited and for the political orientation of the government in their homeland does not concern International Law.

Under International Law envoys and the persons associated with them (§ 27, II) enjoy various *diplomatic privileges* in relation to the state in which they are staying, namely:

1. Exterritoriality, see § 27.
2. A special legal protection of their persons, and
3. Exemption from the rules of certain laws in that they are free from all direct personal taxes, personal services, and public offices as well as public requisitions (e. g. income tax, property tax — but not from the tax on real estate — civil guard duty, air defence duty and the like, the office of juror, military billeting and military requisitions). By courtesy they are as a rule also exempted from paying customs duties on their personal effects.

Similar privileges belong to non-permanent political envoys with special missions, particularly with the task of representing the state at a congress, and non-political envoys with ceremonial functions, for instance when they are to represent the state at a coronation, a wedding or the like.

This rule, on the other hand, does not apply to *consuls*. These have nothing to do with international negotiations. They only look after national interests in the service of the citizens of the country they represent. They do not concern International Law, therefore, apart from the rule that the receiving state can refuse an unwelcome person, for which reason approval is also solicited beforehand *(exequatur)*. It follows from the general rule that consuls are exterritorial as far as their official business is concerned. (§ 33). Personally they enjoy no other privileges.[2]

---

[2] By commercial and consular treaties, however, consuls sent out *(consules missi* in contrast to *consules electi*, who are chosen among the inhabitants of the state of residence) are largely exempted from direct personal taxes.

Chapters IX
TREATIES

In this chapter all international agreements are dealt with. In practice they are designated by many different terms such as treaties, declarations, conventions, protocols, agreements, though no special importance attaches to these terms. In scientific usage it is customary to employ the term treaty for any international agreement. This is misleading in so far as no one would in practice think of denoting e. g. the international agreement concluded by the binding declaration of a minister for foreign affairs as a treaty. In practice the word "treaty" is only used about the more important and solemn international agreements. For convenience I shall, however, often in the sequel use the term treaty as a common term, but it must be remembered that besides the actual, more solemn treaties it will also comprise the ordinary international agreements.

§ 37
INVALID TREATIES

With respect to treaties the main task of International Law is to establish when an international agreement is *valid*, that is, when it entails international obligations for the parties to it according to its content.

In conformity with the principle *pacta sunt servanda* a treaty is valid unless there exists a special reason for its invalidity. The causes of invalidity recognised by International Law may be classified into three groups, namely

(1) Incompetence, that is to say, circumstances which deprive the organ or state that has concluded the treaty of the legal power to enter into an agreement of the kind in question (or to enter into any agreement).

(2) Defects in content, and

(3) Defects of origin.

I. *Incompetence*

may occur both with respect to the acting *state* and the acting representative.

In the first case this means that the treaty, according to its content, falls outside the capacity of action of the state. If the latter capacity is complete, or completely non-existent, no doubt can arise. If it is limited — as for instance in a state under partial protection or a state that is a member of a confederation of states (§ 15) — the agreement is only valid if it comes within the range of the capacity of action as this has been defined in the legal rules of the superior community. The decision may of course here give rise to doubts of interpretation, but questions of this rarely occur in practice.

The problem as to the incompetence of the *representative* is more difficult.

The question as to what representatives may validly bind a state is fundamentally one of International Law. But in conformity with the principle of effectivity International Law answers this question by a reference — at any rate as the point of departure — to the rules of competence of national constitutional law. Constitutional law in this case, however, must not be understood to mean the written constitution as expressed in a fundamental law, but the constitution as actually practised when customary constitutional law is taken into consideration. The difference may often be great. It means, which is of great importance in practice, that one need not study laws and theories but may simply take it for granted that a representative who regularly acts on behalf of the state in external affairs is competent to do so both under National and International Law.

As representatives who, according to the usual practice of states, have greater or less competence to bind the state we may then mention

(1) the head of the state (all agreements, particularly treaties proper);

(2) the government, that is to say, the prime minister or the minister for foreign affairs in the name of the government (government agreements);

(3) the individual ministers (each within his special depart-

ment. Agreements of a technical administrative character; departmental agreements);

(4) the military commander-in-chief (during war: agreements concerning armistices, capitulation and the like).

It may be difficult to draw the limit as to which agreements are government agreements and which require the co-operation of the head of the state. Here, too, the usual practice must settle the question.

Then, if an agreement has been concluded by a representative who according to current law and custom *lacks all competence* to act on behalf of the state, e. g. by an ambassador, it is a matter of course that such an agreement has no international validity whatever. As an example may be mentioned the agreement concluded on the 9th of April 1941 between the American minister for foreign affairs and the Danish minister von Kauffman as to the defence of Greenland and the establishment of American naval and air bases there. In a note of April 12th the Danish government entered a protest against the act of the American government which, in a question concerning the exercise of the sovereign rights of Denmark over Greenland, had negotiated and concluded an agreement with the ambassador in Washington though the latter was not by his position or by special authorisation competent to act on behalf of the government.

On the other hand, serious difficulties arise if the agreement has been concluded by a representative who is certainly authorised to act on behalf of the state in external affairs but who in the case in question by doing so has *transgressed internal constitutional precepts* restricting the constitutional authority of the representative. The doubts arising are due to the fact that often these restrictions do not come into play in the external relations with other states. A reference to what is customary, therefore, leaves the question unanswered. The problem then is whether the internal precepts restricting the constitutional competence of the representative also have a bearing on his international competence. The same question may be formulated thus. Does the reference of International Law to national law only concern the individuality of the competent representative, os does it go behind this; that is, does it also refer to the restrictions constitutionally binding upon the representative in the exercise of his function?

As an example of the internal legal precepts that may come into question here may be mentioned a minister's countersignature, the consent of the legislative assembly or one of its houses, treatment in a state council, the opinion of a commission for foreign affairs, a plebiscite.

A comparison with the rules of civil law concerning agency will instructively illustrate the problem arising here.

A representative who acts on behalf of the state may be compared to an agent acting on behalf of the person who has empowered him. Two different questions arise, viz. first, the question as to the legitimacy of the dispositions of the agent in relation to the principal, and second, the question as to the binding character of his dispositions in relation to a third party. According to the rules of Danish law the first question depends on the extent of the real *competence or authorisation* of the agent, the second on the extent of his *authority* as it appears to a third party. This means that in the former relation any instruction which the principal may have given the agent is binding upon the latter so that he is responsible to that person if he exceeds his authority, whereas it is not certain that his dispositions are not on that account binding in relation to a third party. This depends on the character of the authority. If the authorisation is based solely on a verbal agreement, the dispositions of the agent are not binding in relation to a third party. If, on the other hand, the authority has a "special existence", as for instance a written authority or an authority in virtue of position, the authority, externally, is determined solely by this, and a third party therefore acquires a right within this limit, even though the agent may have exceeded his competence — of course on the assumption that the third party is in good faith.

If now we transfer these conceptions to the situation at hand, it may be said that the real competence of the representative in relation to the state is determined by the rules of internal law, and that the question is whether the representative possesses an authority different from this to bind the state in relation to other states. Is the position of the representative to be understood on the analogy of a verbal authority, that is to say so that the representative can only bind the state when he has acted within the competence of national law? Or must the position of the representative be understood on the analogy of a written authority (the constitution) or an authority in virtue of position (the position of the representative) that is to say that the representative may bind the state if only he has kept within the objective limits determined by the constitution or the usual competence of such a representative according to the international conception?

I point out that here the parallel has only been drawn as an instructive illustration of the problem, not for the purpose of deducing its solution on this basis. It must especially be noted that the solution is not limited to the possibilities indicated by the analogy.

This question has given rise to a very extensive discussion in the literature on International Law, but no agreement has been reached as to the reply. The current view is to the effect that the rules of constitutional law are also relevant to International Law, that is to say, an authority under International Law has no wider scope than a competence under constitutional law. Conversely, others take it for granted that the representative, by virtue of his position, has an unlimited authority to represent the state if only the agreements made come within the field of activities connected with the representative's office (the head of the state is supposed to have *jus repræsentationis omnimodæ*). Others again have in different ways assumed an intermediate solution.

On the other hand, the problem has given rise only to very few conflicts and decisions in the practice of states. Apparently this is strange enough since it might be thought that in practice clarity would be required with respect to the validity of treaties. The explanation is to be found in the fact that under normal circumstances a state *would* not — even if it might — contest a treaty concluded by the head of the state (or another competent organ) because this would also mean an unpleasant disavowal of the state's own representative. It is preferred to keep such things in camera. The question, it may be supposed, will most readily come up in connection with revolutions. Thus a restoration government may contest the validity of a treaty concluded in (supposed) conflict with the constitution of an intermediary revolutionary government or dictatorship.[1] — The few decisions available are inconsistent with one another.

---

[1] As a recent example we may mention that when Marshal Mannerheim had succeeded Ryti as president of Finland the Finns disputed the validity of an agreement not to conclude a separate peace with the Soviet Union which Ryti had made without the co-operation of the parliament, see Prime Minister Hacksell's radio speech 2. Sept. 1944, reported in N. T. 1944 p. 25.

Under these circumstances the question is merely of academic interest. Until a fixed legal practice has developed the solution must be based on general principles.

The current view draws support especially from a reference to the fact that this solution is most in accord with the constitutional desire to create certain democratic guarantees for the exercise of the competence of the head of the state in international affairs. Some few constitutions directly mention or imply the international effect of the precepts. A formal objection to this is that the question, being international, cannot be solved directly on the basis of constitutional precepts, and a real objection is that the co-contractor must also be considered. The same state which, as the party giving the promise, is interested in the restrictions of the constitution being effective in International Law, if receiving the promise in another situation is interested in the opposite.

The theorists who would assign to the representative an authority unlimited by internal precepts point out especially that this is the only way in which security can be created in international negotiations. In the opposite case it would be necessary to make extensive and difficult investigations concerning the position under state law of the co-contractor. In many cases doubts might arise both as to the content of the guarantees offered by state law and as to their actual fulfilment. Remonstrances on this point might be regarded as an undue interference with the internal affairs of another state.

Probably the question should not be solved by a clear alternative.

In the first place it follows from the fundamental view of the international competence of the representative that in those cases where the constitutional guarantee *manifests itself externally* in relation to the co-contractor so that the latter is by custom prepared for it, an international effect must also be ascribed to this guarantee. This applies to the demand for a minister's countersignature.

In other cases similar considerations to those determining the rules for agency in civil law should probably be applied. This means that only such restrictions in the competence which are either *usual* in a given situation, or *objectively recognisable* by the co-contractor, are binding in relation to the latter. Applied to interstate affairs these views will lead to the result that importance is only attached to such internal precepts as *are either customary* in the practice of constitutional states *or clearly stated in the constitution of the states*. According to the special nature of these cases it should further be required that it is possible for the co-contractor to *find out* whether or not the requirement has been fulfilled.

Applied, again, to the concrete precepts that come into question in practice this leads to the result that international effectivity must be ascribed to

— Definite constitutional precepts for the consent of the legislative assembly or one of its houses or for a plebiscite, but not, on the other hand, to

— Precepts for the matter to be dealt with in a state council (as secret)

— Precepts for the verdict of a commission concerned with foreign affairs (secret)

— Demands for the consent of the politically leading house, not in consequence of a particular precept but in accord with general political maxims.

In the judgment of the Permanent Court of 1933 on the *legal status of Eastern Greenland* it is said (with reference to the declaration of the Norwegian minister for foreign affairs of July 22 1919 to the Danish ambassador) that the Court considers it beyond all dispute that a reply given by the minister of foreign affairs on behalf of his government in response to a request by the diplomatic representative of a foreign power, in regard to a question falling within his province, is binding upon the country to which the minister belongs.[2] In view of the procedure in the case this enunciation must be understood to mean that the authority of the minister for foreign affairs is unaffected by possible constitutional precepts. This is indeed stated expressly in judge *Anzilotti's* dissentient vote.[3]

Another judgment (the *Free Zones judgment*) presupposes that constitutional rules are relevant in questions as to the competence of an organ, but at the same time it establishes that the agent of a party to a case may during the proceedings in court make statements which according to the circumstances are binding upon his state, irrespective of constitutional obligations.[4]

---

[2] Perm. Courts Series A/B no. 53, p. 71.

[3] loc. cit. p. 91—92.

[4] Perm. Court Series A/B no. 46, 169—70.

II. *Defects of content.*

In private law it often happens that an agreement between two parties is invalid because its contents are inconsistent with legal rules which the parties cannot vary. Such rules express a social policy by which the community protects individuals even against their own will. Nothing similar occurs in International Law. Every state must protect itself and there is no limit to the validity of what two states may agree to between themselves.

That the agreement may be invalid because it is inconsistent with *the rights of a third state* raises considerations of a different kind.

The matter is quite clear if the rights of the third party are founded on general International Law and may claim to be respected by all; thus if two states were to conclude an agreement excluding the ships of a third state from the open sea.

The case is less clear if the rights of a third state are founded on *a treaty* with the state now bent on establishing a right for another state in conflict with this treaty.

For instance: A has concluded a treaty with B that all ships passing through a certain canal on A's territory are to pay the same dues. Later on A, in a treaty with C, allows the ships of that state a preferential position. Is in that case the latter treaty invalid as conflicting with the former?[5]

In private law the main rule in the laws of civilised states concerning a conflict of rights is as follows. If the conflicting rights concern the same individually determined object or service, the first acquirer takes precedence of the second, at any rate if the latter was in bad faith; if the rights are merely quantitatively determined claims on property (monetary claims), on the other hand, they compete on an equal footing.

There does not seem to be any reason to depart from this principle in International Law in which — since monetary claims are not typical here — it must lead to the result that C cannot acquire a right conflicting with the right which the co-contractor (A) has already established for another state (B). (Bad faith must presumably always be assumed to be present).

---

[5] See the conflict between the *Hay-Pauncefote* Treaty (U. S. A. — England, 1901) and the *Hay-Varilla* Treaty (U. S. A. — Panama, 1903), cf. *Anzilotti*, Cours de Droit international, 417. — On a special aspect of the question as to the rights of a third state see Max Sørensen's interesting paper: The Modification of collective Treaties without the consent of all contracting parties, A. S. I. G. in N. T. 1938, 150.

The opposite view seems to prevail, but appears to me to conflict with all sound sense of justice. It is based on the dogma, clearly false in other respects, that treaties cannot have a burdensome effect on a third state.

B. Further, a treaty is invalid if its performance at the time it is concluded, is *impossible*, for instance if a person whom it has promised to surrender has died. Whether the impossibility may involve a duty to pay an indemnity must be decided by general legal principles relating to this question.

C. Finally, it is generally taught that a treaty is invalid if its content is *immoral* according to international views.

III. *Defects of origin.*

A. It is generally recognised that *compulsion* exercised against a state (war) does not render a treaty invalid.[6] On the contrary view no peace treaty would be valid under International Law.

On the other hand, it is usually said that compulsion exercised against negotiators renders a treaty invalid. Since, however, the negotiators only make a draft for the treaty (cf. § 38), this will merely be of importance in the rather improbable case that the treaty is ratified without knowledge of the compulsion. But the reason for its invalidity is then delusion or fraud, not compulsion.

B. *Delusion* and *fraud* may in rare cases be conceived to render a treaty invalid, for instance if the preceding negotiations concerning the fixing of a boundary have been based on incorrect or fraudulent maps.

IV. *Form.*

International Law prescribes no special form for a treaty. In the judgment on the *legal status of Eastern Greenland* (1933) it is laid down that a mere *verbal* pronouncement is binding. It

---

[6] Perhaps we may here with *Verdross* and others maintain that the same rule holds good here in principle as in civil law; the decisive factor is whether the compulsion exercised is in concflict with the law. War, however, is not normally unlawful, hence peace treaties are valid. Otherwise, if compulsion is exercised in conflict with a treaty, e. g. a provisional peace agreement. On this view the peace treaties after the first world war are branded as voidable dictates (*Verdross*, Völkerrecht, § 20 IV).

may also happen that agreements are concluded by *other than linguistic symbols* (e. g. a flag of truce during a war). Finally in this field too there may be *tacit* agreements without any express declaration. In that case there must be conduct on the part of the state (action or failure to act) which owing to the general view of the practice of states involves obligation for the state exactly as if a declaration had been made.

But by far the most frequent case is of course — owing to the seriousness of the circumstances — that international agreements are made *in writing*.

A comparison of the reasons for the invalidity of treaties with the doctrine of civil law concerning invalid promises will show that there are much fewer reasons for invalidity in International Law. Moreover the circumstance that treaties are normally concluded by the heads of states or other high organs of state in solemn forms and after careful preparation affords a substantial guarantee for the validity of the agreement. An invalid treaty is therefore a rare phenomenon.

§ 38
THE RATIFICATION OF TREATIES

I. *The legal significance of ratification.*

An international agreement, like any other agreement, is normally brought about by the exchange of declarations to that effect by the parties.

It may happen that these declarations are the result of direct negotiation between the competent organs.

The usual procedure, however, is that the competent organs (especially if they are two heads of states) do not enter into direct negotiations but leave it to expert negotiators to draft a treaty. The treaty itself is then concluded by the competent organs each on his part making the draft his own declaration. This does not take place, however — as might be expected from the custom in private law — by the head of the state signing and dispatching the draft to the other party. For reasons to which I shall revert presently the procedure is adopted of letting the expert negotiators sign the draft as if the treaty had already been concluded by this procedure, after which the head of the state then in a succeeding declaration ratifies the "treaty" which in reality is only a draft for a treaty.

Thus the ratification is a declaration from the competent organ (the head of the state) which *appears in the form of a sanction* of a treaty already concluded by others, but is *in reality the unilateral treaty declaration* of that state. In conformity with general rules it becomes binding by being brought to the knowledge of the other party. This takes place by the handing over of a document containing information of the ratification. When the ratification documents have been exchanged the treaty is perfect.

In order to understand clearly the reasons for ratification and its legal significance it may be instructive to compare the conclusion of treaties with other cases in which agreements are made between collective units.

Let us suppose that an agreement is to be made between two joint stock companies. We take it for granted that their respective directors are competent to do so. The agreement may be conceived to be brought about in various ways.

(1) The two directors meet, talk things over, and make a direct agreement.

(2) If it is a more extensive and complicated transaction that is to be carried out, for instance the amalgamation of the two companies, the two directors will probably feel that they do not possess the requisite legal kowledge and will therefore call in solicitors and request them to negotiate and make a draft for a contract. If they succeed in finding an arrangement to which both parties can agree, the contract is made by the directors signing the draft.

(3) Finally, the two directors may be conceived to choose the procedure of each of them authorising a solicitor to negotiate on their behalf about an arrangement with the other party. In that case the contract is made directly by the agreement of the solicitors.

For states the procedure is exactly the same.

(1) The treaty is brought about *directly* by negotiation and agreement between the competent organs.

If these are the respective heads of states, this method is rare. As a rule it is excluded because the consent of the body representing the people to the most important treaties is usually required. From recent times, however, we may mention several examples of treaties concluded directly between the leaders of states ruled by dictators.

If the competent organ is the government, a direct agreement can be concluded by an exchange of notes presented by envoys.

Similarly agreements may be concluded directly between ministers of the various state departements or military commanders.

(2) When conditions are more complicated it is usual for treaties to be prepared by negotiation *between intermediaries without authority,* with a succeeding *ratification* by the competent organs. This procedure may be employed no matter who is the competent organ. Thus the military commander-in-chief may send officers to negotiate about an armistice while the agreement itself requires the ratification of the commander-in-chief.

(3) Finally, it is conceivable that the treaty is concluded directly between *authorised intermediaries.* The treaty is then binding immediately when these have signed it. This procedure, however, implies that the competent organ can lawfully delegate its competence to others. In constitutional states this is largely excluded by the constitution.

The common procedure in more important affairs is therefore that mentioned under (2).

Now these clear facts, which show in what cases ratification is required and explain that ratification in these cases is the actual treaty declaration, are obscured by diplomatic linguistic usage and ceremonies which are grounded in historical tradition alone.

Firstly, in those cases in which the treaty is concluded by the head of the state, the negotiating intermediaries are according to old custom furnished with an "authority" (Full Powers), though this is not intended literally.[1] Further, the "authorised persons" "sign" the draft without their signature being intended to be binding.

---

[1] In Denmark the following formula is generally used:

Nous Christian Dix

Par la grâce de Dieu Roi de Danemark etc.

SAVOIR FAISON: qu'ayant resolu d'entamer des negociations avec Sa Majesté .... afin de conclure un Traité de .... Nous avons choisi, nommé et autorisé, comme par les présentes nous choisissons, nommons et autorisons pour Notre Plénipotentiaire Monsieur .... pour negocier, conclure et signer, sauf Notre ratification, avec le Plénipotentiaire de sa majsté .... un Traité de .... promettant en foi et parole de Roi d'avoir pour

Secondly, ratification is mostly referred to in those cases only where it is the head of the state who confirms a draft for a treaty.

These strange modes of expression and customs are reminiscences from the days of absolutism preserved by diplomatic conservatism. In those days the absolute monarch could and would really give the negotiators an authority. Ratification was then a real ratification, that is to say, the sanction of an agreement made by others. This sanction meant an admission that they had not exceeded their authority and that consequently the agreement was binding. In accord herewith ratification could not as a rule be refused.

As previously stated, in our day the practice of furnishing the negotiators with authority has been retained, even though in constitutional states it is generally excluded that the authority can be seriously meant.

In the first place, the king as a rule *cannot* under the constitution delegate his treaty-making competence to others. At any rate this is clearly excluded in all cases in which the king must have the consent of a parliament to conclude the treaty.

In the second place, even if the king in certain cases could delegate his competence, he is according to the nature of the case *not really intended to do so.* It is difficult to give instructions to the negotiators except in very broad outline. They must have considerable liberty with respect to the proposals set forth by the other party. It will then be the task of the competent representative to form an opinion on the result of the negotiations as a whole. The head of a democratic state is in any case bound by public opinion and must therefore be free to sound it before taking his stand.

Several unfortunate consequences follow from this.

(1) The term "ratification" is *misleading* and deceptive. What takes place is not a sanction of a treaty already concluded, but the making of the treaty declaration itself. The treaty is only binding from the moment the ratification documents have been exchanged. The ratification is the actual responsible decision as

---

agréable tout ce que Notre dit Plénipotentiaire aura conclu et signé en vertu des présents Pleins Pouvoirs.

En foi de quoi Nous avons signé de Notre propre main ces Pleins Pouvoirs et y avons fait apposer Notre sceau Royal.

Donnée a Copenhague de ....

As will be seen, ratification is here stipulated.

to whether or not the state will bind itself. According to the constitution the competent organ cannot as a rule take that decision itself but must have the consent of the people, usually in the shape of the assent of the legislative assembly or one of its houses, or sometimes even in the form of a plebiscite. In this way democratic control is secured for the more important foreign affairs.

(2) Diplomatic usage mostly refers to ratification in those cases only in which it is the head of the state who makes a decision about a drafted treaty. In this way the fact is concealed that the selfsame legal phenomenon is also present when other competent organs have acted by the agency of representatives without authority to conclude a binding agreement.

(3) In some few cases it may be constitutionally possible and is really intended to give the negotiators full authority to bind the state. In those cases, then, the treaty is binding without ratification. Owing to the above-mentioned usage it will, however, be difficult in practice to distinguish the cases in which the authority is seriously meant from the usual situations where it is of a ceremonial character. The result is that ratification must be demanded in all cases in which it is not expressly waived, or in which it does not appear unambiguously from the circumstances that a real authority to bind the state has been given.

The question, when does a treaty require ratification in order to be binding, may then be answered as follows. Ratification is required, and only required, in those cases in which the competent organ has prepared a treaty through intermediaries without authority to conclude a binding agreement, no matter who the competent representative is. Intermediaries must — regardless of the diplomatic formulas — be looked upon as lacking such authority, unless the reverse appears unambiguously from the circumstances. In practice, however, it is assumed that minor additions to a treaty, for instance about its coming into operation, may very well be made by the negotiators in the shape of a protocol without ratification. If the signed draft dispenses with ratification, not expressly reserved in the Full Powers, the signature must presumably be binding on the state and not subject to the objection that the negotiator had no authority to dispense with ratification.

It follows from the legal nature of ratification that it may freely be *refused* without grounds being given and without explanations or apologies. Refusal of a ratification is no rare phenomenon. The more complicated the subject of negotiation is and especially in cases of collective treaties, the more difficult will it be to give the negotiators exhaustive instructions, and the ratification may therefore fall to the ground because the draft does not win the approval of the government. But even apart from this, ratification may become impossible because the government does not succeed in gaining the necessary democratic consent (for example, the United States refused to ratify the Versailles Treaty of 1919 with the incorporated Covenant of the League of Nations for which the American president, *Wilson*, worked with special energy).

II. *The form of the ratification.*

International Law prescribes no form of ratification. Usually it is a document duly signed by the head of the state or some other competent organ. Ratification may also be tacit, by the competent organ beginning the performance of the treaty.

III. *Exchange of the ratification documents.*

Normally this takes place by the documents being delivered by envoys at the same time as the delivery is confirmed in a protocol. In cases of collective agreements this procedure would lead to great inconvenience. Therefore it is usually decided that the ratification documents shall be deposited in the foreign office of one of the contracting countries which will then inform the other parties.

No time limit is prescribed within which the ratification must take place.

IV. *Conditional ratification.*

Conditional ratification or ratification with a reservation is in principle the same as a refusal with a fresh proposal Such a ratification is thus without significance if the other party does not — explicitly or tacitly — accept the proposal, e. g. by proceeding, with full knowledge of the circumstances, to rati fy the treaty or, if the reservation was made later, to its performance. Otherwise, if the contracting parties have agreed beforehand or tacitly understood that ratification may take place with reservation. Such a ratification is then binding on the opposite party without renewed acceptance. This is probably frequently the case upon the conclusion of collective treaties. For in concluding collective treaties it has turned out that in practice it is difficult to obtain consent without reservations, for instance with respect to some clauses, the sphere of application and the like. Of the 14 Hague Conventions of 1907 only 2 were ratified by all parties without reservations. In order to avoid the uncertainty and inequality in legal status that might otherwise occur it has in certain cases been decided either that ratification with reservations shall not be allowed, or only allowed with respect to certain points. It is a mere question of convenience whether it be found wise thus to exercise pressure to obtain unreserved consent at the risk of losing some adherents who might otherwise have been gained.

V. *The coming into force of treaties.*

The moment when a treaty comes into force will normally be expressly stated. Failing this, there is no agreement as to whether it comes into effect when the ratifications are exchanged or whether these have a retroactive power from the moment of signing.

If it is provided in the treaty that it is to come into operation at some time prior to the ratification, which must still take place (e. g. immediately after it is signed), this must be understood to mean that the effect of the ratification is intended to date back to this earlier time.

§ 39
THE PERFORMANCE OF TREATIES

On this subject see § 6.

§ 40
CAN TREATIES CREATE RIGHTS AND DUTIES FOR A THIRD STATE?

I. *Rights for a third state.*

A treaty between two states A and B may of course often contain provisions which are in fact of advantage to a third state, C. But normally the latter will not acquire any legal claim thereby which it may assert independently. It is not entirely excluded, however. It depends on the intentions of the contracting parties. But if the terms are not unambiguous in that respect it is presumed not to be the intention to create rights for others than the contracting parties. This has now been clearly expressed by the Permanent Court: "A treaty only creates law as between the States which are parties to it; in case of doubt, no rights can be deduced from it in favour of third States."[1]

In any case, however, the right aquired by C can be destroyed by a new agreement between A and B.

II. *Duties for a third state.*

The general view is that a treaty can never create duties for others than the parties to it.

It is a question, however, whether a third state has not the "duty" of respecting the right acquired in so far at any rate as it is excluded from acquiring rights by a later agreement inconsistent with the acquired right. On this point the reader is referred to § 37 II.

Certain treaties, for instance those that limit a state's capacity of action, can be maintained towards all states.

Finally we may remind the reader that a treaty may create such a general legal opinion that it becomes binding on all, cf. § 10. I.

§ 41
THE TERMINATION OF TREATIES

The termination of treaties depends on general legal principles, partly influenced by the special nature of international conditions. We may distinguish between termination based on the treaty itself, on the autonomy of the parties in general, and on general International Law.

I. *Termination based on the treaty itself.*

(1) *Performance* of the treaty.

(2) Expiration of a *time limit,* when the treaty has been concluded for a definite period of time. In recent years it has become customary for treaties to be concluded for a certain number of years, often with rules for a simplified renewal.

---

[1] In the case concerning *certain German interests in Polish Upper Silesia,* 1926, Permanent Court Publ. Series A. No. 7, p. 29, see also the judgment in the case concerning the *Factory in Chorzow,* Series A. No. 17, pp. 43—46 and the *Free Zones judgment,* Serie A/B No. 46 p. 147.

(3) The non-fulfilment of a *condition* precedent or the occurrence of a condition subsequent, when the treaty has been concluded on conditions.

(4) *Notice of withdrawal,* when such notice has been stipulated in the treaty. This must be presumed when the treaty concerns matters which owing to their nature can only be settled provisionally, as for instance commercial treaties.

(5) *Default.* It is natural to assume that each of the parties will only be bound if the other party fulfils its obligations. Therefore, if one of the two parties to a treaty breaks the obligation which the treaty imposes, the other party will as a rule be discharged from such performance as may still be due from him. It is controversial whether every breach of obligation gives the other party a right to rescind the treaty or not. The treaty will only be dissolved upon the request of the offended party.

(6) *Frustration* by failure of an assumed essential state of facts. If it appears from the negotiations or the circumstances when the treaty is concluded that one of the parties only desires to be bound on the assumption that certain facts exist and the other party cannot fail to understand this, the failure of the assumed facts entails the right to rescind the treaty.

II. *On the basis of the autonomy of the parties.*

(1) Each of the parties may *renounce* its rights.

(2) A *later agreement* between the parties conflicting with the first one will as a rule cancel the first treaty. It is a question of interpretation how far a different construction must be put on this. If for instance two states have first concluded a special treaty concerning the settlement by the Permanent Court of certain disputes and later on agree upon general arbitration the earlier agreement must probably be supposed to remain unaffected.

III. *On the basis of general International Law.*

(1) *clausula rebus sic stantibus.* According to an old doctrine it is taught that every agreement is concluded with the tacit reservation that it is valid only as long as there is no vital change in the circumstances, which would make the performance of the treaty a serious danger to the party. Indeed, the practice of

states shows many examples of a state withdrawing from an agreement on the plea of changed circumstances.

It is clear, however, and also generally recognised in theory, that very narrow limits must be set to this right, if the fundamental principle of the inviolability of law and justice is not to be rendered illusory *(pacta sunt servanda)*. Anyhow, this method of termination must be distinguished from others to which it bears some relation.

If it is a question of facts which were assumed by the parties when the treaty was concluded the case comes under what was said above about frustration by the failure of an assumed essential state of facts.

If such changes take place that a continuing duty of performance would seriously threaten the existence or welfare of the state, exemption may under certain circumstances follow from general principles of self-preservation (§ 51. IV).

Thus the question will only become of special significance in a case of unanticipated changes falling outside the scope of the right of self-preservation.

In spite of the great dangers connected with the clause its recognition within narrow limits cannot, we should think, be denied. The desire for this is connected with the fact that treaty obligations are often pressed upon states, sometimes by force, and are valid for ever without any chance of lawful revision. Under such circumstances an absolute principle of the sacredness of treaties would be strained to breaking-point and would not be able to prevent a state from onesidedly freeing itself from the unreasonably irksome bonds of obsolete treaties. On the other hand, the recognition of the clause is dangerous, especially in International Law, because there does not exist any general duty to seek a legal decision in a dispute. If a party takes the application of the clause into its own hands the result will easily be that it will serve as a cloak for an arbitrary neglect of duty.

The view that a state cannot onesidedly free itself, but only after the other party to the treaty has refused legal settlement, may seem right and reasonable but can hardly be asserted to be current law, because there exists no general duty to go to law about it.

As already stated, the clause has often been invoked in the practice of states, but in no single instance, we think, has the right of the state to free itself in the case in question been recognised either by public opinion or by any court of law. Conversely, in several instances when a state has freed itself by invoking that clause it has actually been branded as a violation of law. Thus in 1870 when Russia took advantage of the Franco-German war to declare itself released from the obligations it had undertaken by the Paris treaty of 1856 — after the Crimean war — with regard to neutralising the Black Sea and not keeping a fleet there, England protested, and the year after a conference was held in London. By a treaty of London in 1871 the original signatory powers agreed to release Russia from these obligations but added to this a solemn condemnation of the Russian procedure in the following protocol: "It is an essential principle of the Law of Nations that no power can free itself from the engagements of a treaty, nor modify its terms except with the assent of the contracting parties by means of a understanding". The Council of the League of Nations referred to this protocol in a condemnation of German conduct when Germany in 1935 and 1936 onesidedly repudiated the clauses of the Versailles Treaty concerning disarmament and the demilitarisation of the Rhineland.

It cannot be denied, however, that in its categorical form the London protocol of 1871 goes beyond the mark. According to its wording it absolutely forbids every onesided release from a treaty, but this cannot be right (e. g. discharge on account of the other party's breach of terms). It can therefore only be intended that the state should first by negotiation try to come to terms with the other party. This is a special application of the general principle of International Law that in every international dispute an attempt shall first be made to adjust it by diplomatic negotiation (§ 58).

Nevertheless, even with this reduced content, the London protocol opens one's eyes to a vital problem, the *claim for a revision of burdensome obligations and in general of the existing balance of power* which is no longer in harmony with the political development. Brierly justly says: "The problem of oppressive or obsolete treaties is essentially part of a wider problem. Indeed the danger to international order comes more often from oppressive conditions, and especially frontier conditions, whether these were or were not originally created by a treaty, than from oppressive obligations in a still executory treaty. But the "sanctity of treaties" will never be more than a

cant phrase so long as the law is too weak to deny the validity
of a treaty entered into under coercion, or to lay down canons
of international public policy, comparable to those of municipal
law, which shall be conditions of any treaty's validity ab initio.
In part the ultimate solution can probably be found only in
some quasi-legislative international action, comparable to the
legislative interferences which modify the obligations of private
contracts within a state in the interests of social order. This
method of attacking the problem is foreshadowed by Article 19
of the Covenant, which, if only as a recognition that there is a
problem to be solved, at least marks an advance on the declaration of the powers in 1871, which has been quoted above."[1]

(2) Subsequent *impossibility* of performance entails the disso-
lution of the obligation. Whether subsidiary obligations arise as
a consequence, must be decided on general principles of law.

(3) A treaty also is dissolved if the state bound by it *ceases to
be an independent state*, unless the rules of succession (§ 19)
involve its transfer to another state.

(4) It may happen that a treaty is so antiquated that it can
no longer be performed or invoked by the parties to it. It is then
said to have *passed out of use* or lapsed by *desvetudo*.

(5) Finally, general International Law to a certain extent
ascribes to *war* the effect of making treaties between belligerents
void or suspending them. The rules concerning this point do
not come within the scope of the present work.

---

[1] *Brierly*, Law of Nations, 207—08. Art. 19 of the Covenant of the
League of Nations contained the following provision: "The Assembly of
Delegates may from time to time advise the reconsideration by Members of
the League of treaties which have become inapplicable and the consideration
of international conditions whose continuance might endanger the peace of
the world".

Chapter X
CO-OPERATION OF STATES FOR THE PURPOSE
OF SAFEGUARDING COMMON INTERESTS

§ 42
THE DEVELOPMENT AND FORMS OF CO-OPERATION

It has already (§ 31) been stated that general International Law is in the main restricted to an individualistic delimination of the living space of the states, and leaves social co-ordination to be organised by treaty. Such treaties as unite the states in co-operation for the safeguarding of common interests or the combating of common dangers have grown up in great abundance since the middle of the last century. The rapid development of international intercourse, rendered possible by modern technique, made it impossible for states to go on living in splendid isolation but forced them to co-operate for the promotion of common cultural aims. It was the invention of the modern technical means of communication (telegraph, railway) which were first made the subject of international regulation. By their nature they break through the national boundaries and require an international administration for their completion. Later on followed a great number of other domains, an indirect result of closer communication, because certain purposes pursued by the individual states in the national interests could not be effectively carried out without their endeavours being combined with those of other states in the same direction. As examples may be mentioned the protection of public health from certain dangerous infectious diseases (the plague, cholera, typhoid fever etc.). The sanitary arrangements which individual states could make for this purpose would be largely ineffective if these diseases were allowed to spread freely elsewhere. Often it would even have the effect of deterring individual states from the pursuit of certain cultural aims for their own part unless they could obtain a guarantee of co-operation, since otherwise such states would occupy an inferior position in the international economic competition. This applies for instance to the social protection of workmen.

This chapter of the international co-operation for the promotion of a great number of common humanitarian objects is practically one of the most important in International Law. Results have here been achieved of invaluable significance. Any one who condemns International Law off-hand because its efforts to prevent war have hitherto totally failed should consider this chapter before passing judgment. The same applies more especially to the League of Nations. Whatever one's opinion about this as a political organisation may be, one cannot shut one's eyes to the fact that in many respects it has displayed a fruitful activity for the decelopment of international administrative co-operation.

Sometimes the co-operation here concerned merely takes the shape of an agreement to *co-ordinate* the administrative apparatus of the various states. But in many cases a *common international organ* is actually established for the safeguarding of mutual interests. We have then an administrative union.

Administrative unions as a rule comprise three kinds of organs: partly a general state conference (general conference, congress) consisting of representatives of the contracting powers. It often assembles at regular intervals and its task is to revise the fundamental convention and so adapt the union to the changed conditions. Its resolutions therefore have the character of new international conventions. Partly a board of administration (executive committee, commission) conducts and supervises the work of the union; and, finally, there is a permanent office, generally called bureau or secretariat for the execution of the current business.

It is of fundamental importance to note that direct administration is not normally taken charge of by the union organs (the bureau) but by the usual national administrative authorities. The international organs have no power to pass resolutions and no power to take measures of coercion. Legally their task is restricted to *preparing, guiding,* and *stimulating* the national administrations in the spirit of the international union. Thus the administrative unions restrict neither the self-government nor the capacity of action of the member states and are not, therefore, real state unions. There is no international community of administration but only an internationally organised co-operation between national administrations. (An exception to this is, for instance, the European Danube Commission, see § 29).

As an example of an administrative union may be given the *Universal Postal Union,* founded in Berne in 1874, and now embracing practically all the world. The supreme organ is the universal postal congress consisting of representatives from all the member states who meet regularly every five years. The conventions concluded (revisions of and additions to the treaty of the union) are to be ratified in the usual way. In the meanwhile purely administrative questions can be treated at special postal conferences and the individual administrations may make proposals which are distributed and put to the vote. The International Bureau at Berne functions as the permanent organ. Its task is to collect and publish information of every kind which is of importance for the international postal service; on request to give an opinion on disputes; to treat applications for changes in the acts of the congress; to notify members of changes and altogether make such studies etc. as it has been decided should be assigned to the Bureau.

International administrative co-operation embraces the most heterogeneous fields. The rules laid down are manifold and detailed. Here we can only survey the chief subjects. Their arrangement is difficult and somewhat casual.

§ 43
INTERCOURSE, i. e. THE CONVEYANCE OF PERSONS, GOODS, AND COMMUNICATIONS

For the intercourse between nations we find a series of conventions the object of which is to establish international freedom of intercourse with equality for the various parties.

The invention of the *telegraph* gave rise to the first international administrative union *(Union telegraphique universelle)* founded in Paris in 1865, now replaced by the Telecommunication Convention Madrid 1932. It rests on the principle that the telegraph should be open to everybody. No uniform tariff has been introduced. Recently radio telegraphy and broadcasting have been made the subject of international agreements relating to the use of wave lengths etc.

The international *postal* traffic is organised in the Universal Postal Union whose organisation was mentioned above. It rests on the principle of freedom of transit which does not, however, exclude certain rates payable for this. The whole union constitutes a common postal district with the same postal rate, no matter what the distance. No balancing of the postal returns takes place, each country keeping the returns undivided.

About *railways* there are a number of conventions which secure international traffic by rules concerning the standardisation of rail gauges, the sealing of trucks, frontier control at common frontier stations, continuity of service on international routes, exchange and mutual use of rolling stock, the use of through-bills of carriage etc.

For *road traffic* (motor vehicles) several conventions have been concluded concerning marks of identification, drivers' licences, traffic signals etc.

With respect to the traffic on *international rivers* the reader is referred to § 29.

Curiously enough, there are only few international conventions concerning navigation and navigation signals on the *open sea*. This is due to the dominant position of England as a seafaring nation. The Commercial Code of Signals for the Use of all Nations published by England in 1857 (new edition 1934) was very soon voluntarily accepted by all seafaring nations. After the catastrophe of the Titanic in 1912 a convention was concluded in London in 1914 (renewed 1929) concerning the safety of life at sea which contains a number of provisions relating to the build and equipment of ships, the meteorological service, control of icebergs etc. In this connection, finally, may be mentioned a convention concerning the use of ports.

The traffic in *the air* has been regulated by the Paris Aerial Navigation Convention of 1919, revised in 1929. In times of peace it allows the contracting parties the rights of inoffensive flying over land and territorial waters with the exception only of war-customs- and police-aircraft. This includes the right of landing according to detailed rules. Every state has unrestricted jurisdiction over its own air space. An International Air Navigation Commission has been established which in certain domains possesses both legislative, jurisdictional, and executive power.

§ 44
INTERSTATE COMMERCE

It is a deplorable fact that the economic life of states, their conditions of production and trade with each other has not so far been the subject of international regulation. In this we must presumably see one of the chief causes of war. Each state autonomously pursues its own commercial policy. In the struggle for raw materials, markets and employment every state aims at its own objectives, and the conflict of interests arising in this way may, even when there is peace in a military sense, lead to trade wars. One of the major tasks after the recent war will be to put an end to these anarchical conditions.

It is true that since 1860 an immense number of *commercial treaties* have been concluded, but these are virtually all bilateral agreements, instruments for negotiations adapted to circumstances, concerning concessions and promises, not for an international co-ordination. After most countries had abandoned the orthodox free trade doctrine they have mainly been concerned with the fixing of certain limits to tariff rates and similar protective measures.

Nevertheless, in the years before the first world war no mean result was achieved by these measures of unorganised adaptation. The commercial treaties wound their web all round the globe and opened up possibilities of a world commerce which reached great heights. The standing *most-favoured-nation-clause*, which secures to the co-contractor as favourable a position as the nation which is at the moment or will in future be the most favoured, did in fact give rise to a certain generality within the multiplicity of commercial treaties.

A complete change in this development towards free trade set in after the first world war. On military grounds, amongst others, various states adopted *a policy of self-sufficiency* which must necessarily produce a corresponding reaction among states which actually favoured free trade. Everywhere a control of imports was introduced and the commercial treaties not only became concerned with the fixing of customs rates but developed into agreements about export contingents and prices. This development was crowned when, by the Ottawa Treaties of 1932, England definitely gave up free trade in favour of an imperialistic protective policy. The most-favoured-nation-clauses were undermined and partly replaced by the idea of *preference*, according to which the states within a certain group mutually concede trade advantages to each other.

Simultaneously, the ideals of international regulation underwent a change. The earlier ideal of a world economy based on liberty and equality was replaced by the idea of an organised planned economy assigning to every state a particular role within a delimited economic system. The Geneva Convention of 1927 concerning the abolition of all restrictions on imports and exports which was signed by a great number of states stands as a memorial to the liberalist ideas. But owing to the later developments it never became of practical importance.[1] How the future will shape itself in this field I am unable to say. In any case it may no doubt be taken for granted that there will be no return to a state of free unorganised play of forces.

Under these circumstances it will be understood that in the field of economics international co-operation has so far only been concerned with unessential details, mostly of a technical nature. We may mention various conventions on the metrical system, on the publication of tariffs, and the simplification of customs formalities, on the publication of commercial statistics and the like.

§ 45
SOCIAL AND NATIONAL PROTECTION

I. *Workmen.*

On the view that social injustice and the misery and distress connected with it are a danger to the peace of the world and the

---

[1] The convention of 8. Nov. 1927 was signed by representatives of 24 states but did not attain ratification to the extent stipulated as a condition for its coming into operation (supplementary agreement of 11. Jan. 1928, Art. C). For this reason a group of states, among them Denmark, concluded a special convention to give effect to it of 20. Dec. 1929, according to which the convention was to come into operation from 1. Jan. 1930. But a number of states made the fulfilment conditional on stipulations which were not complied with. The result was that the convention became operative only for Denmark, the United States, Japan, Holland, Portugal, and Great Britain. Denmark gave notice of withdrawal from the convention as from 30. June 1933. At that time restrictions on imports under the laws for the protection of the Danish exchange (from and incl. Act No. 8 of 30. Jan. 1932) were already in full development.

good understanding between nations the 13th chapter of the Treaty of Versailles established an independent permanent institution, the *International Labour Organisation,* with the object of working for an improvement in the conditions of labour. States outside the League of Nations may also be members of this organisation.

Its organs are:

1. The General Conference consisting of 4 representatives for each member, two chosen by the government and one representative each of the workmen and the employers. The Conference assembles at least once annually. With a majority of two-thirds it may adopt proposals for international conventions, which, however, only become binding after the usual ratification. There is no obligation to ratify, but before the expiry of a year the members must submit the draft proposal to the competent national authorities for decision.

2. The International Labour Office managed by a council of administration which carries on the preliminary administration in the usual way.

In case a member does not duly perform a convention agreed upon, an organisation of workmen or employers may complain to the Office, or another member state may complain to the Permanent Court.

Since the first General Conference in 1919 the International Labour Organisation has displayed a very lively activity. Up to 1937 it had adopted no less than 62 proposals for conventions, many of which have attained ratification on the part of a considerable number of states. The provisions concern the regulation of the hours of work; prevention of unemployment; protection of children, young persons, and women; minimum wages; the right of association; night work; old-age and accident insurance; repatriation of seamen; holidays with pay etc.

II. *Black slave traffic.*

It was after the discovery of America that the slave trade began to flourish in the shape of the importation of cheap labour for the American colonisation work. International efforts to suppress this traffic first found expression in a supplementary declaration to the Vienna Congress Act of 1815. At that time it was not possible, however, to obtain general adherence to the campaign against the traffic in slaves. In the course of the first

half of the 19th century, however, Great Britain in the main
succeeded in attaining this object by a number of separate
treaties granting the right to search vessels and exercise jurisdiction. Later on slavery was prohibited in the United States' national laws and the slave trade thus stopped of itself.

These efforts had been solely directed against the slave traffic
between Africa and America over the Atlantic Ocean. But now,
instead, there arose a slave traffic from the interior of Africa
over land to the Asiatic states. Directed against this was the
General Act of Brussels of 1890, abrogated by the Convention of
St. Germain and replaced by a Convention of 1919 (revised in
1926). In our day slave traffic is no longer of importance.

III. *White slave traffic.*

This cannot unfortunately be said about the so-called white
slave traffic, i. e. the traffic in women for purposes of prostitu-
tion. To combat this several conventions have been concluded to
which a large number of states have agreed. The League of Nations has also concerned itself with this question.

IV. *National minorities.*

General International Law imposes no duties on states towards
their own citizens. The treatment of these comes entirely under
the "reserved domain" which does not concern other states. If
there are national (linguistic, religious) minorities within a state
this condition is unsatisfactory. The state of origin, (the state
with which the minority feels itself to be associated in
nationality), will be interested in extending protection to the
minority for the preservation of its national peculiarity; and
the community of nations as a whole will be interested in a legal
regulation on general humanitarian principles and for the maintenance of peace. For experience has shown that minority problems are one of the most lively sources of hatred between nations and thus of war between states. It has therefore been
attempted at different times to remedy this by the making of
treaties concerning the protection of certain national minorities.
But such a special arrangement will never be satisfactory. The
general interests connected with the problem are of such grave
import that a universal solution is required.

While in earlier times religious differences were the decisive
factor in the formation of minorities, in our day it is national

feeling which occupies this place. In Europe, at any rate, purely
linguistic or religious minorities rarely occur.

The question as to what is the decisive factor in the *birth and
existence of a nation* and by what criteria a person's nationality
can be determined is a far-reaching and difficult problem which
I shall not go more deeply into here.

"Any attempt to define and delimit the term "nation" (from a
socio-cultural, not a political point of view) by some universally
valid criterion is wrecked both on theoretical and practical
difficulties. What conception of culture should be made the
point of departure — the socalled "higher" literary, or the
popular culture? In the former case the limits must be much
wider than in the latter. And to what cultural similarities must
we attach decisive weight? Race and descent as the foundation
have long since been exposed as myths as far as the mixed po-
pulations of Europe are concerned. The higher intellectual
culture can hardly be used as the basis for a collective unit
which is also to include the lay population which has no immediate share in these cultural treasures. Religion which has
been much stressed by earlier authors is no longer any strong
influence, and a national feeling of solidarity is able to conquer differences of creed. As a rule the language is now emphasised as the most important factor from a cultural point of
view. The "culture nation" is defined as a nation having a
certain language. To this the following objections may be
raised: a) For the broad masses dialect is undoubtedly more
important than the standard languages which to a certain extent are artifical products; tribal states, not national states
would correspond to this. — b) Other cultural factors such as
customs, a common material culture etc. form a strong tie among
the general public, and national feeling often finds it difficult
to overcome these differentiating tribal and local forces (the
traditional contrast between Bavaria and Prussia). c) Linguistic
differences may be of subordinate significance (Switzerland) or
at least less strong than the national solidarity (Belgium).

We do not for that reason mean to deny the reality of the
"culture nation". It certainly exists as a social psychic reality,
and E. Schopenhauer swept it aside with too easy a gesture when
he designated nationalism as "the passion of fools". But a
nation in this sense is a unit based on will, as to whose foundation of facts no universally valid judgment can be passed.
Many historical factors may contribute to make a number of
people feel that they are a nation and the decisive factor is not
the same everywhere. The Frenchman H. Hauser rightly calls

the will to national unity "les residu de l'histoire commune", and Zangwill with a very picturesque expression calls the psyche of a nation "a palimpsest of cultures and religions". The one-sided stressing of the language has no theoretical warrant, but is due to political and practical reasons and so only occurs under special circumstances. The French, German, and Italian Swiss do not think of associating cultural or national claims with their different mother tongues ..... linguistic differences need not separate the people of a state (Switzerland); but a will to political unity or independence fed by other sources uses the language as a rallying point for assembly or opposition (the Czechs in the Austria of the Hapsburgs, the Danes in the former Northern Slesvig) — It depends to a great extent on the policy of the state whether linguistic differences become topical as problems of nationality.

We can go a step further. The positing of state and nation as two different quantities which are to be made to harmonise is not right in this absolute form. The historical factors that lead to the rise of a nation do not work independently of the state, but the state unit may itself as a strong factor contribute to the formation of a nation. The Swiss at any rate are so strongly marked by their special form of democracy that we must ask whether they are not for that very reason an independent nation isolated from Frenchmen, Germans, and Italians". (*Theodor Geiger*, Sociology 540—41 and 541—42, author's translation).

After the first world war an attempt was made to create a European law for minorities. Geographically, however, it had no great extension, especially because the chief victorious powers did not themselves assume any obligation, and by its content, too, it was not very satisfactory. Later developments have indeed turned this chapter of the growth of International Law into mere history. As, however, we are here concerned with an interesting new formation relating to a problem which will undoubtedly come up again in the reconstruction of Europe, it will nevertheless be in place to give in its main lines the European law of minorities during the epoch of the League of Nations.

This was in the main[1] based on the four peace treaties with the conquered countries with the exception of Germany (Austria, Bulgaria, Hungary, Turkey), partly on five special treaties concerning protection of minorities between the Principal Allied and Associated Powers on the one side and various of the states

---

[1] *Verdross*, Völkerrecht § 62.

established or stabilised by the aid of these powers on the other side, viz. Poland, Czecholovakia, Yugoslavia, Roumania and Greece. In addition six states have by declarations made to the Council of the League of Nations in connection with their admission to the League undertaken similar obligations, viz. Finland, Albania, Lithuania, Latvia, Esthonia, and Iraq. Finally a number of bilateral treaties have been concluded between various central European states. The treaty with Poland of June 28. 1919 can be regarded as the model treaty the contents of which have in the main set the standard for the rest of the obligations towards minorities. The remarks that follow refer to this standard content.

A. The *form* of protection. — By these treaties a number of obligations were imposed on the states in question with respect to national, religious, or linguistic minorities within the territory of the state. But these obligations were formulated in such a way that *no corresponding rights* were created either for *the minority* as such, *its individual members,* or the *state of origin,* if by rights in this connection we mean the right to institute proceedings for the purpose of demanding that the obligation be fulfilled or responsibility be asserted. For the right to institute proceedings belonged solely to a power that was represented in the League of Nations. The treaties must therefore be regarded as agreements in favour of the minorities as to interests, but in favour of the powers which are at any time represented in the Council of the League as to proceedings.

The members of the minority themselves, their state of origin, and likewise any other state only had a so-called *right of petition,* i. e. a right to call the attention of the Council of the League to supposed encroachments. But their appeal was an act without legal effects. If the Council or one of its members did not want the matter pursued the plaintiff had no means of obtaining a decision. On the other hand, the Council was invested with authority to give instructions if its assistance was requested so that, if a dispute arose, the case could be referred by the Council or one of its members to the Permanent Court for a binding decision.[2]

It is easy to see that, if only for this formal reason, the protec-

---

[2] The treaty with Poland of June 28. 1919; Art. 12.

tion must be defective. The interests of the minorities were subjected to the administration of the powers represented in the Council and subject to political arbitrariness. They had not even any guarantee that their complaints would be thoroughly and impartially examined, and notably they had no means of being informed of the allegations of their opponent in the usual forms.

B. The *content* of the protection. —The treaties contained no definition of the term minority. This gave rise to great uncertainty with respect to the important question as to how it should be determined that an individual belonged to a minority. The choice here lies between a purely *subjective* criterion, a declaration that one belongs to a certain nationality; purely *objective* criteria (birth on a certain territory or descent from persons born there, notorious inclusion under a nationality at a certain time or descent from persons thus included, the language etc.); or a *mixture* of subjective and objective criteria, the declaration being made the foundation but in such a way that it can be tested. A survey of the practice of various states, especially in connection with the education laws would seem to show that at first there was a disposition to start from purely subjective criteria but that the development has moved towards mixed or even purely objective criteria.[8] This leaves the way open for arbitrariness and abuse on the part of the ruling state.

---

[8] Under the German-Polish Treaty on Upper Silesia of May 15. 1922, Arts., 74 and 103, the possibility of belonging to a minority depends on a declaration which cannot be tested; likewise under the agreement between Poland and Czechoslovakia of April 23, 1925, Art. 13. Under the Danish Elementary National School Act for the South Jutland provinces, No. 192 of March 15. 1939 § 16, the language used in the schools depends on the language spoken by the people in that district, but if 20 % of the voters who have the right to elect the members of the School Board in the school district, representing at least 10 children bound to attend school, vote in favour of German as the language of instruction, arrangements are made that this can take place for those who wish to take part in it. Such instruction is, however, also to be established even if the request for it is only made by a smaller number of the above-mentioned electors of the school district, if on the other hand these represent at least 24 children bound to attend school, unless distances are such that these children can be referred to another school where the German language is used.

In the towns (§ 17) the elementary school is divided into two sections, of which one uses the Danish, the other the German language and parents and guardians can freely choose between them.

The treaties only deal with the protection of *persons* belonging to a minority and thus do not recognise rights for minorities as juridical persons. Notably minorities are given no right of self-administration within the state.

The protection was formulated partly as *relative* rights, that is to say, merely as claims for equality with the rest of the citizens of the state, in such a way that a discrimination because a person belonged to a minority was excluded; partly as absolute rights.

As to the first point we may mention the maxim that all citizens were to be equal before the law, enjoy the same civil and political rights, and altogether the same treatment and guarantees legally and actually — all without any difference being caused by race, language, or religion. Notably the minorities were to have the same rights as others to establish and maintain at their own expense, social institutions, especially *private* schools, with the right to use their own language and with liberty of worship.[4]

Of course it was of importance to have this *maxim of equality* firmly established. Its recognition excludes obvious discrimination. Nevertheless such a rule does not mean much in practice. For it will always be possible, where good will is lacking, to evade such a claim by setting up other criteria which would in reality lead to a discriminating treatment, for instance criteria attaching weight to domicile, education, linguistic proficiency, the possession of landed property etc. It is merely necessary to find some criterion, the application of which, in most cases at any rate, would give the members of the minority a lower status than others. It is true that the demand that the equality shall be not only legal but also actual implies a prohibition of evasion. The Permanent Court has repeatedly had occasion to emphasise this point of view and to establish that a measure which is formally universal but actually directed against the minorities means a violation of the treaty.[5] But the demand for actual

---

Thus Denmark has introduced an exceptionally liberal education legislation for the minority, which rests entirely on a purely subjective decision (voting and parents' or guardians' wishes).

The Prussian school law of Dec. 31, 1928, was also based on a declaration which could not be tested or disputed, but after the national socialists came into power in 1933 this principle was no longer recognised.

[4] The treaty with Poland of June 28, 1919, Art. 7, 1st and 2nd clauses, and Art. 8.

[5] See *Oppenheim*, International Law, I. 572, Note 1.

equality can never exclude the setting up of technically well founded criteria, even though these may actually be detrimental to the minorities, for instance a demand that an applicant should know the chief language of a country in order to obtain a post in the service of the state. But this makes the limits vague, and the violation of law is rendered dependent on an intention to evade which often cannot be proved.

As *absolute* rights may be mentioned:

1. Full protection of *life and liberty*.[6]

2. Liberty of *worship*, that is, the right to the free exercise of religion, both privately and publicly, if it is not incompatible with public order and decency.[7]

3. Liberty of *language*, that is, the right to use any language in private as well as in commercial and ecclesiastical affairs, both in the press, in publications of all kinds, and at public meetings. This is not meant to exclude the recognition of an official state language, but persons speaking a foreign language are then to be provided with suitable facilities for using their own language in law courts.[8]

4. In towns and rural districts where a considerable part of the population belongs to a minority the following rights must further be secured to them:

a. *Instruction* in the elementary school in the minority's own language (but not necessarily by their own teachers).

b. A suitable share in the *public means* granted for education, ecclesiastical purposes, or social aid.[9]

§·46
HEALTH

I. *Infectious diseases.*

Modern man lives longer than his ancestors did. An improvement in public health is a characteristic feature in modern history. The plague — the black death — once ravaged the countries periodically as an unpreventable natural catastrophe. We who know the nature of infectious diseases can only with difficulty picture to ourselves the terror of the plague in those

---

[6] The treaty with Poland of June 28, 1919, Art. 2 Clause 1.
[7] l. c. Art. 2, Clause 2.
[8] l. c. Art. 7, clauses 3 and 4.
[9] l. c. Art. 9.

days; the ever lurking danger which came out of the unknown, spread according to unknown laws, and in the presence of which men were quite powerless. It is computed that in the 14th century about one-third of the population of Europe perished from this disease. Great epidemics of plague devastated Europe in 1599, 1626, and 1657.

Till well on in the 19th century every country tried to protect itself from the worst infectious diseases — especially plague, cholera, and yellow fever — by rigorous quarantine measures which, as a kind of local barriers, were to guard the territory. Gradually it was understood that the common foe must be fought in common and the campaign must begin in the countries where these diseases originated. The opening of the Suez Canal (1869) and the resulting livelier communication with the Asiatic sources of infection were the signal for various international conventions by which an international sanitary police was created for the superintendence of the sanitary arrangements in the East, as well as a co-operation among the various states as to precautionary measures. The *International Office of Public Health* in Paris is at once to be notified of every case of the plague, cholera, or yellow fever.

By the Covenant of the League of Nations, Art. 23. f, the members bound themselves to take international precautions for the prevention and repression of disease. To fulfil these provisions the League of Nations has created a *sanitary organisation* which can support the various governments in their efforts and promote international co-operation. This organisation has further studied the ways of combating the most widespread diseases such as malaria, tuberculosis, syphilis, leprosy, sleeping sickness, and various infantile diseases.

The disease which was once a scourge to Europe, the plague, has now been driven back and is confined to a narrow area of Asia.

II. *Intoxicating drugs.*

An important task has been the protection of man against the destructive forces in man himself. The abuse of alcohol, cocaine, morphine, heroine, and other narcotics, has in certain countries caused even greater havoc than the worst diseases. It is a well-known fact that already at the beginning of the 19th century China made strenuous efforts to wrest its population from the clutches of the opium habit, but that these efforts were power-less in the face of commercial interests and the utter corruption of Chinese officials. In 1906 another attempt was made by China, this time with more success. The result was the International Opium Convention of 1912, later, under the auspices of the League of Nations, supplemented by the conventions of 1925 and 1933 (accepted by a great number of states) which bind the member states to a gradual suppression of the production of and trade in opium and at the same time introduce a certain inter-national control.

The six North Sea powers are signatories to the Hague Con-vention of 1887 for the suppression of the trade in spirits on the North Sea (floating inns). Agreements have also been concluded prohibiting the importation of and trade in spirits in the greater part of Africa.

§ 47
PRIVATE INTERESTS

I. *Literary, artistic, and industrial proprietary rights.*

As previously mentioned (§ 28. II), the general law does not prohibit discrimination to the detriment of foreigners. But while the development fairly quickly led to foreigners being largely put on an equal footing with the country's own citizens in civil law, the prevailing state of things until towards the close of the 19th century was that foreigners were without legal pro-tection of their literary, artistic, and industrial proprietary rights. In order to remedy this state of affairs, a *Union for the Protection of Works of Literature and Art* was founded at Berne in 1886. It is based on the maxim that the members extend to the citizens of other states the same protection as falls to the country's own citizens under the national laws, regardless of whether or not the work is protected in the homeland.[1] Later on the convention, which has gained general adherence, has been revised several times, the last time at Rome in 1928. The Union has a permanent Office at Berne.

On the same principle a *Union for the Protection of Industrial Property* (patent and trade mark rights) was founded in Paris

---

[1] Arts. 4 and 5. The Convention also directly guarantees the author various rights.

in 1883, likewise with its office at Berne. The convention was last revised at the Hague in 1925.

Thus these conventions have the character of extensions by treaty of the general law relating to aliens.

II. *Measures for the promotion of agriculture and other industries.*

Common interests have led to international co-operation for the combating of certain dangers especially to agriculture. For this purpose an *Agricultural Institute* has been founded (Rome 1905) and conventions have been concluded for the suppression of grasshoppers, aphides, and plant diseases. Further we may mention agreements concerning the regulation of the hunting of seals and whales.

§ 48
IDEAL CULTURE INTERESTS

For the promotion of mutual understanding various states have made special contracts concerning co-operation, especially with respect to university, archival, theatre, film, and radio matters. Between Argentina and Brazil an agreement has been made concerning the revision of schoolbooks on history and geography, by which the states bind themselves to remove from these books such narratives as are apt to "create antipathy in the defenceless mind of the young against another American people."

Further an attempt has been made to organise a universal intellectual co-operation. With the aid of the League of Nations an *International Institute for Intellectual Co-operation* was founded in Paris in 1925.

In this connection we may also mention various conventions for the suppression of obscene publications.

§ 49
ASSISTANCE IN THE CONDUCT OF LEGAL PROCEEDINGS

The states generally give each other assistance in the conduct of legal proceedings, both in civil and in criminal cases, for instance by the copying of legal documents, the hearing of evidence, or other procedural acts, police co-operation for the tracking and surrendering of criminals. A great number of bilateral treaties deal with these subjects, especially treaties concerning the *execution of sentences* and the *extradition of criminals*.

In addition, there are some few collective treaties, such as the Civil Procedure Covention of 1905 which have laid the foundation of inter-European legal assistance in civil cases.

Chapter XI

VIOLATION OF THE LAW. RESPONSIBILITY

§ 50

LEADING VIEWS

In the preceding chapters we have mentioned the — preliminary and central — international rules of law that regulate
the intercourse between states. They are derived partly from
general International Law, partly from treaties between two or
more states. In the last analysis they all aim at laying down a
certain conduct as a duty for a state. As previously mentioned
(§ 2. II), a legal duty to act in a certain manner means that this
conduct is "demanded" of the party bound, in the sense that if
he does not comply he may (under certain conditions) be made
responsible. The primary rules stating the duties are therefore
actually only fragments which — if they are to be real norms
— must necessarily be supplemented by *secondary norms which
establish responsibility*. It is the latter which will be dealt with
in the present chapter. That a state is actually responsible if it
fails in its duties appears unambiguously from the practice of
the states and is implied in many judicial decisions. To deny
this would indeed be the same as denying to International Law
all character of law.

A. Since all legal duties "demand" a certain human conduct,
and since all international legal duties are incumbent on states
(we here disregard some few other subjects of International Law),
the fundamental ground for a responsibility is that a state
should have performed an action (or failed to perform an action)
which objectively — that is to say, viewed apart from certain
concomitant psychological circumstances (cf. below) — conflicts with the primary rules imposing the duty and thus violates
certain interests intended to be protected by these rules. Such an

act is called an *objectively illegitimate act* and the violation of the interest caused by it is called an *objective violation of the law*.

In order to decide when this condition is fulfilled it is of course in the first place necessary to know the norms that impose duties. For it is these which are supposed to be violated. But this is not enough. And that for two reasons. First because these only apply with a number of general, objective, reservations which it would be too much trouble to detail at the mention of each separate norm and which are therefore given here once for all as correctives which must be applied by the reader himself to each individual rule presented in the preceding part. Our concern is here with circumstances which exclude the normal objective illegitimacy of an act. Secondly, because it is necessary to know what human acts are ascribed to a state as performed by it. All acts without exception are, we know, performed by individuals. If we are to be able to speak of the state as a collective unit there must be certain human actions in contradistinction to others which according to certain rules are ascribable to the state and therefore can form the basis of responsibility.

Hence, summing up, we may say that the fundamental condition for an international responsibility is the occurrence of an objective violation of the law, for which it is required:

1. that an act (omission) should have been performed which is *objectively* in conflict with the primary norms of International Law imposing duties not covered by the general *reservations*. The norms have been mentioned in the preceding part. The general reservations are presented here (§ 51).

3. that the action should have been performed by a person under such circumstances that it is *ascribable* not to himself but to a state (§ 52); and

3. that this has caused a *violation of interests* which the international legal rules are intended to protect (§ 53).

B. But even if this fundamental condition has been fulfilled it cannot be taken for granted that it will give rise to international responsibility. In certain cases at any rate guilt (*culpa*, i. e. intention or negligence) on the part of the state is further required, that is to say, on the part of the person whose action is ascribed to the state. We may then distinguish between the state's responsibility for injury by guilt, and its responsibility for injury without guilt (§ 54).

C. When the above-mentioned conditions are present, that is to say, when there is an objective violation of the law which may perhaps be ascribed to the state as a delinquency, it is a matter of course that some one will be held responsible. This gives rise to two more questions:

1. *Who incurs* the responsibility? Normally of course that state is responsible which has committed the violation of the law. But this is not always the case. A distinction may be drawn between the state's responsibility for its own acts and the state's responsibility for the acts of other states (§ 55).

2. Who can *make* the state *responsible*? (§ 56); and

3. What is the *substance* of the responsibility? (§ 57).

§ 51
OBJECTIVE VIOLATION OF THE LAW
CIRCUMSTANCES WHICH EXCLUDE THE NORMAL
ILLEGITIMACY OF AN ACT

Normally an act is illegitimate when it conflicts with the international norms that impose duties. These norms, however, are only valid with certain general reservations, that is to say, there may be special circumstances which abrogate the normal illegitimacy of an act. These are:

I. *Consent.*

While in internal law consent only to a very limited extent cancels the normal illegitimacy of an act, it must be assumed that in International Law any violation may be made legitimate by consent. Thus for instance occupation of the territory of another state is prohibited, but becomes legitimate if consent is given. It is a condition, however, that the consent should be given *prior to or simultaneously* with the illegitimate act. A succeeding consent cannot do away with the fact that a violation of the law has taken place. It only means that the offended state waives its right to enforce responsibility in the case.

As to the *validity* of the consent the same rules apply as for treaties. Thus especially consent is valid even if compelled by war. If, on the other hand, the compulsion itself conflicts with the law the enforced consent is without significance.

In all cases it is a condition that there should be real consent and not merely passivity in the face of inevitable facts.

Consent has no influence on the possible illegitimacy in relation to other states of the act committed.

Consent may in itself be in conflict with the law in relation to other states or at any rate may involve the loss of rights.

II. *Self-defence.*

Even internal law recognises that acts committed in self-defence to avert an *illegitimate attack* which has *commenced* or is *impending* are legitimate. In this situation it would evidently be impossible to expect that the party attacked should wait and try to obtain his rights by asserting them before the courts.

The same must be all the more valid in International Law where there is no organised administration of justice to turn to. This is, indeed, generally recognised even if the rule is often erroneously masked as a fundamental right to self-assertion or existence (§ 34). A state therefore can meet any attack on its territory, citizens, ships, etc. with force.

The prerequisite for legitimate self-defence is that the attack should be objectively illegitimate. It follows that the attack must be ascribable to a state. On the other hand, it is not required that the attack should impose responsibility. This is of importance in cases where responsibility is conditioned by guilt.

If the act of self-defence goes farther than to avert the attack we have excess of self-defence, which may sometimes be legitimate as a reprisal.

III. *Reprisals.*

If an attack has been *terminated* internal law demands — apart especially from pursuit *in continenti* — that the offended party should not take the law into his own hands but should seek redress through the state's organised administration of justice. The same demand cannot be made in International Law, seeing that there is no such administration here. It is therefore generally recognised that a state which has been exposed to attack is allowed to counter the violation by another violation for the purpose of enforcing reparation, and/or preventing future repetitions. Such an act is called an act of reprisal. An act of reprisal is thus different from a simple act of revenge. It must be based on an intention to protect the rights of the state. This entails various limitations to its legitimacy.

In the first place, there must be grounds for claiming reparation, that is, there must be a violation which is not only objectively illegitimate, but also *imposes responsibility.*

In the second place, the use of force naturally implies that the delinquent will *not voluntarily* accept the responsibility. It is therefore indispensable to the legitimacy of reprisals that the offended party should first in vain have requested the other party to make reparation. If the responsibility is disputed, it would further seem reasonable to demand that the offended party must not have rejected a proposal for legal settlement.

Finally, the object being legal protection, it is required that the act of reprisal should not be *out of all proportion* to the violation that has given rise to it. On the other hand, it is not required that the act of reprisal should be directed against benefits of the same kind that were the object of the violation that gave rise to it.

These conditions, which were formerly only based on a general sense of justice, have now been expressly affirmed by an arbitral award pronounced in 1928 between Portugal and Germany (the *Naulilaa* case). In 1915, while Portugal was still neutral in the first world war, an incident occurred in Naulilaa — a Portuguese station on the boundary of German Southwest Africa — in which three Germans were killed. As an act of reprisal the Germans sent an expeditionary corps on to Portuguese territory, attacked several frontier stations and drove the garrison out of Naulilaa. In connection with this event a rising occurred among the natives, which the Portuguese had great difficulty in putting down. The tribunal denied the legitimacy of the German action because none of the three above-mentioned conditions for the legitimacy of the act of reprisal could be considered to be fulfilled. The incident must be considered to have arisen by a misunderstanding without responsibility on the part of Portugal; Germany had not applied to Portugal for redress; and the German repressive measures were obviously out of proportion to the cause.

Besides the above-mentioned conditions laid down by general International Law, narrower limits to the right of reprisal may be drawn by treaty. Here we may especially mention the 2nd Hague Convention of 1907 (the *Drago-Porter Convention*) according to which the use of armed force — that is to say, military reprisals, especially pacific blockade — for the recovery of debts must only take place when the debtor state refuses to agree to settlement by arbitration or fails to carry out the arbitral award.

Measures of reprisal may naturally be of many different kinds. They need not be directed expressly against the offending state and its interests, but may also be aimed at the citizens of that state and their interests. Much employed in practice are embargo on ships of the nationality of the opposed party, temporary occupation of parts of the territory, especially a port, perhaps in connection with seizure of customs revenues or of property, especially ships on the open sea belonging to citizens of the delinquent state; and finally the so-called pacific blockade. The latter, which has especially been used by strong maritime powers, consists in an express interdiction against sailings to and from the blockaded area, maintained by force by means of warships, so that ships breaking the blockade are seized and detained. It is now recognised that the blockade cannot legally be maintained towards the ships of a third state, but this limit can be transgressed by establishing a state of war.

Reprisals may consist both in positive intervention and in the failure to carry out obligations, for instance the payment of national debts (negative reprisals).

It follows from the purpose of the act of reprisal that the property that has been seized is restored to the owner if the offending state gives satisfaction. In the opposite case the property may be confiscated for damages.

Sometimes it may happen that military reprisals assume dimensions similar to what is generally understood as war. This may give rise to difficult problems as to where the line should be drawn between reprisals and war in an international legal sense, which, however, do not come within the scope of this work.

Reprisals are naturally most frequently carried out by stronger states towards weaker ones and may be regarded as an *intervention* (§ 32) backed by the intention of legal protection. But this intention cannot alter the fact that reprisals, like all other intervention and exercise of force, approach the limit of the province of law, with a tendency to pass into pure politics. Viewed from the angle of legal ideals it is at the outset an anomaly to extend a legal sanction to private arbitrary power. But if once this has been found necessary, as in International Law, it is, on the other hand, difficult and a source of fresh anomalies to set legal limits to the exercise of absolute power. An enforcement of justice which is in the hands of the offended party and depends on his physical resources is difficult to distinguish from a quite arbitrary exercise of power without any legal drapery. The anomaly lies in the fact that International Law stands powerless in the face of such exercise of violence as war. Hence an illegal act of reprisal can always be made legal if the state unilaterally declares that there is a state of war. Thus when in 1901 America protested to England and Germany because of certain measures which these states thought of taking towards Venezuela in the shape of a pacific blockade these states evaded the protest by declaring that there was a state of war between themselves and Venezuela.

The role of the law, if it tries to regulate political forces without possessing any real power, will easily be to serve as a decorative drapery when that is most convenient and to be trampled upon when that seems more convenient.

IV. *Self-preservation in emergencies.*

The common fact which, in the two above-mentioned cases — self-defence and reprisals — caused a suspension of the usual restrictions on the liberty of action is an objectively illegitimate attack on the part of another state. This fact explains, on the one hand, that the extension of the liberty of action *depends on its direction:* it can only be resorted to against the attacking state; and, on the other hand, that its extension in that direction then indeed *goes very far.* Its range is mainly determined by the consideration for what is necessary in order to resist the attack or obtain reparation, regardless of whether the injury caused by the counter-attack exceeds the benefit violated.

Good grounds can also be given for a suspension of the restrictions on the normal liberty of action even though there may be no illegal attack, if this action is necessary *to avert an impending injury* to the interests of the state. We can then speak of the exercise of the right to self-preservation in emergencies. In that case it does not matter whence the danger comes. It may be an illegitimate attack on the part of a third state, human attacks that cannot be ascribed to a state, or danger simply following from the laws of nature without the interference of man. As examples of the two latter situations may be mentioned an attack by private individuals during a riot which the state is not able to avert, and a famine threatening the population.

It follows, on the one hand, that, in contrast with the above-described situations the act of self-preservation in emergencies *is not determined as to direction:* the intervention may be directed against any one. On the other hand, its range is *very limited.* Of course a state cannot be allowed to fail to fulfil its normal obligations merely because it would be inconvenient to it. In conformity with general legal principles it must be demanded that there should be urgent, immediate distress which cannot be relieved in any other way, and that the threatened benefit should patently and considerably exceed in value the benefit sacrificed. On the other hand, it cannot be demanded that the existence of the state should be imperilled. Finally, the blamelessness of the other party demands that an *indemnity* should be paid for the intervention. With respect to the three above-mentioned situations the following may be noted.

If the danger comes from the attack of a third state the belligerent may, for instance, in case of urgent necessity requisition and use rolling stock belonging to neutral states (5th Hague Convention 1907, Art. 19). The belligerent may likewise, if lacking tonnage, requisition neutral freighters present on its territory (right of angary). In both cases we have special positive applications of the principle of self-preservation in emergencies which will also cover other violations of neutrals.

If the danger springs from natural causes, for instance famine, the seizure of food-stuffs will be justified as a measure of self-preservation. Such a case occurred in 1795 when a British cruiser, during a threatening famine in England, seized the American ship *Neptune* and brought the ship with its cargo into an English port.

Finally, if the danger is due to private individuals it will often be difficult to draw the line between self-defence and self-preservation in an emergency. Since the state is objectively bound, as far as lies in its power, to avert attacks against other states or their citizens on its territory (§ 28. II), the distinction depends on whether or not the state has been able to do so. In the former case we have an objectively illegal act (whether or not the state is without guilt and so not responsible) and so we have self-defence, in the latter case we have an attack which cannot be ascribed to the state and so self-preservation in an emergency. In practice, however, there is probably no reason to attempt to draw this difficult distinction, as it seems reasonable to treat all cases of attack, even on the part of private individuals, according to the principle of self-defence.

In practice these cases occur especially in two typical situations. Either a gang is formed on foreign territory for the purpose of attacking a foreign state. Or foreign citizens in a state are molested by private individuals (internal disturbances, revolts and the like, cf. § 28. II). In both cases it is recognised in practice that in an emergency the threatened state may itself intervene on foreign territory to protect its own interests.

As an example of the former situation we may mention the well-known *Caroline* case in 1838. During a rising in Canada a group of rebels had armed and organised themselves on the American side of the Niagara river, and prepared to attack Canada from there on a small steamer called the Caroline. The British authorities received news of the matter, started an expedition which took the offensive on American soil, in which procedure some American citizens were killed and the ship sent down the falls. On that occasion a dispute arose between the British and American governments, but the parties agreed as to the principles on which the legitimacy of an act of self-defence must be judged, namely that there must have been "a necessity of self-defence, instant, overwhelming, leaving no choise of means and no moment for deliberation"; and that the act do not exceed what is necessary for self-defence. (Formulated by the American minister for foreign affairs *Daniel Webster*). This situation was judged on the principle of self-defence not on that of the right of self-preservation in an emergency, and it was indeed quite beyond doubt, as shown by the circumstances, for the American state would not only have been able objectively to avert the attack but had even been guilty of neglect.

As an example of the latter situation may be mentioned a number of instances in which British and American men of war sailed up Chinese rivers to protect the life of their citizens during riots. In the Spanish civil war, too, several maritime powers sent men of war to the Spanish waters to protect their nationals.

I think it beyond doubt that both groups must be judged according to the principle of self-defence, even though the state concerned was unable to protect the foreigners. This is of importance partly with respect to the extent of the admissible measures of defence and partly with respect to the question of compensation.

V. *Legitimacy of otherwise prohibited acts by their usefulness.*

In relation to internal law it has been shown in Scandinavian theory that prohibition of acts which imperil benefits to which others are legally entitled must be interpreted with the general reservation that when the danger is slight, illegitimacy can be abrogated owing to the usefulness of the act in other respects. Thus many of the ordinary avocations of life and the pursuit of many an occupation are not entirely without danger to others. Nevertheless these acts, because of their usefulness, must be regarded as legitimate. In the concrete case they are judged on the one hand by the greater or less usefulness ("importance") of the act, on the other by the greater or less probability of danger. In the same degree as the usefulness of the act increases, the greater must be the probability of danger if a duty to omit the act is to be demanded. This is the true core of the Scandiavian doctrine of illegitimacy. Only, it has not been realised that here we have one more general reservation in addition to the others for the exclusion of the normal illegitimacy laid down by the legal rules, but it has been thought possible to base the concept of illegitimacy directly on the principle of balancing usefulness against danger.

Owing to the primitive and formalistic character of International Law (§ 31) a reservation of this kind will hardly play any important role in international questions.

§ 52
OBJECTIVE VIOLATION OF THE LAW: ASCRIPTION TO A STATE

As states alone are capable of international duties the existence of an objective violation of the law, as we have already pointed out, implies that the act which by its effects conflicts with the international norms imposing duties — interpreted with the reservations indicated — shall have been performed by a person under such circumstances that the act is ascribed, not to himself but to a state. The question then arises what human actions can be ascribed to a state, or — since the ascription normally involves responsibility — for the actions of what persons is the state responsible?

In principle this question is generally answered by enquiring through what persons the state usually expresses its *will*. A state, it is said, expresses its will through its organs, and it is then held that in so far as a state according to International Law is responsible for other than lawful actions by its organs, it must be held responsible for the acts of others.

This view is objectionable. As we have previously seen (§ 2, VI), the notion of a collectivity as a subject of law furnished with its own "will" only means that the subject imposing and the subject incurring the responsibility are different persons associated in a community of interest. An act performed by X involves a sanction against Y. In that case the collective whole (X, Y) is said to be the subject of law and X the organ of the collective whole.

If it is taken for granted that only acts carried out by the organs of a state can be ascribed to that state, this actually means that the basis is the *constitutional* rules of state law concerning the solidary connection between action and responsibility. For the organs of the state mean precisely those persons who accord-ind to their legal status in the state and the rules of state law are able to act effectively on behalf of the state, that is to say, with responsibility for others than themselves. But the question as to whose actions the state is responsible for — exactly like the question as to what agreements are binding upon the state (§ 37. I) — is a question directly concerning *International Law*. It is a question of "competence to violate the law", exactly like the "competence to conclude treaties".

The question must then be answered directly on the basis of International Law. It is the latter which determines whose actions can be ascribed to a state in the sense that they constitute the normal basis of the international responsibility of that state. (The normal basis, because it may happen that the state becomes responsible for the actions of other states, i. e. for such human actions as normally entail responsibility for other states).

Now, International Law answers this question to a certain extent by *referring* to the rules of national law concerning the status of a state organ. The reference, however, does not extend so far as in the case of the competence to conclude treaties. For

while as a main rule a state organ only binds the state by agreement when it has acted within its legal competence, the opposite is the case here.

The starting point is that a state is responsible for its *organs,*
for its organs *only,* and for *all* its organs.

A state organ may act in three different manners:

(1) Within its legal competence. It has carried out just that
function which according to the law in force it is required to
carry out;

(2) Exceeding its legal competence, yet externally as a state
organ, i. e. within the field of that kind of business which it is the
duty of an organ of this kind to take charge of. Examples: A
constable takes a person into custody without a warrant, a man
of war carries out a bombardment without instructions, a judge
passes a sentence in evident conflict with the law of the land.

(3) Entirely beyond the functions of which the organ has been
ordered to take charge, whether pretending to execute a state
function or acting in a private capacity. For instance: A clergyman takes a person into custody, soldiers plunder and rape.

Of course a state is responsible in the instances mentioned
under (1). Further it is a fixed rule in the practice of states that a
state is also responsible in the situations mentioned under (2).[1]
In certain cases the responsibility is even extended to group (3).

At the outset it may seem unreasonable that a state should be
held responsible for actions carried out by its organ beyond that
organ's legal competence. The reason is to be found in similar
considerations to those underlying the rule of the responsibility
of an employer for his servants. The decisive factor in both cases
is that the action has been performed during the service. The
responsibility must, then, go with the interest, whether or not
the organ (the servant) has exceeded its competence (his instructions).

If the action has not been performed in its service, on the
other hand, the state as a rule will not be responsible. Thus a
state is not responsible for manslaughter committed for private
reasons or similar actions which fall outside not only the actual
but also the apparent competence of the organ.[2] However, by
the Hague Convention of 1907 on the Laws and Customs of

---

[1] See *Eagleton,* Responsibility of States, § 18.
[2] See *Strupp,* Das völkerrechtliche Delikt, 42, Note 6.

War on Land, Article 3, it is expressly laid down that a belligerent power is responsible for all actions committed by persons belonging to its armed forces — hence also for acts, which, like looting and robbing, have nothing to do with the military service. There is, I think, a tendency to let the same strict rule of responsibility apply in peace time to military organs.[3]

As previously mentioned, the state is responsible for all its organs whatever state function they perform, and whether they are regarded as organs of the state or of a subordinate community (municipalities and the like). The notion sometimes met with, according to which a state is only directly responsible for its international organs, is just as baseless as the one that the government alone and the organs controlled by it should be able to make the state responsible, and after the Codification Conference at the Hague in 1930 both must be regarded as conflicting with the view of the states themselves.

According to this a state is in the first place responsible for its *legislative power*, either because it has made laws conflicting with International Law or — more frequently — because it has failed to enact the laws necessary if the state is to fulfil its duties. With respect to the first point it should be noted that a law does not conflict with International Law because it renders possible an act conflicting with International Law and that, altogether, international interest attaches less to legislation as such than to the concrete actions resulting from it (administration and jurisdiction). It will therefore be relatively rare that a law viewed in isolation will constitute a violation of International Law.

On the other hand, a state will in many instances become responsible for actions carried out by the *executive* (and thus, in so far as the action is legitimate, indirectly for the legislation of which it is a result). Most frequently it will be the actions of the executive which will conflict with foreign interests, for instance: police invasion of the rights of foreigners, encroachment on foreign territory, the failure of the administration to fulfil treaty obligations, the exercise of compulsion against exterritorial persons, etc. etc. The responsibility is incurred both for superior and subordinate organs, but only for the exercise of actual

---

[3] See *Oppenheim*, International Law I, 163; *Strupp*, Das völkerrechtliche Delikt, 39. Note 5.

governmental power, thus it does not apply to officials in the economic concerns carried on by the state, such as railways, forestry and the like.

In the same way, though less frequently, the state may also incur responsibility for its *administration of justice* (and thus, in so far as the acts of the courts are legitimate, for the state of law conditioning these). The courts are state organs as well as all others and the conception that the responsibility of the state should be excluded owing to their independence of the government is based on the erroneous implication that the state is only directly responsible for its government.

In so far as the courts keep to the law of the land a judgment conflicting with International Law is merely a concrete manifestation of a state of law conflicting with International Law. In the opposite case we have an independent judicial violation of the law. In this connection it is usual, in textbooks on International Law, to give an account of the demands that International Law must make on the courts of a nation in the exercise of their function in relation to aliens. It is clear, however, that this question does not concern the formal rules of responsibility, but the material rules of conduct, and it has therefore been treated above in the international law of aliens (§ 28).

Conversely, the state is only responsible for its organs, not for the conduct of *private individuals*. The medieval view of the state as solidary with each of its citizens has since the time of *Grotius* been superseded by the view that the state is an organisation of the group, not the group itself, and that it is therefore only responsible for its organs. If nevertheless responsibility can be incurred by the state owing to the injurious acts of private individuals, for instance during internal disturbances, (assaults on foreigners, civil war and the like) this is due to the fact that the state has a certain duty to prevent such actions and failing this, afterwards to prosecute the delinquents. If the state neglects its duties it incurs responsibility for the omissions of its organs. But the responsibility is then a responsibility for the state's own organs, not for the actions of private individuals. These are only the external occasion that calls into being certain duties for the state.

Here too it is usual in the current doctrine to continue with an account of the duties of the state for the protection of aliens against encroachments on the part of private individuals. But these rules also belong to the material law and have therefore been dealt with earlier in that connection.

§ 53
OBJECTIVE BREACH OF THE LAW:
VIOLATION OF INTEREST

The condition essential to international responsibility is not only that an action should have been committed which, conflicting objectively with the law, can be ascribed to the state, but further that by this means such interests have been violated as were intended to be protected by the norm trangressed. Only then is there an objective violation of the law in relation to the state which represents the violated interest, and only then therefore can the latter make any claim to reparation. Hence it is necessary that an injury should have been done which is objectively caused by the action conflicting with the law. No more is required of this causal connection for a violation of the law to have come into existence. It is otherwise when later on it is to be decided for what consequences of the illegitimate act the state is responsible.

It follows that a state cannot hold another state responsible merely by referring to the fact that the latter has violated general International Law or a collective treaty of which the other state is one of the signatories. If, for instance, a belligerent state violates another state's neutrality only the neutral that has been injured can hold the other party accountable, not other neutrals by a reference to the mere fact of a violation of the principle *pacta sunt servanda*.

On the other hand, it is by no means necessary that the damage done should be of a *material* kind. Notably the violation of the dignity of other states will also be taken into account. According to the circumstances it is even conceivable that any assault conflicting with International Law may have the effect of a violation of the dignity of the assaulted state, in which case any question of further consequences will fall away.

§ 54
SUBJECTIVE IMPUTABILITY: GUILT AND INJURY

Whereas in the theory of civil law it is agreed that the normal basis of responsibility is determined by the *culpa* rule it is highly controversial whether the same applies to International Law. The current doctrine since *Grotius* holds that culpability in International Law too is normally indispensable to responsibility. But recently various authors, especially the Italian *Anzilotti*, have maintained that this is an unwarranted transference to International Law of the rules of civil law. According to the principles of International Law the element of culpability is unimportant; the state is quite objectively responsible for any damage caused in conflict with the law.[1] Others, however, as for instance *Strupp*, hold that culpability is a prerequisite in violation of the law by omission, not by positive acts.[2]

The explanation of this disagreement about a point theoretically so fundamental, is partly to be found in the special nature of the facts of International Law. The typical estimate of culpability expressed in ordinary linguistic usage by such terms as "neglect", "due diligence" and the like only comes into play in cases in which there are norms *materially limiting the liberty of action,* with due consideration for the consequences of the action for the interests of others. The practical *bonus pater familias* estimate, then, is at the same time concerned with a weighing of the objective justifiability of the action and a subjective estimate of the psychological attitude of the performer of the action at the moment of action. Often culpability has one-sidedly been identified with the subjective element, and it is then said that there is culpability when the acting person at the moment of action realised or ought to have realised that the action had the qualities which made it conflict with the law (unjustifiable). But in whatever light this theoretical factor is viewed it is clear that the practical determination of culpability in contrast with the accidental *(casus)* only acquires its actual typical significance in instances in which the justifiability of the action depends on its immediate or more remote consequences for the interests of others. In the case of actions which are *formally* prohibited by certain direct signs of the action itself, for instance

---

[1] *Anzilotti*, Droit international I, 496 f.
[2] *Strupp*. Das völkerrechtliche Delikt, § 7.

a prohibition against walking on a lawn, the problem of culpability is much simplified and in most instances does not arise at all in practice.

Now, as previously shown (§ 31), the facts as regards International Law are generally as follows. The rules of general International Law have the character of such formal norms of competence as outwardly delimit the living space of the states without respect to the further consequences of the action. Thus for instance the rules concerning territorial supremacy.. Encroachments on foreign territory are formally prohibited. This will in great part explain that there can be such disagreement in theory about the problem of culpability, though seemingly the question has not given rise to similar difficulties in practice.

To this must be added that the opponents of the rule of culpability do not appear to have realised in what the problem consists. Since the action conflicting with International Law has always been committed by a person who is an organ of the state, the question must be whether the action is to be ascribed to the organ as his culpa, that is to say, whether the organ has acted in a manner unjustifiable under International Law and at the moment of action realised, or ought to have realised, that the action was of a kind that made it unjustifiable under International Law. This has nothing to do with the evaluation of the action according to national law. Both *Anzilotti* and *Strupp* overlook this, each in his own way. Anzilotti thinks that culpability is excluded when the organ has acted legitimately according to national law, because in that case it is not to blame according to national law. Conversely, Strupp is of opinion that culpability is excluded when the organ has gone beyond its lawful competence, because in that case the action and the culpa cannot be attributed to the state according to national law. Thus both points of view lead to a groundless denial of the importance of the element of culpability in certain circumstances.

It is probably right to say that International Law — through the acceptance of a generally recognised legal maxim — *as a main rule* makes the culpa rule the basis of responsibility, though it *does not acquire the same practical importance* as in civil law, partly because many of the norms of International Law are formal norms of competence in which the question of guilt in most cases falls into the background; partly because in international relations due diligence must be strictly demanded so that responsibility is often taken for granted without any special discussion of the question of culpability. The latter question is of special importance for the legal acts of a state (laws, decrees, acts of administration, judgments, etc.), since it must be assumed that the organ ought always to realise the international significance of these acts, so that the result will practically be the same as a quite objective responsibility.

As a matter of fact, it is obvious from the practice of states and international judicial decisions that a number of cases may be mentioned in which the responsibility of the state is plainly associated with negligence on the part of its agent. As an example may be mentioned the responsibility of a state for offences against aliens where the decisive factor clearly is whether the organs of the state have failed to do what was required in the circumstances in order to protect the aliens in a satisfactory manner from threatening dangers or to prosecute delinquents (§ 28. II). It would be quite arbitrary to restrict culpability to apply to omissions only (Strupp). And, as a matter of fact, it was stated by the British-American commission in the *Cadenhead* case (1914) that the state does not incur responsibility by a police organ's accidental killing of an alien. Conversely, examples may also be given of decisions which establish responsibility without guilt. In the *Costa Rica Packet* case[8] (England—Holland 1891) an English captain was charged with and imprisoned for the theft of some cases of gin etc. from a derelict boat by a court in the Dutch East Indies. It turned out, however, that — contrary to the information given to the court — the theft had taken place outside Dutch territorial waters. The Russian authority on International Law, von Martens, who was arbitrator, sentenced Holland to pay damages on that occasion. The decision has, however, been severely criticised.

The culpa rule does not of course exclude that International Law — like civil law — in certain cases recognises responsibility for damage without culpability, as for instance in the 4th Hague Convention of 1907, Article 3, according to which a belligerent state is responsible for all acts committed by persons belonging to its armed forces.

---

[8] *Moore*, Intern. Law, § 148.

§ 55
VICARIOUS STATE RESPONSIBILITY

When a state has, in the manner above-described, violated International Law, international responsibility will arise. Normally of course this responsibility is incumbent on the state which has committed the breach of law. For the function of the rule of responsibility is to create a motive for refraining from conduct which is in conflict with International Law. Normally, therefore, it will be absurd to hold one state responsible because another has committed an illegitimate act.

There are instances, however, in which, according to International Law, a state incurs vicarious responsibility. In these cases, then, the subject of the delinquency and the subject of responsibility are not identical.

I. *Delimitation of the problem: Vicarious responsibility is present even if the acting state is without international capacity of action.*

According to the current view the problem does not include those cases in which the acting state, for instance a member of a federal state, has no international capacity of action. It is then held that the member state does not come into consideration at all as a subject of International Law, and that the responsibility of the federal state is responsibility for an action of its own.

This view is due to a misinterpretation of the conception of international capacity of action. As already mentioned in § 15, that concept signifies capacity to binding oneself in relation to other states by one's own legal acts, especially treaties, and the capacity conditioned thereby to send representatives to these. A state may lack capability of action. On the other hand, *no state can lack capacity of delinquency*, that is to say, capacity to bind itself (or in exceptional cases others) by its own breaches of the law. So far as the state is self-governing it is the state and the state alone which has the power of action and is thus able to comply with the law or break the same; it is necessarily the subject of conduct and also normally the subject of responsibility. And, indeed, there are obviously no grounds for concluding from the fact that a member state cannot conclude

17*

treaties that it cannot, either, be held responsible for a violation of the law.

Hence, if in such circumstances the federal state is nevertheless made responsible we are confronted with a case of vicarious state responsibility.

On the other hand, *only states* are capable of delinquency. Thus if the act has been committed by a municipality or another subordinate community without self-government, it must be ascribed to the state to which the municipality belongs and there is no question of vicarious responsibility.

II. *Delimitation of the problem: Vicarious responsibility does not occur in cases of complicity owing to coercion or leadership.*

On the other hand, a number of situations must be segregated in which there is apparently vicarious responsibility and which are also often treated from this angle. It follows from general principles of complicity that a state becomes responsible for its own acts if it *compels* another state to violate the law. This point of view holds good whenever there is a relation of dependence which has actually abolished the liberty of action of the state coerced, whether the coercion has a narrower or a wider application. As steps in a sequence may be mentioned: coercion aimed at an isolated act of a nation otherwise independent (as when Russia in 1911 forced Persia to dismiss the American reconstruction expert Morgan Shuster); coercion temporarily directed against liberty in certain domains of life (e. g. a military occupation in which the country's own government is retained); coercion as an expression of a permanent and comprehensive dependence so that actually there is only a pseudo-state without real self-government (e. g. Holland under Napoleon in 1810). Whether the state thus coerced is in these cases at the same time freed from its responsibility must depend on the character of the coercion in the circumstances.

What has here been said about coercion must likewise be true if one state appears as the lawful *leader* of another state, that is to say, if the first state not only externally represents the other state and carries out independent political decisions but also conducts its foreign affairs according to its own judgment and in its own interest. The leading state is then directly co-responsible for the acts, e. g. illegal withdrawal from a treaty, which it carries out on behalf of the other party. It follows that the protector state in the complete protectorate (§ 15) is directly responsible for the acts which it commits in the name of the protégé state, and similarly the federal state, in so far as it acts on behalf of the member state.

III. *Vicarious responsibility may be based partly on control, partly on protection.*

There are two leading points of view which may explain that in exceptional cases a state A may be held responsible *without complicity* for actions committed by a state B.

A.   One is that B is in such a relation of dependence on A — legally or actually — that the latter is able to exercise regular *control* of the actions of B, at any rate within a certain domain. Even if A has not in the given case directly co-operated in the performance of the act — on which assumption there would be complicity and direct responsibility — it would nevertheless be reasonable to hold A responsible because A has the real control of the action. The party who has the power must also accept the responsibility (the *control theory*).

B.   The other point of view is that there exists a relation of dependence between A and B, A *protecting* B's interests as his own, and therefore any attempt on the part of a third state to force responsibility on B must count on meeting resistance on the part of A also. Because A thus bars the way to making B effectively responsible A must accept the responsibility itself. When the fleet and army of the U. S. A. prevent the effective assertion of responsibility for Louisiana, the U. S. A. must itself bear the responsibility *(protection theory)*. This point of view is of special importance for a federal state in which any violation of the rights of a member state — whose population and territory constitute parts of that of the federal state — must necessarily at the same time be an invasion of the rights of the federal state. Nevertheless, it is not as supposed by *Verdross*[1] and several others (in the so-called *encroachment theory, Eingriffstheorie*) this circumstance in itself which underlies vicarious responsibility. If this were the case we might with the same

---

[1] *Verdross*, Theorie der mittelbaren Staatenhaftung, Zeitschrift für öff. Recht, Bd. XXI (1941) 302, 308.

right deduce a vicarious responsibility for the member-states
with respect to the actions of the federal state. The political
protection is the really decisive factor.

C. These points of view will explain the recognition in the
practice of states and in international judicial decisions of the
vicarious responsibility of a *protector state,* a *federal state* and
a *suzerain* state respectively for the protégé state, the member
state, and the vassal state.[2] In the two latter cases the responsibility is unlimited according to the protection theory. In the
first case the responsibility will be restricted to the extent to
which the protector state actually has protected or been able to
exercise control of the protégé state. (It will be recollected that
the protector is directly responsible for acts it has performed
itself in the name of the protégé state, cf. above under II).

In practice, however, there would seem to be a tendency, in
protectorate relations also, to make the responsibility unlimited
on the ground that to the outside world the protector state *represents* the protégé state.[3] This practice is evidently inspired by
the current doctrine motivating vicarious responsibilty, the
decisive feature — according to *Anzilotti* — being that a state
taking charge of another state's foreign affairs represents that
state to the world (the *representation theory*). Apart from the
circumstance that this theory obviously does not cover all cases
of vicarious responsibility it is in itself without any convincing
power. The mere fact that a state A acts towards the outside
world on behalf of a state B cannot, according to ordinary legal
principles, afford grounds for a responsibility for A, any more
than the fact that a guardian or agent acts on behalf of another
can make these persons responsible for the minor or the person
assigning the authority. If weight is attached to the fact that A
undertakes the representation on his own judgment and in his
own interest, this, as already stated, will lead to a direct responsibility for A with respect to the representative acts. Beyond
that only the control or protection underlying the representation can afford grounds for a vicarious responsibility. The
theory has insisted on a normal external symptom and not gone

---

[2] Cp. l. c. 285 f.

[3] See l. c. 290 and the arbitral awards mentioned there in the cases *Adolph
G. Studer v. Great Britain* (1925) and *Reclamations britanniques dans la
zone espagnole du Maroc* (1925).

to the heart of the matter. The above-mentioned tendency in practice is therefore only justifiable if it can be considered to be sufficiently grounded in the control or protection theory.[4]

The correctness of these points of view will appear from a consideration of a relationship such as that which existed between Denmark and Iceland under the Danish-Icelandic law of union (1918—44). Denmark represented Iceland to the outside world, but it was in the interests of that country itself and according to its own instructions, cf. § 15. B. Since Denmark did not, either, exercise any control or protection in Icelandic affairs, it would have been absurd to impose responsibility on Denmark for violations of law on the part of Iceland.

§ 56
WHO CAN MAKE STATES RESPONSIBLE?

As previously mentioned (§ 2. IV), according to the concept of International Law there is nothing to prevent individuals from being recognised as subjects of rights. Actually individuals are also to a great extent subjects of interest. On the other hand, according to current International Law individuals are not, apart from a single exception, recognised as subjects of legal proceedings (§ 16).

This means that according to the current law *states and states only* are competent to make other states internationally responsible, and especially to appear as parties in proceedings.

But even through it is thus established that individuals cannot themselves hold states responsible, nevertheless various associated questions will arise in this connection which can be solved in different ways. We refer especially to the following:

(1) When it is assumed that not the individual himself but only his home state can hold another state responsible, what point of time is then decisive for the national status which determines what state is the competent home state?

---

[4] Denmark was the only state to, in her reply to a questionnaire as the basis of the Codification Conference of 1930, accept with reserve the theory that international responsibility always must be ascribed to the state which represents another, even though in her reply she did not see clearly the relations determining when there is responsibility and when there is not. See Société des Nations, conference pour la codification du droit international, Bases de discussion t. III, p. 122.

(2) Can the individual with binding effect renounce his right to protection and the claim to responsibility resulting from it?

These questions are generally answered on the basis of metaphysical suppositions as to who possesses "the right itself" as something which is different from the functions of positive law and supplies the basis in which these rest. There are supposed to be two alternatives. Either "the right itself" belongs to the state. In that case the nationality at the moment when the violation of law was committed is decisive, since otherwise the state has not been injured through its citizen. And the individual cannot renounce protection. Or else "the right itself" belongs to the individual and the part of the state is restricted to the representation demanded by the law. In that case the nationality at the time when the proceedings are instituted must be decisive, for otherwise the state does not represent the plaintiff. And the individual may renounce his right to protection. The consensus of opinion is in favour of the first possibility, evidently on the metaphysical view that rights are the substantial counterpart of duties; when the international duties are incumbent on a state it must also possess the international rights.[1]

However, to a practical view of the law these ideas are without any justification. The questions put above should be answered on the basis of practical considerations alone, which may favour one or the other arrangement, while no interrelationship between them is necessary.

On the position in practice the following comments made be made:

I. *What point of time is decisive for the national status?*

The views indicated are *combined* with the result that it is demanded both that the injured person should be a citizen at the moment the damage was done, and that he should since have preserved his citizenship up to the moment when the proceedings were instituted. This rule of course is very inadequate. In case a change of nationality occurs in the interval, no state, either the original home state or the succeeding one, will be competent to take proceedings.

---

[1] Cf. the judgment of the Permanent Court No. 2, p. 12, and the Danish government's reply to the questionnaire Point XIII in the publication quoted in § 55, note 4, p. 141.

II. *Can the injured party renounce his right to protection or his claim against the injuring state?*

Independently of dogmatic constructions general legal maxims would seem to indicate that a *renunciation at the outset* of protection of one's rights is invalid. Hence the *Calvo clause* named after the South American statesman Calvo, is invalid, in so far as it states that a foreigner renounces the right to call upon the diplomatic protection of his home state against the state in which he is resident. This is indeed now recognised in practice. On the other hand, in so far as the clause states that diplomatic protection must not be called upon before the local remedies have been exhausted, it is superfluous, as this follows already from general International Law.

III. *The rule of local redress.*

We have here touched upon an important maxim for the possibility of making a state responsible as a result of a violation of the law. According to this, opportunity is to be given to a state that has violated the law to repair the damage by means of its own law machinery before it is made internationally responsible — of course provided the local legal system warrants legal remedies for this purpose. If for instance a foreigner thinks that his property has been illegally confiscated, diplomatic intervention cannot on that account be called for before his appeal for redress through the courts of the country in which he is resident has proved without avail. This can also be expressed thus. A violation of the law is only regarded as temporary and without international consequences as long as the culpable state has not had an opportunity to redress the wrong through its own judicial organs. This rule must be considered a happy one, since it gives the culpable state an opportunity of freeing itself in a convenient way, while it avoids making the matter an international question.

There are, however, limitations to the rule. If the offence is aimed *directly at a foreign state* (invasion of territory, offences against its dignity and the like) it is not to be expected that the latter will first seek redress in the courts of its opponent — quite apart from the fact that in such cases there will often be no legal way of obtaining redress. This limitation is a natural counterpart to the rule of the exterritorial rights of foreign states.

Further the rule does not of course apply where there is *no (further) legal remedy*[2] because the offence has been committed by a supreme state organ against whose actions there are no legal means of redress, for instance if the offence consists in a denial or distortion of the law by a court whose judgment cannot be appealed.

Finally, it is acknowledged that the plaintiff need not go to law when experience of similar cases has shown that it must at the outset be regarded as *hopeless* to appeal to the local courts. It is absurd to refer any one to the law when there is no law. You cannot gather roses where no roses grow.

§ 57
IN WHAT DOES THE RESPONSIBILITY CONSIST?

I. *Reparation or compensation.*

International responsibility consists in a duty either to repair the damage done or yield compensation, usually determined as an equivalent of the loss suffered, though it may also at the same time have a penal character.

While, according to the maxims of civil law, an injured party may incertain cases, but far from always, obtain a decree for specific performance, a state is always under International Law, so far as it is possible, bound to make restitution in kind. Thus for instance an act conflicting with the law must be repealed, a person unlawfully imprisoned must be set free, occupation of a country must be discontinued etc., and the state is not able to free itself by offering compensation instead. International claims are always in principle of such a political character that they are incompatible with a compulsory transformation into a pecuniary claim. An exception must be made, however, when the offence does not concern important state interests if redress would entail disproportionate disadvantages. This might be conceivable, for instance, if a foreigner had been subject to an illegal judgment, final according to national law, the repeal of which would therefore imply a change in the constitution (cf. *City of New Orleans v. Abbagnato* (1894), § 6 III).

If full redress in kind is not possible or would involve ex-

---

[2] For further light on this question see *Algot Bagge's* arbitral award in the *Finnish-British shipping dispute* given on May 9, 1934.

cessive disadvantages, or if the injured party agrees, compensation may be substituted for it.

II. *The extent of the liability for compensation.*

This must be decided according to general legal principles. Both by theory and practice there has, especially formerly, been a tendency to distinguish between direct and indirect injury. Some have held that the liability for compensation only comprises direct injury and think that the well-known *Alabama* award lends support to this view. Others have disputed that interpretation and asserted that the liability for compensation applies to every injury which can be demonstrated to be causally connected with the violation of the law that has taken place. As has been realised in recent civil law theory, this distinction is erroneous. It expresses in the wrong way the right feeling that responsibility cannot include every remote and accidental consequence of the illegal act. It is probably right to say in accordance with the recent Northern doctrine of compensation that the responsibility comprises the consequences which are a normal realisation of the visible injurious tendencies of the action. Consequences which were not to be reckoned with at the moment the damage was done, as well as consequences brought about by causal elements of the same kind, therefore fall outside the responsibility. The idea appears to be the same as that which is expressed by the mixed German-American Claims Commission when it says that "all indirect losses are covered on the assumption only that Germany's action from a juridical point of view was the decisive and nearest cause and source from which they flowed."[1]

It is for the consequences of its internationally illegal actions that the state is responsible. When the action consists in the failure of the state to prosecute individuals who have committed injurioius acts it will as a rule be difficult or impossible to demonstrate damage as a consequence of the negligence of the state. Nevertheless, the responsibility of the state has as a rule in practice been measured by the damage caused by the private individual. If for instance a murder has been committed, to which the state is not an accessory owing to negligence, the state is nevertheless responsible for the loss of the breadwinner if it

---

[1] Cf. *Eagleton*, Responsibility of States, 201.

does not in due course prosecute the perpetrator in order to punish him. The compensation has here the penal character of an expiation.

III. *The nature and estimation of the compensation.*

In cases of *material* damage a pecuniary compensation is fixed, measured by the general economic value of the damage.

In *immaterial* injuries — which are of much greater importance in International Law than in civil law because many directly material offences at the same time involve offences against the dignity of another state — the compensation may take many different shapes. No fixed rules exist either for its kind or its estimation. The shaping of the claim must be left to the judgment of the injured party, within reasonable limits determined by general international ideas (the international standard).

We are here in all cases concerned with acts or contributions which in one way or another are suited to satisfy the outraged sense of justice and may act as a moral reparation. As examples from the practice of the states may be mentioned: An *apology,* often in a ceremonial form, for instance by sending special envoys of expiation, the rendering of *honours* to the outraged state or the offended individuals (salutes to the flag, a funeral service with military honours, trooping of the colours, erection of a monument); *punishment* (dismissal) of the delinquent and proclamation of this to the population; *preventive* measures (the enactment of laws and interdictions to prevent repetition); measures of *control* (access to control of the prosecution and bringing to justice of the delinquent and the like); *a penalty,* i. e. a pecuniary reparation which besides being a compensation for damage done has also a penal character.

It is clear that the stronger the wronged state is compared with the delinquent the wider can it be tempted to open its mouth, and it may be difficult to distinguish a legal claim on the other state from purely political claims.

To illustrate the way in which claims for redress are formed in practice we may quote — from *Eagleton* — the claims made on Greece by the Conference of Ambassadors on the occasion of the murder of General *Tellini* and others in 1923. He was an Italian who had been charged by the Conference of Ambassadors with co-operating in the demarcation of the boundary between

Greece and Albania. He was murdered on Greek territory by unknown persons from ambush (the *Corfu* affair).

(1) Apologies shall be presented by the highest Greek military authority to the diplomatic representatives at Athens of the three Allied Powers, whose delegates are members of the Delimitation Commission;

(2) A funeral service in honor of the victims shall be celebrated in the Catholic Cathedral at Athens in the presence of all members of the Greek Government;

(3) Vessels belonging to the fleets of the three Allied Powers, the Italian naval division leading, will arrive in the roadstead of Phaleron after eight o'clock in the morning of the funeral services;

After the vessels of the three Powers have anchored in the roadstead of Phaleron the Greek fleet will salute the Italian, British and French flags, with a salute of twenty-one guns for each flag;

The salute will be returned gun by gun by the Allied vessels immediately after the funeral services, during which the flags of the Greek fleet and of the three Allied Powers will be flown at half-mast;

(4) Military honors will be rendered by a Greek unit carrying its colors when the bodies of the victims are embarked at Prevesa;

(5) The Greek Government will give an undertaking to ensure the discovery and exemplary punishment of the guilty parties at the earliest possible moment;

(6) A special commission consisting of delegates of France, Great Britain, Italy and Japan, and presided over by the Japanese delegate, will supervise the preliminary investigation and enquiry undertaken by the Greek Government; this work must be carried out not later than September 27, 1923;

The Commission appointed by the Conference of Ambassadors will have full powers to take part in the execution of these measures and to require the Greek authorities to take all requisite steps for the preliminary investigation, examination of the accused, and enquiry;

The Greek Government will guarantee the safety of the commission in Greek territory. It will afford it all facilities in carrying out its work and will defray the expenditures thereby incurred.

The Conference of Ambassadors is forthwith inviting the Albanian Government to take all necessary measures . . ."

(7) The Greek Government will undertake to pay to the

Italian Government in respect to the murder of its delegate, an indemnity, of which the total amount will be determined by the Permanent Court of International Justice at the Hague, acting by summary procedure ...[2]

The case, however, was never brought before the Court but the Conference of Ambassadors fixed the indemnity at the sum of 50 million Italian lire, a sum, the exorbitant size of which proves the predominantly penal character of the contribution.

If it is once recognised that pecuniary reparation can be imposed as a punishment, the question arises whether other interventions can be used for the same purpose (the occupation of an area etc.). We have here come to the germ of an international penal law.

---

[2] l. c. 187—88.

Chapter XII
THE SETTLEMENT OF STATE DIFFERENCES
(International Process Law)

§ 58
LEADING POINTS OF VIEW

I have mentioned how, in International Law as in any other system of law, the primary norms, i. e. the norms imposing duties, can in the first place be segregated. They describe directly, in terms of rights and duties, the conduct of the subjects of rights which it is attempted to enforce through the legal system.

I have also explained how these primary norms must necessarily be supplemented by secondary norms establishing the responsibility following from the contravention by a subject of rights of the primary norms (Chapter XI).

But a well-developed system of law cannot stop at this. It is not enough to have rules concerning duties and responsibility. The parties will only too readily disagree as to the consequences in the particular concrete cases. Such a disagreement will easily lead to disputes and contentions. If the social peace is to be preserved, it is necessary, therefore, that the discussion between the parties should be brought to an end by a settlement which establishes with authority whether there is responsibility and, if any, of what kind it is in the concrete situation. This settlement should then be given effect with the support of a superior power, to that any attempt on the part of the party declared responsible to continue his dispute with the opponent and offer resistance must at the outset be considered hopeless and doomed to failure.

It is necessary, therefore, that the primary and secondary norms should be supplemented by *tertiary* or *processual norms* establishing the procedure to be adopted in cases of disputes in order to put an end to them by a *settlement* (judgment) which with irresistible power can be *enforced* towards the party involved. These procedural norms imply the existence both of organised courts of law, and of an organised apparatus of coercion (police, prison authorities etc.) which are actually able, at any rate under normal circumstances, to overcome any other manifestation of power in the community in question. It is, in the first place to these state organs, not to the parties to the case, that the procedural rules refer. The courts and the apparatus of coercion act in conjunction as a machinery which, controlled by the procedural rules, bring about legal settlements and enforce them. Sometimes when the rules are contravened this machinery is set going "automatically" — i. e. *ex officio*. Sometimes it is only set going if a party having a right to institute proceedings so desires and takes the necessary steps towards it (citation). But in no case is the function of the machinery dependent on the consent of the opponent to submit to it. The jurisdiction is never "optional".

In International Law this is quite different. There exists no similar interstate legal machinery which guarantees the settlement of every dispute and the fulfilment of every responsibility. But when a dispute cannot be brought to an end there is no guarantee for peace. One day the dispute will break out into open hostility: war.

The attempts that have been made in the course of time to create an international process, that is, rules concerning the procedure in a pacific settlement of disputes, are exceedingly modest compared to the machinery of internal law. In the first place — apart from an abortive attempt in the Covenant of the League of Nations — there is no organisation whatever of the power to enforce the judicial decisions given. Hence all fulfilment of them is voluntary. But further, under general International Law there is no obligation to submit a dispute to decision by a court. Thus all jurisdiction too is voluntary. There are exceptions, however, the states having to a certain extent bound themselves to go to law (obligatory jurisdiction: *arbitral settlement* and *decision by a court*, see below §§ 59—61).

In addition various modes of procedure have developed which without including a legal settlement yet aim at the adjustment of the difference and the maintenance of peace, namely by diplomatic-political methods (*mediation, inquiry, conciliation*, see below §§ 62—65).

Common to all these modes of procedure, legal as well as political, is the circumstance that in principle, that is to say, according to general International Law, they are optional. The only obligation which general International Law imposes on contesting parties is the self-evident and modest one that before they take arms they shall have made an attempt to compose the quarrel by *diplomatic negotiations* with each other.

Thus all international process is based on the *autonomy* of the parties. In order that a certain procedure may be adopted it is implied, without exceptions, that the parties should agree about it. But this agreement may here as elsewhere be more or less direct, consent being given in advance to the carrying out of some arrangement. By previous general treaties a state can undertake an obligation to make certain disputes liable to a certain mode of settlement which thus, viewed in relation to the particular dispute, is of an *obligatory* character. The more comprehensive this obligation is and the more the procedure has been institutionally fixed in advance the more will the autonomous arrangement in practice approach a purely authoritative arrangement. Though it is in both cases in principle based on the autonomy of the parties, there is an enormous difference between the situation in which the parties voluntarily agree to submit a dispute to a mode of settlement stipulated for that particular case, and one in which a state is cited before the Permanent Court in conformity with a general jurisdiction agreement.

In order to supplement the autonomy of the parties general International Law has in addition developed a number of declaratory rules which likewise contribute to raise the settlement above spontaneous agreement.

Thus two procedures differing in principle are at the disposal of the contesting parties for the settlement of the dispute: the legal way or the political way. The difference between them is in the *remedy:* judicial procedure (arbitration, judgment) on the basis of law (or at least according to the principles of justice and equity, § 59. IV) aims at establishing the legal position and the responsibility; political procedure (mediation, inquiry, conciliation) aims at finding the solution which in the circumstances is regarded as the most opportune, amongst other things because it has the greatest political prospect of being accepted by both parties. The two different modes of procedure need not, as is often supposed, differ in that one is binding on the parties, while the other is not. On the one hand, there is nothing to prevent a party from requesting a judicial decision merely as an advisory opinion; and on the other hand, there is nothing either which can prevent the parties from binding themselves to submit to a decision based on purely political opportunism. This follows from the autonomy of the parties. It can merely be said that according to International Customary Law, failing any other express stipulation, recourse to legal procedure involves an obligation to submit to the decision, while recourse to political procedure does not. Moreover, this is expressly laid down in the Hague Convention of 1907 concerning the Pacific Settlement of International Disputes, articles 37 and 6 respectively. An appeal from the contesting states to the International Court will always make the decision binding.

There is some vagueness of terminology. If we combine the basis of the treatment with its binding or non-binding character, four types will emerge which may be grouped as follows.

	binding	non-binding
legal treatment	arbitration (ad hoc) adjudication (institutional)	advisory opinion
political treatment	"political arbitration" (ad hoc) "political adjudication" (institutional)	mediation inquiry conciliation

The vagueness is due to the fact that the term "arbitration" is also used about binding decisions of a political nature, e. g. the arbitral award pronounced in Vienna on November 2. 1938 by v. Ribbentrop, minister for foreign affairs to the Reich, and Count Ciano, minister for foreign affairs, Italy, on the cession of Czechoclovak areas to Hungary. To avoid confusion the term arbitration in this exposition is used exclusively about the binding decisions of a legal nature. For want of a better term the other form will be called "political arbitration" and "political adjudication".

§ 59
JUDICIAL SETTLEMENT

I. *Its forms.*

As already stated, a judicial settlement may have two forms, *arbitration* and *adjudication* (decision by a court).

Their common object is, as we have previously mentioned, to obtain an opinion on the dispute on the basis of *current law.* Hence there is no question of the tribunal of arbitration as such having greater liberty than a court of law to decide *ex æquo et bono* or to give a frankly political solution. This has not always been recognised. In earlier times a tribunal of arbitration, especially when it consisted of the head of a state, felt freer to act. But gradually the view gained ground that, in the absence of other rulings, reference to arbitration meant that the decision was to be given on a strictly legal basis. This development was confirmed at the 1st Congress at the Hague in 1899, where it was laid down in the Convention for the Pacific Settlement of International Disputes that arbitral awards must be based on respect for the law (Article 15, Conv. 1907 Art. 37). It is another matter that the parties, in virtue of their autonomy, may instruct the court as to the basis on which it must give its verdict. In principle there is nothing to hinder the parties from an even quite arbitrary fabrication of a code. But the more this is done the farther do we get from arbitration as a judicial settlement. If it appears from the character of the dispute in connection with the composition of the deciding body or the other circumstances that the parties wish for a decision of a purely political nature, there will be no legal decision but a "political arbitration". The Statute of the International Court permits the parties to authorise the Court to decide *ex æquo et bono* (Art. 38), but otherwise excludes autonomy of the parties with respect to the basis of the decision.[1]

---

[1] The Permanent Court of International Justice has in an Order of the Court in the case concerning *The Free Zones of Upper Savoy* laid down that the parties cannot in their individual compromise depart from the Statute of the Court (Ser. A No. 22, p. 12). The question as to whether the parties can prescribe the legal principles to be applied by the Court in its adjudication, will therefore depend on an interpretation of the Statute. Art. 38, last paragraph, allows the parties to decide that the settlement should be made *ex æquo et bono.* By way of contrast it seems to me most natural to infer from this that the parties cannot otherwise prescribe the legal principles to

The difference between arbitration and adjudication lies in the *institutional character* of the adjudicating organ; arbitration is the term used when the organ is selected by the parties with a view to the dispute under consideration. Its members are called arbitrators, the organ itself an arbitral tribunal and its decision an arbitral award. A decision by a court is the term used when the organ is a permanent institution established once for all which functions with unchanged composition in all cases coming within its competence. Its members are called judges and its decisions judgments.

Further the Statute of the Court naturally contains fixed rules of procedure which largely evade the autonomy of the parties, whereas the procedure in arbitration can be fixed *ad hoc*. At the Hague Conferences, however, a number of declaratory rules of procedure have been laid down which on this point have contributed to give arbitration a similar institutional character to settlements by a court.

Arbitration and adjudication have each its special advantages and this explains that even after the establishment of the Permanent Court of Justice at the Hague, both institutions exist side by side (Statute of the Court Art. 1). Arbitration offers the advantage that it is possible to choose arbitrators who either possess the confidence of the parties in a special degree or are in possession of special technical knowledge with respect to the case under consideration. The great advantage of decision by a court lies in the fact that it and it alone offers a possibility of creating a continuous practice which will further the consolidation of International Law. Moreover, it is clear that the existence of the instrument prior to the dispute facilitates the institution of proceedings. An arbitral procedure always implies that the parties to the concrete case first agree about the composition of the arbitral tribunal. This is a rock on which the whole procedure may easily be wrecked. The automatic starting of proceedings, that is to say, citation, is only possible before an existing court.

------

be applied. The practice of the Court in this respect does not seem quite unambiguous. In the *Oder Commission case* (Ser. A No. 23, p. 19) it is said that it is for the Court to decide *ex officio* in legal problems. But in other cases (the *Oscar Chinn case*, Ser. A/B No. 63, p. 80, and the *Meuse Waters case*, Ser. A/B No. 70, p. 16) the Court seems to have departed from this principle.

II. *Agreement as to jurisdiction.*

Both forms imply that the parties agree to litigate. An agreement as to jurisdiction is therefore a prerequisite. In cases of arbitration the term arbitration agreement is used. In cases of decision by a court there is no fixed terminology. A jurisdictional agreement would seem a suitable term. But the necessary agreement may be brought about in various ways.

The concord is *spontaneous* when the contesting parties agree to let the question at issue be settled by law. The agreement to do so is called a *reference*, the jurisdiction (arbitration, judicial settlement by a court) *optional*, spontaneous, or isolated.

The concord is *institutional*, that is, it expresses a general arrangement or institution when the parties have bound themselves in advance to let certain disputes be settled by law. In that case the jurisdiction is termed *obligatory* or institutional. The agreement may take the *s h a p e* either of a *clause* in a treaty dealing mainly with another subject (compromise clause) or it may be an *independent* agreement (arbitration agreement, jurisdictional agreement). As to its *c o n t e n t* it may be either *unlimited* or more or less *limited*. According to the contracting *p a r t i e s* it may be either *individual*, that is, concluded between two states only, or *collective*, that is, concluded between a number of states.

As stated above, an institutional arbitration agreement always implies a renewed spontaneous agreement between the parties in connection with the reference of a case to arbitration. For it is necessary to agree as to the establishment of the arbitration court, the subject of the dispute, and in addition, if it has not been previously agreed upon or settled by precepts which the parties can vary, the rules of procedure, the dates for delivering of the pleadings, the basis of the settlement, disposition of money to cover the costs etc. This agreement too is called a reference and might conveniently be called a secondary reference.

III. *What disputes are justiciable?*

A. *Treaties.* — There exist treaties concerning obligatory jurisdiction which are unlimited in their terms. But they are rare and are for the most part restricted to disputes between small states on opposite sides of the globe. Usually agreements as to obligatory arbitration (or jurisdiction) are limited by more or less vague and wide reservations.

Often, especially in treaties concluded before World War I, we find reservations based on the view that the limitation expresses a limitation of the *will* of the contracting states to submit to judicial decision. Thus for instance in the earlier typical conventional reservations with regard to questions touching the national honour, independence, and vital interests of states, likewise reservations concerning constitutional questions, the Monroe Doctrine, territorial integrity, earlier disputes etc.

But since Hague Convention I of 1899 it has become customary to formulate the reservations more in the nature of principles which imply that there are certain disputes which according to their *inner nature* are not suited to be settled by law. The Hague Convention I declared that arbitration was the most effective and suitable means of settling *legal* disputes. Since then this turn of phrase has been embodied in a great many treaties on obligatory arbitration either in combination with or without the conventional reservations. The criterion has especially been adopted in the Statute of the Permanent Court of Justice which, in Art. 36, limits the normal competence of the court to certain specified legal disputes.

This is based on the theoretical view prevalent nowadays that a well-founded distinction may be made between disputes that, according to their inner nature, are suitable for legal settlement and such as are not. The former are called *legal disputes* the latter *political disputes* or disputes as to interests. In accordance with this view it is considered appropriate that agreements as to jurisdiction should be limited to include legal disputes. All such disputes, and such only, are justiciable.

This gives rise to another problem. By what criterion should the justiciable disputes be delimited? Here the agreement ends.

B. *The objective theories.* — An earlier view was based on the idea that the factor deciding whether a dispute was legal or political was whether there existed an international legal norm by which it could be settled. On this view it is the incompleteness of International Law, its "gaps", which is the true reason why certain disputes are not suitable for judicial decision and therefore must be withdrawn from the domain of jurisdiction.

There is a growing tendency to admit that this view is not tenable. The general theory of law teaches that it is a mistake to believe that there can be "gaps" in a legal system in the sense

that it will not apply to a given case, and that the judge must
therefore give up the case with a so-called *non-liquet*.[1] Any
legal claim brought before a court ends in the assertion of a
certain legal duty based on current law. Now either there is a
warrant in the legal system for the duty asserted, — in which
case judgment must be given against the defendant. Or there is
no warrant — in which case the action must be dismissed. Thus
logically the absence of a norm leads to a dismissal of the action,
not to a *non liquet*. The idea in speaking of "gabs" in the legal
system is that the dismissal of the action is offensive to the sense
of justice. The gap therefore is not a real "gap in the law" but
merely a deficiency viewed from a political angle. This theoretical consideration finds support in the practical experience that
no instance has ever yet been registered in which a judge has dismissed a case on the ground that it was impossible for him to
settle it on the basis of current law.

C. *The subjective theories.* — An attempt was then made to
give the criterion a subjective trend. The decisive factor, it was
said, is how the parties formulate their assertions. If they
mutually dispute each other's rights — whether this be due to a
disagreement about the facts or about the interpretation of the
legal rules — the dispute is a legal dispute, whereas it is a
political dispute if the claim put forward has for its object
a change in the existing legal situation or takes no account
of any legal considerations at all. In that case the dispute
can certainly be formally settled by law, but a judicial decision
is of no value because the question at issue does not concern
current law at all. If for instance a state claims the cancellation
of a burdensome treaty, the formal legal validity of which is not
disputed in itself, it is clear that this dispute cannot be put an
end to by a judicial decision which could only confirm once
more that the treaty was legally valid.

In this connection it is worth pointing out that disputes
between states cannot quite simply be compared to disputes between private individuals which, in a state, are referred to the
obligatory settlement of the courts. It is true enough that, if a

---

[1] Cf. *Ross*, Towards a Realistic Jurisprudence, 137—38; Theorie der
Rechtsquellen, XIII, 7—9.

tenant quarrels with his landlord, the courts and the courts alone are competent to settle that dispute. But if all tenants as a group of the population disagree with landlords as an opposed group about the reasonable terms of leases the courts neither can nor will give an opinion on this dispute. The same is true of disputes about wages, taxation, maximum prices, the defence of the country, the system of government, public relief etc. etc. Here as elsewhere, where the interests or views of groups of the population clash — it is for the legislative power to bring the tension to an end by suitable political regulation. If it cannot be done by legislation the antagonism will break out into open strife (labour conflicts).

We learn from this that even if it can perhaps be said that there is a legal way for the solution of every conflict within the state, it is far from true that this legal way always consists in an appeal to the courts in order to obtain a settlement of the dispute on the basis of current law. Not all civil disputes are justiciable in this sense.

This comparison lends support to the view that international disputes also are not all justiciable and that the non-justiciable conflicts are precisely those in which the parties do not dispute each other's rights but for political reasons demand a change in the existing conditions. Thus defined the political conflicts correspond precisely to those which, in a state, are dealt with by legislation. As there is not, unfortunately, within the society of nations any legislative instrument which can smooth out the political difference by adjustment, the result — as they are not suited for judicial settlement — is one of two alternatives: either the two parties come to a political understanding (perhaps employing political means of settlement) or the tension remains until it may break out into open hostilities, war.

In state documents the subjective theory here described was first expressed in the Locarno Acts of 1925 — a number of agreements on mutual guarantee and arbitration, which were to ensure the good understanding between Germany and the western powers. For here the domain of obligatory jurisdiction accords with the subjective criterion defined as "controversies with regard to which the parties are in dispute as to their respective rights". And later on the same subjective formulation has been accepted in a long series of more recent arbitration and conciliation treaties.

It will often happen that one and the same subject of dispute between two states presents a legal as well as a political aspect. That is the case if both parties put forward legal arguments and one or both of them political ones as well. The legal aspect of the dispute is then justiciable, but not the political one.

Further it may happen that a concrete situation of conflict comprises several issues, some of which are justiciable or have a justiciable aspect, while others have not.

D. *Lauterpacht's criticism.* — Among writers on International Law the theory was for a time widely accepted but has since been subjected to a radical criticism by *Lauterpacht*.[2] This author denies every limitation of justiciability ("the function of law") grounded in the nature of the dispute itself. The objective theories are not tenable. But the subjective theories also offer no solution. If justiciability and thus obligatory jurisdiction is to depend on the claims of the parties it will mean that the obligation is rendered illusory. It will then always be open to any party to disregard the legal claims and thus to make the dispute a political dispute, and withdraw it from jurisdiction. A modern treaty on obligatory arbitration in all legal conflicts is in reality not one whit more advanced than the treaties of the old type with the reservations for honour, independence, and vital interests. Then it was merely declared openly that each of the parties could avoid arbitration by reference to these clauses. Now the same arbitrariness is concealed under cover of the theory that according to their inner nature certain disputes are political. The truth is that a dispute is political and cannot be settled by arbitration merely because the parties to it *refuse* to submit to a judicial settlement.

From this Lauterpacht, if I understand him rightly, would draw the further conclusion that as true law International Law must ignore a will that will not submit to law. The law must refer all disputes to be settled in court and cannot make concessions without compromising its own nature.[3] Therefore the author ends by recommending the concluding of unlimited arbitration conventions on the Danish model.[4] He does not

---

[2] Cf. *Lauterpacht*, The Function of the Law in the International Community.
[3] l. c. 372—73.
[4] l. c. 370—71.

indeed think that it will be possible to settle every dispute in this way. But the legal system cannot itself at the outset recognise a will to override its commands. That is logically and legally impossible. Further, the author is of opinion that a good many so-called conflicts of interests might be smoothed out by arbitration or adjudication if the judge could, in greater degree than is now the case, decide *ex æquo et bono*.[5]

E. *Criticism of Lauterpacht.* — In my opinion Lauterpacht is not right in his view that the subjective criterion leads to the arbitrary evading of legal settlement. For if for instance Norway in her dispute with Denmark had wished to avoid a judicial settlement of this dispute, it could only have been done by Norway admitting the correctness of the legal arguments put forward by Denmark. Otherwise the dispute must have been a legal dispute suitable for judicial settlement, which was indeed the way it was settled. But it is clear that it is another and far more dangerous matter for a state openly to admit the right of its opponent than to refuse jurisdiction point-blank. Actually states will ordinarily be afraid to give up a legal basis for their contention and in so far they will be compelled to accept a judicial settlement.

In addition I believe it is unrealistic to maintain that owing to "the nature of law" International Law must logically ignore conflicts of interests and demand a judicial decision in all cases. What is the good of rigorously asserting the duty of a judicial settlement when it cannot be assumed that this duty will be effectively respected? The result will merely be that the law will commit itself by its own powerlessness. It will be a sounder procedure to set narrower and more precise limits to the obligation to submit to arbitration in the hope that the obligation will really be fulfilled.

What the result will be if, inspired by unrealistic idealism, extravagant claims are made for obligatory jurisdiction, is shown by the sad experience gained from the Central American Court established in 1907. Its competence was unlimited. As events turned out, the Court, owing to cetain plans in Nicaragua for giving Japan a concession for the building of another canal to compete with the Panama Canal, became involved in disputes of

_____

[5] l. c. Chapter XV, especially §§ 30 and 31.

a highly political nature. The Court remained true to its judicial function, with the inevitable result that its authority went by the board in the attempt to decide conflicts by law which could not possibly be settled in that way, and so expired with the expiration of the 10-year period for which it had originally been established.

Even if the courts were furnished with the power to settle conflicts of interests *ex æquo et bono*, that is to say, according to free discretionary principles, this way would hardly be practicable. It is not conceivable that the states would be willing, in important matters, to let questions of great political concern be settled by a small circle of juridical experts whose decisions were supported neither by political insight nor by power.

On the other hand, it must be admitted that the criterion "legal dispute or political dispute" which is used in a great many treaties is so vague that much too often it opens up possibilities of arbitrary interpretations and evasions. It would be desirable that it should be more precisely defined by an enumeration of a number of conflicts which at any rate must be regarded as legal. This enumeration must however be much more detailed and precise than the very general and vague categories mentioned for instance in the Statute of the International Court, Art. 36.

Nor will it of course be disputed that it would be desirable that there should be instruments for a binding settlement of pure conflicts of differing interests. Only it must be realised that such a conflict cannot be put an end to by a legal judgment passed by a judicial organ and that the instrument therefore cannot be looked for among courts of justice. What is required is an authoritative adjustment of interests through a powerful political body, acting as an instrument for the common community, i. e. a. "political arbitration" or "political adjudication" which is actually more like a legislative act than a judicial act.

IV. *The basis of judicial settlement.*

It has already been mentioned that when the parties to a dispute submit a matter for settlement they can, by virtue of their autonomy, themselves determine on what the decision is to be based. But when nothing else has been fixed, or if quite general terms have been used, it holds good that the decision, whether it be an arbitral award or a judgment, must be based on International Law. The statutes of a court, however, will generally restrict the autonomy of the parties in this respect.

The parties may specially authorise the court to give a decision *ex æquo et bono*. Such authorisation must at least[5] be tacitly implied as soon as a political dispute is submitted to settlement by arbitration or adjudication. It may then be considered doubtful whether there can be said to be a judicial procedure and settlement at all, and whether such cases should not rather be counted among the political means of settlement, even though they are tried by the usual forms of legal procedure. The reply to this must be that a settlement *ex æquo et bono* does not mean the same as a purely political settlement. The political evaluation merely considers what is opportune and practicable in the circumstances, but a settlement *ex æquo et bono* means a settlement according to the principles of what is fair and just. Even though this settlement is not bound by the rules of positive law it is at least in the spirit of the law, that is, it is based on evaluations of a legal and moral character. In practice this is manifested by the fact that the authority to judge *ex æquo et bono* is given to an organ which is otherwise created to function in the settlement of legal disputes. The fact that several treaties impose first a conciliation treatment of political disputes and then, if this proves abortive, decision by arbitration *ex æquo et bono*, must imply that such a settlement is essentially different from a political settlement. Or else there would be no sufficient reason to transfer the binding settlement from the conciliation commission to the arbitration court.

A settlement *ex æquo et bono* too must therefore be regarded as, in principle, a judicial settlement, even though it only borders on it and, owing to the great freedom of judgment, approaches a political settlement. It is another matter that, as previously mentioned, it can hardly be regarded as a well-suited means of smoothing out political conflicts of a more serious nature.

V. *The binding power of the settlement.*

It has also been mentioned that the obligation to submit to the decision is not conceptually necessary but is, nevertheless, implied if nothing else has been expressly stipulated. A court

---

[5] Cf. above p. 275 on "political arbitration".

will not as a rule, according to its statutes, be able to give advisory opinions to litigants.

An arbitral award, if nothing else is agreed upon, is *final.* The judgments of the International Court are always final. They cannot be appealed.

On the other hand a decision may be *invalid,* and thus lose its binding force. The difference lies in the fact that, while an appeal is only based on the plea that the decision is not right and provides regular access to have the case tried by a higher instance, an objection on grounds of invalidity implies special circumstances which provide a cause for disputing it on general legal principles. In the national administration of justice the question of invalid judgments is practically of no importance owing to the regular access to appeal.

As grounds for invalidity the following are generally recognised:

(1) Acting *ultra vires,* which may occur with respect to:

a. the *matter of the case.* The decision may purport to deal with affairs on which the court is not competent to pass judgment.

b. the *basis* of the decision. The case may be decided without authorisation *ex æquo et bono,* not according to current law. As an example we may mention the arbitral award which the Dutch king in 1831 pronounced in a boundary dispute between the U. S. A. and England. Though the dispute related to the interpretation of a treaty of 1783, the arbitrators decision was based on general considerations of convenience. In this connection it must be called to mind, however, that a decision based on current law warrants the right to take into account general legal principles as well (§ 10. III).

c. the directions for the *procedure in the case,* e. g. the rules of procedure in the Hague Convention or the statutes of a court. It must be supposed, however, that only the contravention of essential rules of procedure, for instance the duty to hear the parties and give grounds for the decision, entails invalidity.

d. The *pleas* of the parties, as it must be supposed that the decision must be kept within the limits determined by these.

e. *Other* instructions the parties may have given for the execution of the task.

The question which, in practice, will most frequently give rise to doubts is certainly that mentioned under a, viz. the problem as to the material scope of the competence. But precisely here a special circumstance will prevent this objection on grounds of invalidity from being raised very often. It is the rule expressly laid down with respect to the International Court of Justice and the Permanent Court of Arbitration which must now be regarded as current customary law, viz. that in the absence of an opposite ruling the Court is competent to decide questions as to the scope of its own material competence.[7] This means that if a protest against its competence is put forward while the case is being tried and the court or the tribunal declares itself competent the matter is settled with binding effect. The final judgment or award cannot then be called in question — apart from the rare case that the temporary decision of competence is itself rendered invalid by one of the other causes of invalidity mentioned below (essential error and patent distortion of the law).

If, on the other hand, the protest is not made till after the case has been settled, it must be possible to dispute the decision and test it in conformity with the existing authorisation. As no pleading has taken place we cannot assume that the decision itself contains a tacit yet binding settlement of the question of competence.

(2) Essential *error*, which may be present with respect to:
a. the legal rules.
b. the facts.

In the last respect the Hague Convention and the Statute of the International Court contain fixed directions for access on certain conditions to a *revision* of the award or judgment if, after the pronouncement, new facts come to the knowledge of a party which may have a decisive influence on the issue.

(3) *Manifest injustice*, that is to say, bribery and other evident corruption.

If a party disputes the validity of a decision and no agreement with the opponent is arrived at this dispute is itself a fresh legal dispute which must be decided in the forms both parties have agreed upon for the settlement of legal disputes. As previously stated, reservations must be made with respect to protests, during the trial, against the material competence of the Court, which are settled at once by the court itself.

---

[7] The Hague Convention for the Pacific Settlement of International Disputes 1899 Art. 48, 1907 Art. 73, Statute of the International Court Art. 36.

§ 60
SPECIAL REMARKS ON ARBITRATION

I. *Historical survey.*

Arbitration was already of considerable importance in the relation between the co-ordinate Greek city states. During seven centuries we know of more than 80 cases of arbitration.

On the other hand, the dominant position of the Roman Empire was not favourable to the idea of arbitration. It was only towards the close of the Christian Middle Ages, from the 13th to the 15th century, during the attempt of the emperor and the pope to exercise a mediating supremacy, that arbitration again came into play. During the succeeding centuries, in the age of the absolute rule of princes, arbitral awards are again very rare.

The modern development of the idea of a legal settlement of disputes between states is rooted in the conceptions of the French revolution concerning individual and national equality and fraternity. In the young American nation especially these ideas met with sympathy, partly in the relation between the states and partly in the relation to the mother country. In 1794 the famous *Jay Treaty* was concluded between the United States and Great Britain. It referred various differences which remained after the secession to arbitral settlement. Since then the idea of a pacific settlement has grown continually in spite of many setbacks. It has been calculated that, in 1913, 139 arbitration treaties and 154 clauses of reference were in force, and that in the period 1794—1913 more than 200 arbitral awards had been given[1]. One of the most famous is the *Alabama* award given in 1872. Nevertheless, it can hardly be supposed that very many of the 200 verdicts have been concerned with questions of such significance that the judicial settlement has prevented a war. But even if arbitration has perhaps not been of very much importance as a measure to prevent war, its value must not be underestimated. At any rate a legal solution has been found for conflicts which would perhaps otherwise have remained unsolved or have had a more arbitrary issue.

At first arbitration was optional, that is, founded on the

---

[1] *Ch. L. Lange,* L'arbitrage obligatoire en 1913 (Bruxelles 1914) cf. *Politis,* La justice internationale, 227, 34.

voluntary agreement of the parties to refer a conflict that had already arisen to legal settlement. A further development was the endeavour to make arbitration *obligatory*, that is, to found it on a binding agreement with respect to future conflicts. In the first half of the 19th century a good many clauses of reference saw the light, but only in 1876 was the first independent treaty on obligatory arbitration concluded between Salvador and other American states.

At the same time another line of development endeavoured to replace the individual treaties by a comprehensive *collective* treaty which was intended to replace at one stroke numerous treaties already existing. Attempts were made in this direction at the two Hague Conferences of 1899 and 1907 convened on the initiative of the Russian Czar. Twenty-six states took part in the first, forty-four in the second. Although the participators proceeded with caution and only contemplated obligatory arbitration for certain particular legal disputes or at any rate with far-reaching reservations for national honour, independence, and vital interests, the attempt was wrecked in both cases on the resistance of Germany. While in 1899 Germany was opposed to obligatory arbitration altogether, it accepted the principle in 1907 but would not agree to a collective arrangement. Both congresses therefore closed with only a general recommendation of arbitration in legal disputes, especially such as relate to the interpretation or application of treaties. The states that in 1907 had declared themselves adherents of a collective treaty on obligatory arbitration attempted to carry the plan into execution themselves but failed, and shortly afterwards the first world war put an end to further developments.

Under these circumstances the institution of arbitration could only continue its development through a great number of individual treaties. The Covenant of the League of Nations also did not contain any rules as to obligatory arbitration for the members. By the Statute of the Permanent Court of International Justice a possibility was opened of common obligatory jurisdiction but no arbitration in the proper sense was here intended. Only the General Act for the Pacific Settlement of International Disputes, adopted by the Assembly of the League of Nations in 1928 and later on ratified by more that twenty states, introduced common rules as to obligatory arbitration in political disputes. In 1929 the American states concluded a collective treaty in Washington on pan-American arbitration. Apart from this the institution of arbitration is still based on individual treaties.

II. *The tribunal of arbitration.*

It follows from the autonomy of the parties that they can make up the tribunal of arbitration as they like. The leading idea of arbitration in contradistinction to decision by a court is precisely that the tribunal can be made up of persons who enjoy the special confidence of the parties or possess special expert knowledge in reference to the case in question.

Formerly it not rarely happened that the head of a foreign state was chosen as arbitrator. The case was then of course prepared by authorised assistents. It turned out, however, that in this way arbitration tended to depart from a judgment on a strictly legal basis and become more in the nature of a politically coloured mediation. This mode of procedure has therefore now been generally abandoned. The usual method at present is for the tribunal to be composed of a mixed commission consisting of an equal number of arbitrators selected by each party under the presidency of an umpire chosen by these arbitrators or, in case of disagreement, elected according to special rules.

The election of the arbitrators, especially of the umpire, may often give rise to difficulties which delay or entirely prevent the submission of a case to arbitration. In order to diminish this difficulty an institution was established by the first Hague Convention in 1899 called the *Permanent Court of Arbitration.* The name is in so far misleading as there is no question of an actual court. The "Court" is in reality only a list of persons suited and willing to undertake the task as arbitrators. At the same time rules are laid down as to how the parties should proceed in the individual cases in order to set up an arbitral tribunal by choosing among the persons on the list. This provides the advantage that the parties, if they agree to refer a case or conclude a treaty on obligatory arbitration, need not lose themselves in the question as to the composition of the tribunal. They can simply refer the matter to be settled by the Permanent Court of Arbitration.

The list is made up by each of the contracting parties pointing out four suitable persons. Shortly before the last war it counted 134 persons representing 41 states. These persons are not arbitrators as such and never meet in pleno as a court.

The parties who wish to submit a matter to the "Court" may themselves decide how the tribunal is to be composed in the case in question by selection from the list. In default of an agreement to the contrary, each party appoints two arbitrators and these in conjunction choose an umpire.

It is a voluntary matter whether the parties will refer the arbitration to the "Court", but the latter is considered competent in all cases of arbitration between the contracting parties in which no other agreement has been reached as to the composition of the tribunal. As the "Court", in spite of the great number of members, yet restricts the liberty of choice in concrete cases, many member states still prefer to establish the arbitration court in complete independence.

The "Court" was not abolished by the establishment of the Permanent Court of International Justice in 1920. A total of 20 awards has been given by it, the last one in 1932.

To the "Court" is attached a bureau at the Hague and a permanent Council for administrative purposes.

III. *Procedure in arbitration.*

This too can be arranged for in every respect by agreement. But it follows from the nature of the case that the provisions relating to procedure in arbitration treaties and clauses of reference are as a rule very few. It is thus necessary to fall back on supplementary rules of procedure derived from legal custom and general principles of law. In order to facilitate and promote arbitration on this point too, a number of rules of procedure were laid down in 1899, simultaneously with the establishment of the Permanent Court of Arbitration. These come into operation if the parties have not agreed to other rules.

The adoption of the rules as such is only binding on the contracting parties, but the main principles of the rules must also be supposed to be an expression of current customary law.

Among the chief rules may be mentioned:

The arbitral procedure falls into two stages: a written inquiry and the oral main proceedings.

The negotiations are as a rule secret.

The tribunal is empowered to decide questions as to its own competence.

The deliberations of the tribunal are secret and the decision is made by the majority.

The award must be accompanied by motives — a rule which is of special importance for ensuring that the verdict is based on current law.

The award is final, but is only binding on the contesting parties. This rule has a special bearing on the interpretation of collective treaties. In such cases each of the signatories has the right to intervene and the award is then also binding on them.

§ 61
SPECIAL REMARKS ON ADJUDICATION

I. *Historical survey.*

Hand in hand with the efforts to develop the institution of arbitration went the endeavour to establish a general Internatiotional Court of Justice co-ordinate with it. Hence it was by no means the intention that such a court should render arbitration superfluous, more especially the Permanent Court of Arbitration at the Hague. The states were still to have liberty to decide what form of legal settlement they preferred. But it was presumably anticipated that if once a court had been established there would be some hope that it would in time win the confidence of the parties and establish its authority to such a degree that arbitration would gradually recede into the background.

It was at the second Hague Conference of 1907 that the plan for the establishment of a real international court was first advanced — by America. The proposal had at first an astonishing success, being accepted by the other great powers, among them Germany also. That nevertheless the plan proved abortive was due to the fact that in spite of many attempts it was not possible for the powers to agree as to how the members of the court were to be elected. The great powers suggested the rotation principle which was later adopted by the League of Nations. According to this, 8 of the 17 members of the court were to be permanently appointed by the 8 great powers, while the other 9 were to be appointed in turn by the rest of the member states according to certain rotation rules which took into account the relative size of the states. But the smaller states, with Brazil at the head, stubbornly insisted on the formal principle of absolute equality and equal rights, which in this situation would lead to each state having its own judge so that the court would consist of 44 members in all. The powers then merely worked out a project for a convention concerning the proposed court — called the Court of Arbitral Justice in contradistinction from the existing Permanent Court of Arbitration — without any rules as to the composition of the court, and recommended the signatory powers to adopt this proposal and establish the court as soon as they should have come to an agreement concerning the election of the judges and the composition of the court. The attempts made later on by a small circle to realise this idea proved abortive, and the outbreak of the first World War temporarily upset all plans.

There would have been a good chance of establishing a universal court of justice already in 1907. It was destroyed by the shortsighted jealousy and rigorous insistence on the false dogma of equality of the small states (§ 34).

At the same congress an attempt was made to establish a special universal court for the settlement of prize cases, *the International Prize Court.* The court was organised as an international court of appeal superior to the national prize courts. It was to be open to appeal from neutral states as well as private individuals. In this case too there was disagreement as to the composition of the court. However, the objections of the small states to a rotation system were overcome, so that 8 of the 15 judges to be appointed were permanently to represent 8 great powers, while the 7 other appointments rotated among the rest of the signatories in compliance with certain rules based on the extent of the maritime interests of the states. The reason for this success is presumably to be found in the fact that the small states in this special case expected considerable advantages from the court, and so preferred to renounce their claim to equal representation. The establishment of the court was then agreed on by the Conference in its 12th convention. It was the first convention in the history of the world on the establishment of a real universal court.

That this convention was never ratified and the court accordingly never came into existence was due to hesitation, especially on the part of Great Britain, in connection with the defective development of material International Law. In the convention it was determined that the adjudication of the court was to be based on the rules of International Law or, if such were lacking, on general principles of justice and equity. Since however there did not in 1907 — any more than now — exist any well-developed generally recognised material prize law, there was a fear of the discretionary power which was thus put into the hands of the court. The court would in reality become on international legislator. In order to make up for this deficiency a conference on maritime law was convened in London in 1909 on the initiative of Great Britain. Its task was to lay down general international rules concerning the position of neutral ships during war at sea (blockade, contraband, unneutral services etc.). The result of this was the London Maritime Law Declaration of 1909 which, however, especially because of the resistance of the British House of Lords, was never ratified. This sealed the doom of the prize court.

Before this, however, the first International Court, though for a very limited group of states, had come into being. It was the *Central American Court* of Justice established in 1907 between Costa Rica, Guatemale, Honduras, Nicaragua, and Salvador, with obligatory competence in all disputes between these states. This comprehensive competence was the very cause why the court broke down while handling tasks which in reality were outside the scope of legal settlement, and so ceased to exist with the expiration of the decade for which it had been founded.

The object, a general international court, was not attained until 1920. According to Article 14 of the Covenant of the League of Nations the Council was to work out a proposal for the establishment of an International Court. Accordingly, a commission of jurists was appointed at the first meeting of the Council for the purpose of drawing up a proposal for the statutes of such a court. The commission gave a unanimous report which, with few changes, was adopted by the Assembly. The establishment of the court under these statutes was adopted in a protocol of December 16th 1920, which was then ratified by a very large number of states.[1]

---

[1] Up to June 15th 1939 the following states have ratified the protocol of 16/12 1920 concerning the establishment of the International Court:

Abyssinia	Canada	Finland	India
Albania	Chile	France	Iran
Australia	China	Germany	Ireland
Austria	Colombia	Great Britain	Italy
Belgium	Cuba	Greece	Japan
Bolivia	Czechoslovakia	Haiti	Latvia
Brazil	Denmark	Holland	Lithuania
Bulgaria	Esthonia	Hungary	Luxemburgh

II. *The International Court of Justice.*

Of international courts, therefore, there only exist at present the International Court at the Hague established in 1920 by the League of Nations, reestablished in 1945 by the Charter of the United Nations.

That it was possible in 1920 successfully to avoid the rock on which the plan of an international court was wrecked in 1907, viz. the claim of the small states for equality in the appointment of judges, was due partly to the pressure exercised directly by the situation after the first World War, partly to the devising of a method of election which, without mentioning anything about the difference between great and small states, indirectly favours the former. For it was provided that the 15 judges of the court were to be elected on an equal footing by the Assembly and the Council, those candidates being regarded as elected who obtained an absolute majority in both assemblies. Since now the great powers had a safe position of preference with permanent seats on the Council, a preferential influence in the appointment of the judges was in this way indirectly secured to them. According to the new Statute the members of the Court are to be elected by the General Assembly and by the Security Council of the United Nations.

Incidentally, it has been attempted in various ways to counteract the idea that the court should be composed of members representing their nations. It has been expressly laid down that the choice must be made regardless of nationality with a view to the technical qualifications of the candidates only. Further, care is to be taken that the main forms of civilisation and the principal legal systems of the world are represented in the court. Again, the members are elected from a list of candidates nominated not by the states themselves but by the national groups in the Permanent Court of Arbitration. No group may mominate more than 4 candidates, not more than 2 of whom shall be of their own nationality.[2]

New Zealand	Poland	Siam	Uruguay
Norway	Portugal	South Africa	Venezuela
Panama	Roumania	Spain	Yugoslavia
Paraguay	Salvador	Sweden	Liechtenstein
Peru	San Domingo	Switzerland	Monaco

[2] See the Statute, Articles 2—12.

With respect to the competence of the court the rule applies in regard to persons that the court is practically open to any state which will submit to its jurisdiction.[3] Thus it is by no means reserved for the members of the United Nations. It is intended to be a real universal court.

In a material respect the rule applies that the ratification of the Charter and thereby of the Statute annexed to this does not entail any duty to submit to the jurisdiction of the court. The warrant for this, according to the Statute, Art. 36 is to be found

either in the fact that the parties to the conflict submit a case to the court for settlement (*optional* jurisdiction);

or in the fact that the competence of the court has been agreed on in advance in a clause or treaty (*obligatory* jurisdiction).

No limit has been set to the nature of the disputes which can be referred to the settlement of the court. Purely political disputes too can be submitted. In that case the court must be considered empowered to decide *ex æquo et bono* (Art. 38, last part). This authority, which has not as yet been invoked, is not without danger for the authority of the court as a legal organ.

Thus the obligatory jurisdiction of the court is based on a separate agreement. Article 36, part 2, of the Statutes paves the way, however, since it provides that the states parties to the Statute may at any time make the *unilateral declaration* that they recognise as compulsory *ipso facto* and without special agreement, in relation to any other state accepting the same obligation, the jurisdiction of the court in all legal disputes concerning:

a. The interpretation of a treaty.

b. Any question of International Law.

c. The existence of any fact which, if established, would constitute a breach of an international obligation.

d. The nature or extent of the reparation to be made for the breach of an international obligation.

The declaration may be made unconditionally or on the condition of reciprocity on the part of several or certain states, or for a certain term.

Declarations made under Art. 36 of the Statute of the former

---

[3] See the Statutes, Art. 35.

Permanent Court of International Justice and which are still in force shall be deemed, as between the parties to the present Statute, to be acceptances of the compulsory jurisdiction of the International Court of Justice for the period which they still have to run and in accordance with their terms (Art. 36, part 5).

Many states have made such a declaration, though often with some reservation, by which an extensive obligatory jurisdiction has been created.[4]

Unfortunately, the delimitation in Art. 36 part 2 of the possible content of the unilateral declaration is anything but clear.

In the first place it is not clear whether the general characterisation as a "legal dispute" is to be regarded as a further qualification or merely as a — superfluous — description of the disputes mentioned under the succeeding letters, the implication being then that these are already characterised as legal disputes in themselves. Logic favours the first interpretation but in practice this will involve that all the uncertainty attaching to the concept "legal dispute" (§ 59. III) will be implicated in the delimitation of the obligatory jurisdiction.

In the second place the enumeration of the four groups is not clear. If group b is not to absorb all the others it must be restricted to the cases in which the dispute only concerns the interpretation of legal rules in contradistinction to disagreement as to the facts. But then it is incomprehensible why no other relevant international legal facts are mentioned under c except violation of the law, for instance the existence of facts creating, amending, or abolishing rights. It does not for instance seem possible to include under the said categories such an obvious

---

[4] Up to June 15th 1939 the following states had made declarations in respect of Art. 36. part 2.

Abyssinia	Esthonia	Italy	Roumania
Albania	Finland	Latvia	Salvador
Australia	France	Liechtenstein	San Domingo
Austria	Germany	Lithuania	Siam
Belgium	Great Britain	Luxemburgh	Spain
Bolivia	Greece	Monaco	Sweden
Brazil	Haiti	New Zealand	Switzerland
Bulgaria	Holland	Norway	South Africa
Canada	Hungary	Panama	Uruguay
China	India	Paraguay	Yugoslavia
Colombia	Iran	Peru	
Denmark	Ireland	Portugal	

legal dispute as whether or not an agreement has been concluded.[5]

This lack of clarity is only in some degree remedied by the final provision that the court itself decides disputes which may arise as to the question of the scope of its own competence.

The rules of procedure are in the main based on the same principles which apply to the Permanent Court of Arbitration (§ 60. III).

As one difference it may be pointed out that while the bringing of a case before the Court of Arbitration always implies a reference, a unilateral citation may here take place if both parties have bound themselves to accept the jurisdiction of the Court. Further the official languages of the Court are to be French and English and the hearing in court is based on the principle of publicity.

Besides giving judgments in interstate disputes the Court will, at the request of the General Assembly or Security Council (or other organs of the United Nations and specialized agencies so authorized by the General Assembly) give an *advisory opinion* on any legal question. This advisory activity has in practice proved more fruitful and important than was originally anticipated. The Court has so far given 27 opinions as against 31 judgments. Strictly, when the Court exercises its advisory activity there are no parties and so there is no pleading. In practice, however, the interested parties appear before the Court and state their case. Since further the opinion of the Court has hitherto always been accepted the difference between the judicial and the advisory jurisdiction is in actual fact not great.

---

[5] That Art. 36 does not include all legal disputes is rightly implied in the General Act for the Pacific Settlement of International Disputes of 1928 (Art. 17) where it is said that legal disputes comprise especially such as are included in Art. 36 of the Statute of the Permanent Court of International Justice.

On the other hand, it appears from the preliminary draft for Art. 36 (the draft of the Commission Art. 34) that the Commission itself regarded the categories enumerated as including all justiciable disputes. It was probably realised that the terms used were not the best, but for political opportunistic reasons it was desired to abide by this formulation taken oven from Art. 13 of the Covenant of the League. There is therefore good reason for interpreting the article with as wide applications as possible. This can be done by interpreting point c in accord with a statement in the preliminary draft as applying to questions concerning any fact from which a legal responsibility may arise.

§ 62
POLITICAL SETTLEMENT

I. *Its forms.*

Apart from simple diplomatic negotiations, political settlement occurs in three types established by custom, viz. mediation, inquiry, and conciliation.

Their common object is to put an end to the dispute by finding the politically most opportune solution; or at any rate, by a procedure conducted by others than the parties to the dispute to tone down the disagreement between them and so delay and perhaps prevent a violent issue.

The difference between them is in the means brought to bear for the promotion of the purpose. *Mediation* is the form in which the intervening party's own *political* activity comes most into play. It is the term used when a co-ordinate power, i. e. in international relations, another state, comes between the contesting parties and by good advice and by virtue of its influence tries to bring them to an agreement. The appeal to them then acts not only by its inherent reasonableness but also by the mediator's authority and the strength of his political wishes, even perhaps by a latent threat behind the appeal. The political power of the mediator helps out his political tact. Even though every mediator will probably maintain that he is an "honest" mediator, a shade of selfinterest will often lurk behind his honesty. As a rule great powers aspiring to a certain territorial political hegemony play the part of mediators; and the small states to whom their good offices are offered have often harboured some fear of accepting them lest the mediation should degenerate into a masked intervention. We need only think of the policy of the Holy Alliance. Owing to this fear the Hague Convention for Pacific Settlement of 1899 expressly, at the initiative of the small states, included a provision that mediation has exclusively the character of advice and never any binding power.[1] This of course will only apply if no other agreement has been made. If other agreements are made, the mediation will be merged in "political arbitration".

It is different with *inquiry* and *conciliation*. In this case the mediating organ is a commission of private individuals. There

---

[1] Conv. 1899 (1907) § 6.

is here no danger of the assistance changing into dictation. It can only act on technical grounds as an appeal to reason and sobriety. But then, on the other hand, owing to the laws governing human nature, its prospect of success is so much the less.

History shows that while mediation in one way or another has often led to a result, at any rate to the maintenance of peace, though the "honesty" may have been greater or smaller, no single case can probably be pointed out in which a commission of inquiry or any of the numerous commissions of conciliation that have been established have come successfully into action. (The inquiry in the *Dogger Bank* Affair (1904) perhaps forms an exception. But here there was an extended investigation of a character approaching arbitration).

Inquiry and conciliation differ from each other in that it is not the task of the commission of inquiry to make a proposal for the solution of the dispute, but merely to issue a report for the true elucidation of what has actually happened. It is then hoped that the delay and the clearing up of the affair in conjunction will be able to pour oil on the troubled waters. For it is often the case that the parties, through onesided accounts, entertain exaggerated ideas of the wrong they have suffered.

II. *The agreement as to the settlement.*

All forms imply that the parties agree to a settlement of the dispute. An agreement to that effect is therefore a necessary antecedent.

But the necessary agreement can be brought about in different ways.

The agreement is *spontaneous* when the contesting parties agree to submit an already existing dispute to settlement. This will be typically the case in *mediation* simply by both parties accepting an offer of mediation. Owing to its pronounced political character mediation is not suited for regulation in advance unless there exists a permanent international instrument of the highest political authority to which it will be natural at the outset to assign the part of the mediator. This is the case under the Charter of the United Nations Art. 37 by which the members have pledged themselves to refer any dispute between them likely to endanger the maintenance of international peace and security, and which the parties have failed to settle by peaceful means of their own choice, to the mediation of the Security Council.

Commissions of inquiry too are conceived by the Hague Convention as appointed *ad hoc,* but according to the nature of the case there is nothing to prevent them from being made into institutions. Actually, however, they have been replaced as such by commissions of conciliation.

The agreement is *institutional* when the parties have bound themselves in advance to refer certain future disputes to political treatment. This will typically be the case with respect to *conciliation.* In a situation of political tension it will facilitate the procedure if the organ has been created by previous agreement. But of course there is nothing to prevent this aid from being called in spontaneously.

III. *What disputes are suited for political settlement?*

All are. Even legal disputes. In civil procedure each case begins with proceedings with a view to conciliation. If a reconciliation can be brought about there is no reason to go to law.

Since, as we have seen, disputes concerning interests are not as a rule regarded as suited for treatment in the forms of jurisdiction the possibility arises of a combination of jurisdiction and political settlement, especially conciliation, either *alternatively,* i. e. disputes as to interests are referred to political treatment, legal disputes to jurisdiction; or *cumulatively,* i. e. all disputes are first submitted to political treatment (conciliation) whereupon, failing results, only legal disputes are submitted to a succeeding jurisdiction.

IV. *The basis of the settlement.*

In political settlement no norms of any kind are applied. Political judgment alone decides what is opportune. Politics are the art of what is possible, success is the only norm of this art, tact and power are its instruments.

If as a rare exception a political dispute is submitted to treatment in the forms of jurisdiction the decision is given *ex æquo et bono.* This maxim, as is well known, is different from the purely political. It indicates a decision in the spirit of the law on the principle of what is fair and just.

V. *The non-obligatory character of the appeal.*

It may well be conceived, but is not very practical, that the parties might bind themselves in advance to comply with the proposal put forward by the mediator or the conciliation commission. In the absence of any rules for arriving at the decision the parties would be unable to known to what they were binding themselves. A binding effect of a political treatment would in reality be a politically creative legislative function. If such an idea were to be realised there would have to be a corresponding organisation of the political power. In the League of Nations an approach was made to giving the mediation of the Council a certain, politically supported, binding effect. In this way it came close to a "political adjudication". The same will be the case with respect to the mediation by the Security Council under Art. 37 of the Charter of the United Nations.

§ 63
SPECIAL REMARKS ON MEDIATION

It is customary to distinguish between good offices and mediation, good offices denoting a mediating activity on the part of a third state which only aims at bringing together the contesting parties for continued negotiation. In practice, however, there is no distinction between good offices and mediation.

Mediation has taken place in all ages. Owing to the ceaseless growth of interdependence the cause of mediation, that war cannot be regarded as *res inter alios acta*, has greater validity today than ever before. War concerns us all. Hence it was expressly established at the first Hague Conference that it must be considered useful that one or more powers, strangers to the dispute, should, on their own initiative, offer their good offices or mediation to the states at variance with each other, and that the exercise of this right shall never be considered by either of the parties to the dispute as an unfriendly act.[1]

There exists *no duty*, however, to offer mediation any more than to request it. The pronounced political character of mediation owing to the lack of an international political organisation of the powers makes it unsuitable to be obligatory. As a matter of fact the Convention of 1899 only states that in case of serious dispute or conflict, before an appeal is made to arms, the powers would have recourse, as far as circumstances permit, to the good offices or mediation of one or more friendly powers.[2]

---

[1] Conv. 1899, Art. 3. At the revision in 1907 the words "and desirable" were added after "useful".

[2] Conv. 1899 (1907) Art. 2.

With the seconds in a duel as prototypes the Hague Convention of 1899 recommended the employment under special circumstances of a special form of mediation. Each of the contesting parties was to choose a second state whose task it would be to enter into communication with the power chosen by the other side.[3] The idea was that in cases where neither arbitration nor ordinary mediation seemed to have any prospect of success, that is to say when matters were strained to breaking point, it would be useful to leave the further discussion to third parties. But this invention, as far as we know, has never been carried into effect.

As previously stated, the Covenant of the League of Nations made an attempt to give mediation an institutional character and to attach a certain political sanction to it. The idea in itself is sound, but the League lacked effective power to carry it into operation successfully. One must hope that the United Nations Organization will prove more effective in this direction.

The organ of mediation is always one or several third states. In the nature of the case there can be no question of rules of procedure.

§ 64
SPECIAL REMARKS ON INQUIRY

In former times it has often happened that neighbour states, on the occasion of some frontier incident where it may often be difficult for each of the states alone to get the facts of the case sufficiently cleared up through its own organs, have agreed to set up a common mixed commission for the purpose of finding out what has actually taken place. This commission is then furnished with the right to make inquiries and especially to hear the parties on both sides of the frontier.

The first Hague Conference of 1899 tried to develop these special technical frontier commissions into a general instrument for the political settlement of disputes between states. A proposal to make the institution of such commissions of inquiry obligatory met with emphatic resistance, although it was well wrapped up in reservations in regard to "honour and vital interest" as well as according to the formula "if circumstances

---

[3] Conv. 1899 (1907) Art. 8.

permit". While the idea of obligatory arbitration was wrecked on the resistance of Germany, it was in this case a number of smaller states which energetically insisted on the voluntary character of the investigation. The result, then, was merely a statement that — with the above-mentioned reservations — the powers regard the setting up of commissions of inquiry as useful. At the same time several declaratory rules were given for the institution, composition, and tasks of such commissions.[1]

Thus the commission of inquiry is highly reminiscent of a tribunal of arbitration appointed according to the rules of the Hague Convention, with the difference following from the different objects of the two organs. The commission of inquiry is made up according to the same rules as a tribunal of arbitration. Its task is to elucidate the actual questions by an impartial and conscientious trial. It ends its work by issuing a *report* which confines itself to stating the facts and lets the parties keep their full liberty with respect to the effect they will give to this statement. As before a tribunal, so also here party pleading takes place before the commission. Detailed rules for this procedure were fixed at the revision by the second Hague Conference of the Convention for Pacific Settlement in 1907.

Commissions of inquiry have not in practice been employed as mush as it was hoped they would. As far as we know, only one case has occurred in which this expedient has been resorted to in an international conflict. It was in the *Dogger Bank* affair in 1904. When the Russian Baltic fleet on its way to the scene of war in the East passed the Dogger Bank in the North Sea in the night it attacked a fleet of English fishing vessels in the belief that it was attacking Japanese torpedo boats. The commission of high naval officers from various countries which was appointed had the task, however, not only of elucidating the facts but also of saying who must be held responsible for the events. Hence it was in reality more than a commission of inquiry.

---

[1] Conv. 1899, Arts. 9—11, Conv. 1907, Arts. 9—36 (rules of procedure were added in 1907.)

§ 65
SPECIAL REMARKS ON CONCILIATION

Thus though the work of the Hague Conferences for the institution of commissions of inquiry did not lead to any appreciable practical result, yet it paved the way for the conclusion of a great number of treaties concerning the appointment of standing commissions of conciliation. The advantage of this mode of procedure is presumably to be found in the fact that states can more easily agree as to the appointment of a permanent commission when on friendly terms than during strained relations. The appointment in a strained situation of a commission without the previous conclusion of a treaty is always a concession. The conclusion during friendly relations of a treaty of conciliation is for the present merely a gesture for the maintenance of peace.

Already before the first world War the United States had, at the initiative of the pacifist *Bryan*, concluded a large number of so-called Bryan treaties (c. 30) with other states, according to which *permanent conciliation commissions* were to be set up consisting of 5 persons, two chosen on each side, and an umpire. But it was not until after the war that the institution grew apace. According to the Covenant of the League of Nations the Council as a central organ was to exercise a mediating and conciliating activity. But instead of further developing the function of the Council by agreements as to an obligatory conciliation treatment before the Council, a decentralisation was commenced after 1922 at the instance of the Scandinavian states. The individual states were recommended to conclude agreements with each other concerning the establisment of permanent commissions of conciliation. Since then several hundred such treaties have been concluded, as a rule in some combination or other with agreements as to jurisdiction. And more than a hundred permanent commissions of conciliation have been established. Despite all these efforts they have virtually played no part in the practice of the states.

INDEX

Aaland Islands *85*, 129.
Abbagnato case *72 f*, 100, 165, 266.
Acquisition of territory 145 f.
Act of state 117, *121 f.*
Adequacy 267.
Administration of justice 54 f, 76, 77, 271 f.
Administrative unions 224.
Æquo et bono 93, *275*, 282, 284, 295, 300.
Agreements, see Treaties.
Agrément 200.
Agricultural Institute 239.
Aircraft 174, 226.
Air space 139.
Alcohol 237.
Aliens Law 138, *159 f.*
Ambassadors, see Envoys
Analogy 92.
Angary, right of, 248.
Animus possidendi 147.
Apatrides 153.
Arbitration 272, 275 f, 287 f.
Armed forces under command 158, 253, 258.
Ascription of violation of the law to a state 250.
Assistance in conduct of legal proceedings 239.
Authority to ratify treaties 213 f.
Autonomy, of parties 23, *84*, 273.
— of state 21.
Aviation 226.

Bancroft treaties, the 153.
Base lines 142.
Bays 142 f, 144.
Bona officia see Mediation.
Bryan treaties 304.

Calvo clause 265.
Canals 144.
Capability of action 26, 36, 42, 44, *104*, 259.
— of delinquency 104, 259.
— of duty 96 f.
— of rights 28, 96[1].
Caroline, case of the 249.
Catholic church 103.
Causal connection *255*, 267 f.
Central American Court 110, 282 f, 293.
Cession 145, 148.
Chargés d'affairs, see Envoys.
Cholera 237.
Citizenship 138, *149 f.*
Civil war 165 f, 249, see Insurgent parties.
Closing of Great and Little Belts 172[2].
Codification conference at the Hague 57, 141, 149, 153, 178, 253, 263[4].
— — in Paris *160*, 163.
Coercion 210, 260.
Communication, means of 226.
Compensation 266 f.

Alf Ross   20

BIBLIOGRAPHY
ONLY OF SUCH LITERATURE AS IS NOT QUOTED IN FULL IN THE NOTES

Anzilotti, Dionisio: Cours de Droit international. Paris 1929.

Brierly, J. L.: The Law of Nations. 2. ed. Oxf. 1936.

Bruns, Viktor: Fontes juris gentium A. II. 1. (Entscheidungen des deutschen Reichsgerichts in völkerrechtlichen Fragen). Berl. 1931.

Cobbett, Pitt: Leading Cases on International Law. I Peace. 4. ed. Ld. 1922.

Eagleton, Clyde: The Responsibility of States in International Law. New York 1928.

Gihl, Torsten: International Legislation. Ld. 1937.

Hägerström, Axel: Der römische Obligationsbegriff I. Skrifter utgivna av K. Humanistiska Vetenskaps-Samfundet i Uppsala. 23. Upps.-Lpz. 1927.

Kelsen, Hans: Théorie générale du droit internationale public (Extrait du recueil des cours). Paris 1933.

Knubben, Rolf: Die Subjekte des Völkerrechts. Stuttg. 1928. (In Stier-Somlo, Handbuch des Völkerrechts).

Kunz, Josef L.: Die Anerkennung von Staaten und Regierungen im Völkerrecht.Stuttg. 1928. (In Stier-Somlo, Handbuch des Völkerrechts).

Lauterpacht, H.: The Function of Law in the International Community. Oxf. 1933.

Lundstedt, A. V.: Superstition or Rationality in Action for Peace? Ld. 1925.

Mirkine-Guétzevitch: Droit constitutionel international. Paris 1933.

Moore, John Bassett: A Digest af International Law. Washington 1906 f.

N.T. = Nordisk Tidsskrift for international Ret.

Oppenheim, L.: International Law. 5. ed. (Lauterpacht). Ld. 1937.

Politis, N.: La justice internationale. 2. ed. Paris 1924.

Rec. = Recueil des Cours de l'Academie de droit international de la Haye.

Ross, Alf: Theorie der Rechtsquellen. Wien-Lpz. 1929.

— Kritik der sogenannten praktischen Erkenntnis. Copenhagen 1933.

— Towards a Realistic Jurisprudence, Copenh. 1946.

Scelle, Georges: Précis de droit de gens I—II. Paris 1932—34.

Scott, James Brown: Cases on International Law. St. Paul 1922.

Spiropoulos, Jean: Théorie générale du droit internationale. Paris 1930.

Strupp, Karl: Das völkerrechtliche Delikt. Berlin 1920. (In Stier-Somlo, Handbuch des Völkerrecht).

— Wörtenbuch des Völkerrechts und der Diplomatie. Berlin-Lpz. 1924 —29.

Suckiennicki, Wiktor: La Souverainété des états. Paris 1927.

Verdross, Alfred von: Völkerrecht. Berlin 1937.

Waldkirch, Eduard von und Vanselow, Ernst: Neutralitätsrecht. Stuttg. 1936. (In Stier-Somlo, Handbuch des Völkerrechts).

Walz, Gustav Adolf: Völkerrecht und staatliches Recht. Stuttg. 1933.

Williams, Sir John Fischer: Chapters on Current International Law and the League of Nations. Ld. 1929.

Lightning Source UK Ltd.
Milton Keynes UK
UKHW012120221121
394427UK00002B/112

9 781584 777076